LAND AND COVENANT

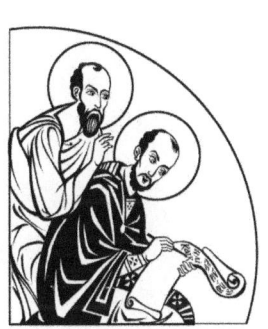

LAND AND COVENANT

Paul Nadim Tarazi

OCABS PRESS
ST PAUL, MINNESOTA 55112
2009

LAND AND COVENANT

Copyright © 2009 by
Paul Nadim Tarazi

ISBN 1-60191-009-6

All rights reserved.

PRINTED IN THE UNITED STATES OF AMERICA

In memory of
my parents
Jamal and Widad

Other Books by the Author

I Thessalonians: A Commentary

Galatians: A Commentary

The Old Testament: An Introduction

Volume 1: Historical Traditions, revised edition

Volume 2: Prophetic Traditions

Volume 3: Psalms and Wisdom

The New Testament: An Introduction

Volume 1: Paul and Mark

Volume 2: Luke and Acts

Volume 3: Johannine Writings

Volume 4: Matthew and the Canon

The Chrysostom Bible

Genesis: A Commentary

Land and Covenant

Copyright © 2009 by Paul Nadim Tarazi
All rights reserved.

ISBN 1-60191-009-6

Published by OCABS Press, St. Paul, Minnesota.
Printed in the United States of America.

Books are available through OCABS Press at special discounts for bulk purchases in the United States by academic institutions, churches, and other organizations. For more information please email OCABS Press at press@ocabs.org.

Abbreviations

Books by the Author

1 Thess	*I Thessalonians: A Commentary,* Crestwood, NY: St. Vladimir's Seminary Press, 1982
Gal	*Galatians: A Commentary,* Crestwood, NY: St. Vladimir's Seminary Press, 1994
OTI_1	*The Old Testament: An Introduction, Volume 1: Historical Traditions,* revised edition, Crestwood, NY: St. Vladimir's Seminary Press, 2003
OTI_2	*The Old Testament: An Introduction, Volume 2: Prophetic Traditions,* Crestwood, NY: St. Vladimir's Seminary Press, 1994
OTI_3	*The Old Testament: An Introduction, Volume 3: Psalms and Wisdom,* Crestwood, NY: St. Vladimir's Seminary Press, 1996
NTI_1	*The New Testament: An Introduction, Volume 1: Paul and Mark,* Crestwood, NY: St. Vladimir's Seminary Press, 1999
NTI_2	*The New Testament: An Introduction, Volume 2: Luke and Acts,* Crestwood, NY: St. Vladimir's Seminary Press, 2001
NTI_3	*The New Testament: An Introduction, Volume 3: Johannine Writings,* Crestwood, NY: St. Vladimir's Seminary Press, 2004
NTI_4	*The New Testament: An Introduction, Volume 4: Matthew and the Canon,* St. Paul, MN: OCABS Press, 2009
C-Gen	*The Chrysostom Bible - Genesis: A Commentary,* St. Paul, MN: OCABS Press, 2009

Abbreviations

Books of the Old Testament*

Gen	Genesis	Job	Job	Hab		Habakkuk
Ex	Exodus	Ps	Psalms	Zeph		Zephaniah
Lev	Leviticus	Prov	Proverbs	Hag		Haggai
Num	Numbers	Eccl	Ecclesiastes	Zech		Zechariah
Deut	Deuteronomy	Song	Song of Solomon	Mal		Malachi
Josh	Joshua	Is	Isaiah	Tob		Tobit
Judg	Judges	Jer	Jeremiah	Jdt		Judith
Ruth	Ruth	Lam	Lamentations	Wis		Wisdom
1 Sam	1 Samuel	Ezek	Ezekiel	Sir	Sirach	(Ecclesiasticus)
2 Sam	2 Samuel	Dan	Daniel	Bar		Baruch
1 Kg	1 Kings	Hos	Hosea	1 Esd		1 Esdras
2 Kg	2 Kings	Joel	Joel	2 Esd		2 Esdras
1 Chr	1 Chronicles	Am	Amos	1 Macc		1 Maccabees
2 Chr	2 Chronicles	Ob	Obadiah	2 Macc		2 Maccabees
Ezra	Ezra	Jon	Jonah	3 Macc		3 Maccabees
Neh	Nehemiah	Mic	Micah	4 Macc		4 Maccabees
Esth	Esther	Nah	Nahum			

Books of the New Testament

Mt	Matthew	Eph	Ephesians	Heb	Hebrews
Mk	Mark	Phil	Philippians	Jas	James
Lk	Luke	Col	Colossians	1 Pet	1 Peter
Jn	John	1 Thess	1 Thessalonians	2 Pet	2 Peter
Acts	Acts	2 Thess	2 Thessalonians	1 Jn	1 John
Rom	Romans	1 Tim	1 Timothy	2 Jn	2 John
1 Cor	1 Corinthians	2 Tim	2 Timothy	3 Jn	3 John
2 Cor	2 Corinthians	Titus	Titus	Jude	Jude
Gal	Galatians	Philem	Philemon	Rev	Revelation

*Following the larger canon known as the Septuagint.

Contents

Abbreviations

Preface

Introduction

Part I – The Book of Genesis

From Adam to Abraham	23
The Patriarchal Narratives	45
Abraham	55
Isaac	71
Jacob	75
The Joseph Cycle	85

Part II – The Law and the Prophets

The Mosaic Law	97
The Book of Joshua	115
The Book of Judges	135
1 & 2 Samuel	141
1 & 2 Kings	151
The Prophets	157

Part III – The Wisdom Literature

The Writings (Ketubim)	189
The Canon of the Writings (Ketubim)	199
The Septuagint	205

Part IV – The New Testament

The New Testament Writings	215
The Mission of Jesus and the Apostles	223
The Absence of Canaan in the New Testament	235
Scripture: History of the Jewish People or Word of God?	241
The Second Coming	259
The Millennium	271

Epilogue　　　291

Preface

"Holiness is not spatial, inherent to a piece of real estate or a building. It is behavioral."

Paul Nadim Tarazi

If you have lived in the Middle East since the inception of the state of Israel, or if you are a student of twentieth century Middle East history, you cannot help but take part in the debate which has produced many books on the ongoing conflict between Jews and Arabs, especially Palestinians. Many people, especially "born-again Christians" took part in this debate, interpreting the Scripture in their own way and dismissing the true biblical understanding of God's promise. This debate has centered on this question: "To whom does Palestine belong, to Arabs or Jews?"

Back in the late 1960s, I held a press conference in Miami Beach, Florida, and presented a new concept of a new state, called "The State of the Holy Land," where Jews, Christians and Muslims will live together in harmony under a secular political system with equal rights for all. Needless to say, my proposal to bring peace to the Middle East was rejected, and the cycle of violence which has resulted in much bloodshed, loss of life, misery and destruction continues, and there is no end in sight.

Three years ago, I asked my friend, Paul Nadim Tarazi, a biblical scholar and renowned professor of theology, to write an objective book on this subject. He complied and produced this volume, "Land and Covenant," which is not written from an historical point of view, but strictly biblical. The Holy Land was inhabited by Philistines, Jebusites and Canaanites when Abraham came to Palestine. Tarazi believes that the Holy Land belongs to all people who keep God's commandments and walk in his way. When I told Tarazi that the reality of this world is a reality of different nations, he said: "Still different nations must keep God's commandments and walk in his ways, if they want to live in a peaceful world."

"Land and Covenant" is a very scholarly and interesting biblical study, and I recommend it to all who seek the truth, objectively and without any prejudice.

+Archbishop Philip Saliba
Englewood, New Jersey
August 20, 2009

Introduction

The necessity for discussing the way the Bible looks at God's alleged promise to secure out of Canaan an eternal deeded property to the Jews of all ages need not be justified. The bloodshed and misery caused by such a misreading of the Bible and carried out throughout the 20th century into ours is, in itself, horrific. Linking it, directly or indirectly, to God's Word and thus his will is, to say the least, blasphemous. In the words of the Apostle: "For, as it is written, 'The name of God is blasphemed among the Gentiles because of you.'" (Rom 2:24) Therefore, I shall limit my Introduction to a few lines concerning the terms referring to the "land" in scripture.

As is clear from the expression "land for sale" in real estate terminology, the noun "land" has the connotation of defined property owned by someone. On the other hand, as can be heard, for instance, in the phrase "the land of the free" in our National Anthem, the same term has come to be used in reference to land that is the defined property of a community of people forming a nation. Consequently, the phrase "land of Israel," found in translations as early in the King James Version, is often misunderstood as the property of a nation called Israel, which is understood to be composed of the "Jews." Hence, the accepted notion that the contemporary Middle Eastern political entity known as the state of Israel is the "Land of Israel," that is, the land of (belonging to) the Jews. That, however, is not the original meaning of "land." The biblical connotation of "land" is merely the expanse of "earth" where a group of human beings live. It is only the rise of nationalism, starting with the 19th century, that viewed "national land" as a defined "property." It is no secret to anyone that the establishment of the state of Israel would not have been possible except within the parameters of modern "nationalism."

In the original Greek as well as Hebrew, however, we have the one word *'eretz* (Greek *gē*) that is translated into either "earth" or "land," the latter virtually systematically found in the phrase "the land of [name of an area or people]." The bias, whether intentional or not, becomes evident when the translations, starting with the King James Version that prides itself on being literal, usually render the Hebrew *'adamah* into "ground" except in the repeated phrase *'admat*[1] *yisra'el* in Ezekiel which it translates into "the land of Israel" instead of "the ground of Israel." As we shall see in my discussion later, this issue is very important for two reasons: (1) once in Ezekiel we find *'eretz yisra'el* (literally "the earth of Israel") which is again translated as "the land of Israel," blurring thus the difference between the two original Hebrew phrases *'eretz yisra'el* (earth of Israel) and *'admat yisra'el* (ground of Israel)," and (2) the close link between the Hebrew *'adam* (human being) and *'adamah* (ground). The foregoing will explain to my readers my decision to keep the original *'eretz* as "earth" since in English the plural "earths" is not used.

---

[1] This is the form *'adamah* takes when followed by a noun complement.

Part I

The Book of Genesis

1
From Adam to Abraham

Much of the misunderstanding regarding critical issues in the Bible, including that of the Promised Land, stems from the lack of consideration given to the first 11 chapters of Genesis. One usually begins the "biblical story" with the call of Abraham in chapter 12.[1] However as in all major literature, the introductory part not only sets the tone for what follows, but also functions as its basis. In this sense, one can refer to the introductory part of a massive literature as the "institutional" or "constitutional" matrix that holds together its entirety into "one story." Take for instance the beginning of the Iliad:

> Sing, O goddess, the anger of Achilles son of Peleus, that brought countless ills upon the Achaeans. Many a brave soul did it send hurrying down to Hades, and many a hero did it yield a prey to dogs and vultures, for so were the counsels of Jove [Jupiter] fulfilled from the day on which the son of Atreus, king of men, and great Achilles, first fell out with one another.[2]

This clearly tells us that Homer's epic is not about the Trojan War per se, but rather that it is woven around Achilles' ire that forms the matrix around which the story revolves. Without it, the story of the Trojan War would have ended swiftly and, consequently, its telling might not have been an epic.

In the same manner, the Book of Genesis forms the matrix of the entire Bible. In it we find all the important elements or

---

[1] Gen 1-3 are used mainly in conjunction with either the value of the human being in general, often without connection with the rest of the Bible, or the texts where Paul refers to Jesus as the new or last Adam.
[2] Samuel Butler's translation: http://classics.mit.edu/Homer/iliad.1.i.html.

topics that will be dealt with in the rest of the biblical books. These include covenant, promise, blessing, curse, inheritance, circumcision, sabbath, Israel, exodus. Within Genesis itself, the first 11 chapters are set apart in that they do not deal with the origins of Jacob-Israel and its subsequent pedigree, as does the rest of the biblical story. These chapters deal with the entire humanity from which Jacob-Israel stems and within which the latter's story is set. Furthermore, this introduction concerning the entire humanity is not done cursively with the mere intention of tracing the genealogy of the children of Jacob; this could have been done with the table of the nations found in chapter 10. Rather, the rendition is much more elaborate and extensive. Not only is biblical terminology established (blessing, curse, commandment, sin, punishment, covenant, salvation from the waters, etc.), but it is also established that the Lord God is the main agent and as such he is dealing with all humanity well before his dealings with Jacob-Israel. Even more, the story of Adam and his descendants, indeed the entire human race, forms the main biblical storyline that, in turn, will be applied to Jacob-Israel as an exemplar of one people of the human family. The intent behind this is to show that *any* given people of the human race will behave toward God in the same unduly manner. As Paul will correctly conclude:

> What then? Are we Jews any better off? No, not at all; for I have already charged that all men, both Jews and Greeks,[3] are under the power of sin, as it is written: "None is righteous, no, not one; no one understands, no one seeks for God. All have turned aside, together they have gone wrong; no one does good, not even one." "Their throat is an open grave, they use their tongues to deceive." "The venom of asps is under their lips." "Their mouth is full of

---

[3] In the original Greek we have the term "Hellenes" which is, along with "ethnies" (*ethnē*), the alternate translation for the original Hebrew "nations" (*goyim*).

curses and bitterness." "Their feet are swift to shed blood, in their paths are ruin and misery, and the way of peace they do not know." "There is no fear of God before their eyes." Now we know that whatever the law says it speaks to those who are under the law, so that every mouth may be stopped, and the whole world may be held accountable to God. (Rom 3:9-19)

Put otherwise, the general premise in Genesis 1-11 regarding the human beings' ungrateful attitude toward God's grateful attention to them is tested in detail in the story of one given people, Jacob-Israel. The result is that even with biblical instruction no people or individual human being is better than the other; all would act in the same way.

The Adamic Story

Looking more closely at Genesis 1 the reader will notice that the earth is not exclusively the domain of human beings, but is a place that is to be shared with the animals as well. This is verified by that (1) both land animals and the human beings are created on the same day, the sixth, to underscore their togetherness; (2) both are intentionally included under the same blessing;[4] and (3) both share the earth's vegetation, together with the fowl[5] that

---

[4] Notice how, whereas fish and fowl are honored with a two-pronged blessing in Gen 1:22 (And God blessed them, saying, "Be fruitful and multiply and fill the waters in the seas, and let birds multiply on the earth"), we hear about only one blessing in the sixth day which is specifically addressed to the human beings (v.28). Since the blessing is connected with the multiplication of the race, it is impossible for the reader not to include mentally the land animals within the same range of the divine blessing uttered on the sixth day. The reason for the omission is to be explained by that the divine words of blessing addressed to humankind include the humans' accountability for the state of the earth and the welfare of its inhabitants. Why not then two separate blessings? The intention is obviously to underscore the togetherness of those who live on earth and from its fruit.

[5] Gen 1:29-30 (And God said, "Behold, I have given you every plant yielding seed which is upon the face of all the earth, and every tree with seed in its fruit; you shall

cannot feed on air, the domain assigned to it. Thus the central topic that holds together the narratives of both Genesis 1 and Genesis 2-3 is not the human being; rather it is the earth, the domain where the human being resides and functions.

This "priority" of the earth over man in God's overall interest is rooted in God's being the creator of all creation and creatures, not only of humankind.[6] The entire movement creating heavens and earth (Gen 1:1) is triggered by God's action, given that before this intervention "the earth was without form and void, and darkness was upon the face of the deep; and the Spirit of God was moving over the face of the waters" (v.2). Actually, the first four days (two thirds of God's activity) revolve around the establishment of the earth, its vegetation, and its seasons. If one adds the sixth day that deals with the earth's creatures and their livelihood from that same earth, then God's dealings with the earth span five sixths of his activity, with the fifth day being just an appendix underscoring that he is the God of all that is. Thus God's primary concern is the earth which He, as the provider, has created for all beings; man is only indirectly God's concern. This is elucidated further in the Psalms:

> All the ends of the earth shall remember and turn to the Lord; and all the families of the nations shall worship before him. For dominion belongs to the Lord, and he rules over the nations. (Ps 22:27-28)

---

have them for food. And to every beast of the earth, and to every bird of the air, and to everything that creeps on the earth, everything that has the breath of life, I have given every green plant for food." And it was so).

[6] Anthropocentrism, which amounts to egocentrism, is actually in scripture the epitome of sin and cause for all evil that besets not only man but God's entire creation.

> The earth is the Lord's and the fullness thereof, the world and those who dwell therein; for he has founded it upon the seas, and established it upon the rivers. (Ps 24:1-2)
>
> The heavens are thine, the earth also is thine; the world and all that is in it, thou hast founded them. (Ps 89:11)[7]

The dependence of the human being on the "earth" is reflected in the terminology of Genesis 1-3. The Hebrew *'adam* (man) is formed (as a potter would form a vessel out of clay from the ground) out of the *'adamah* (ground). Morphologically speaking, *'adamah* is the feminine noun corresponding to the masculine noun *'adam*. The priority of the earth or the "ground" of the earth over man is further underscored in that man is formed "of dust from the ground" (Gen 2:7), to which dust he will return upon his demise: "In the sweat of your face you shall eat bread till you return to the ground, for out of it you were taken; you are dust, and to dust you shall return." (3:19) The clarification that man is formed not directly out of the ground, but out of its dust, goes hand in hand with the pottery metaphor whereby a broken or unused pot may end up pulverized and not look like a vessel anymore.

It is also worth mentioning that the relationship between the ground and man is not specific to Genesis 2-3. It is already deftly introduced in the first account of creation in Genesis 1 in conjunction with God's "making" the animals just before his "making" man:

---

[7] Notice also how the first statement of the Niceo-Constantinopolitan Creed defines our trust in the God of the entire creation: "We believe in one God the Father Almighty, Maker of heaven and earth, and of all things visible and invisible."

> And God *made* the beasts of the earth according to their kinds and the cattle according to their kinds, and everything that creeps upon the *ground* (*'adamah*) according to its kind. And God saw that it was good. Then God said, "Let us make *man* (*'adam*) in our image, after our likeness; and let them have dominion over the fish of the sea, and over the birds of the air, and over the cattle, and over all the earth, and over every creeping thing that creeps upon the earth." (Gen 1:25-26)

That the reference to "ground" was done intentionally can be gathered from the fact that, in the larger context (vv. 24, 27-30), the animals are repeatedly and systematically connected with the earth and not the ground:

> And God said, "Let the *earth* bring forth living creatures according to their kinds: cattle and creeping things and beasts of the *earth* according to their kinds." And it was so. And God made the beasts of the earth according to their kinds and the cattle according to their kinds, and everything that creeps upon the *ground* (*'adamah*) according to its kind. And God saw that it was good. Then God said, "Let us make man in our image, after our likeness; and let them have dominion over the fish of the sea, and over the birds of the air, and over the cattle, and over all the *earth*, and over every creeping thing that creeps upon the *earth*." So God created the man in his own image, in the image of God he created him; male and female he created them. And God blessed them, and God said to them, "Be fruitful and multiply, and fill the earth and subdue it; and have dominion over the fish of the sea and over the birds of the air and over every living thing that moves upon the *earth*." And God said, "Behold, I have given you every plant yielding seed which is upon the face of all the earth, and every tree with seed in its fruit; you shall have them for food. And to every beast of the *earth*, and to every bird of the air, and to everything that creeps on the *earth*, everything that has the breath of life, I have given every green plant for food." And it was so. (vv.24-30)

The latter passage (vv.26-30) is interesting in that it underscores man's dependence on the earth *as one of the earth's creatures,* thus emphasizing the priority of earth and not man in God's plan. Just as the animals were introduced as creatures of the *'adamah* (ground; v.25) before *'adam* (man) is introduced, so also are animals presented as "having the breath of life (a living breath; *nephesh ḥayyah)*" (v.30) before man is formed into a living being [living breath; *nephesh ḥayyah*] (2:7).

Notice also how in the case of Adam, when he transgresses God's commandment, it is not he but the ground, the source of his sustenance and life, which is cursed:

> And to Adam he said, "Because you have listened to the voice of your wife, and have eaten of the tree of which I commanded you, 'You shall not eat of it,' cursed is the ground because of you; in toil you shall eat of it all the days of your life; thorns and thistles it shall bring forth to you; and you shall eat the plants of the field. In the sweat of your face you shall eat bread till you return to the ground, for out of it you were taken; you are dust, and to dust you shall return." (Gen 3:17-19)

Eden

In order to understand the land and its function in the biblical story, one should keep in mind that in Hebrew the same word *'eretz* (earth) applies equally to the entire globe as well as to the land surrounding a given city for use by its entire population.[8] The earth is the property of the sole God and this "earth" and its produce are provided to each human being within the community he or she happens to be a member of. The earth is

---

[8] The same applies, for that matter, to the Greek *gē* (whence our geology, study of the earth).

never an actual property or possession. It is always a patrimony, a place that is inherited and granted as a communal gift. In the Ancient Near East, patrimony was the property of the family[9] represented in the person of its progenitor.[10] Family names did not exist, and the family or clan or tribe was referred to as "sons of" or "children of" followed by the name of the forefather.[11] The land surrounding a city was considered the patrimony of that city's deity and entrusted to the monarch who was the representative of that deity. All the residents of that land, without any discrimination or exception, were under the monarch's protection.

This sheds a light on what is being presented in Genesis 1 and again in Genesis 2-3. The realm within which human beings live is referred to as "heaven(s) and earth," which is their "world" or "universe." This is fully logical from the practical perspective since neither the sea nor the underworld (domain of the dead) is a place where man normally lives.[12] However, from God's perspective, given that he is the maker of all that exists, the expression "heaven(s) and earth" is inclusive rather than

---

[9] And not of the individual; hence "patrimony" that has the connotation of "heritage" in English.

[10] See 1 Kg 21:1-3 (Now Naboth the Jezreelite had a vineyard in Jezreel, beside the palace of Ahab king of Samaria. And after this Ahab said to Naboth, "Give me your vineyard, that I may have it for a vegetable garden, because it is near my house; and I will give you a better vineyard for it; or, if it seems good to you, I will give you its value in money." But Naboth said to Ahab, "The Lord forbid that I should give you the inheritance of my fathers.").

[11] This tradition is pervading. We find it in personal as well as family names in different societies: "ben" in the Semitic languages; "Mac" and "Fitz" (from the French "fils" meaning "son") in the Gaellic; "son" (at the end of the name) in Teutonic and Anglo-Saxon.

[12] Notice how a full day (the second) is consecrated to ensure that the earth that emerges from the "earthly" waters is also protected from the heavenly ones. Moreover, it is the lack of such protection that produces the flood that will threaten "earth" and all that it supports: fauna and flora as well as humans (Gen 6-7).

restrictive or exclusive since it also includes the sea.[13] Although the world of human beings includes heavens (air as well as sky), their domain is actually on earth. And since scripture is addressed to human beings, it stands to reason that the earth (and its inhabitants) gets the lion's share in Genesis 1 (18 out of 31 verses [vv.2, 9-12, 14-15, 17-18, 24-31]), and that the story of Genesis 2-3 revolves around man's life in conjunction with the earth. This concern about the earth becomes even clearer in the narrative of man in the garden of Eden. We are told that it is God, not man, who planted the garden (Gen 2:8). Consequently, the garden cannot be man's possession; it is just a venue granted to him where he is able to spend his life "from dust to dust," while sharing it with the animals that God has formed (v.19), just as he has formed man (v.7).

What applies to man in Eden applies to all mankind, even after Adam was exiled out of the garden (3:23-24). Both the garden and the rest of the world (more specifically, the world in which the biblical story unfolds) are watered—that is, are given the life that sustains the vegetation which, in turn, sustains man and animal—by the same river:

> A river flowed out of Eden to water the garden, and there it divided and became four rivers. The name of the first is Pishon; it is the one which flows around the whole earth of Havilah, where there is gold; and the gold of that earth is good; bdellium and onyx stone are there. The name of the second river is Gihon; it is the one which flows around the whole earth of Cush. And the name of

---

[13] In languages "pairs" (whether complementary such as "heaven and earth," "men and women," "adults and children," "humans and animals," "fauna and flora" or opposite such as "black and white," "light and darkness," "day and night," "rich and poor," "big and small," "good and evil") are intended to speak of the totality rather than the two mentioned elements in an exclusive manner.

the third river is Tigris, which flows east of Assyria. And the fourth river is the Euphrates. (2:10-14)[14]

God, not man, planted the garden and, by extension, the entire earth. Adam, who is neither the creator of the earth nor the planter of the garden, is to preserve this garden and be sustained by it. The status of blessedness lies in that Adam is to enjoy his stay in the garden by just taking care of it, that is, by doing what is required as a caretaker, to preserve God's work: "The Lord God took the man and put him in the garden of Eden to relax[15] by working the earth and keeping it." (v.15) As caretaker, however, Adam is to follow the will of the owner: "And the Lord God commanded the man, saying, 'You may freely eat of every tree of the garden; but of the tree of the knowledge of good and evil you shall not eat, for in the day that you eat of it you shall die.'" (vv.16-17) This commandment is actually a reminder to Adam that he is merely the caretaker of God's earth and all that lives in and on it. Adam is not the actual owner of the earth or the garden, and he is not to act as a deity who would know good and evil, that is, know everything.[16]

The breaking of God's will expressed in his command transposes Adam's state from one under a divine blessing to one under a divine curse. The ground (*'adamah*) of the garden where man (*'adam*) was meant to rest, and which was supposed to

---

[14] This passage clearly looks ahead since the last two rivers are in Mesopotamia where the subsequent revolt of mankind will take place (11:1-9) and where the children of Israel will be exiled.

[15] The Hebrew verb *nuaḥ* found in the original Hebrew is from the same root as the noun *Noah* and means "relax." Its fits the fact that Noah was the first to plant a vineyard from which is made wine (Gen 9:20-21) that is drunk at festivities meant for relaxation and enjoyment.

[16] See footnote 13.

support man as a caring mother would, is now a place where man will have to toil to get the same result (3:17-19).

One should not imagine, however, that Adam was expulsed out of a specific geographical location. Rather, the blessing that man and animal and vegetation multiply and enjoy God's earth is taken away, and all creation—animal (represented in the serpent), human beings, and the ground that supports the vegetation as food for both—will now have to struggle to survive rather than live easily.

One can see how God's blessing in Genesis 1, connected with procreation and the earth as food-producing "mother," is countered by the curse of Genesis 3 concerning woman as child-bearer:

> The Lord God said to the serpent, "Because you have done this, cursed are you above all cattle, and above all wild animals; upon your belly you shall go, and dust you shall eat all the days of your life. I will put enmity between you and the woman, and *between your seed and her seed*; he shall bruise your head, and you shall bruise his heel." To the woman he said, "*I will greatly multiply your pain in childbearing; in pain you shall bring forth children*, yet your desire shall be for your husband, and he shall rule over you." And to Adam he said, "Because you have listened to the voice of your wife, and have eaten of the tree of which I commanded you, 'You shall not eat of it,' *cursed is the ground because of you*; in toil you shall eat of it all the days of your life; *thorns and thistles it shall bring forth to you*; and you shall eat the plants of the field. In the sweat of your face you shall eat bread till you return to the ground, for out of it you were taken; you are dust, and to dust you shall return." The man called his wife's name Eve, because she was the mother of every living one. (vv.14-20)

It is striking that this passage ends with naming the woman Eve (*ḥawwah*), in conjunction with her being "mother of every living one (*ḥay*)."[17] Just as the divine punishment takes away from Adam the "relaxation" in living without taking away his life, so also the same punishment takes away from woman the "consolation" in birth-giving without taking away procreation itself. This allows God's original blessing to continue in spite of man's sin. The intention on the part of the author to show that life as created by God will continue is made clear in the phrasing of the immediately following text that links Adam and the woman, on the one hand, with the following human generation represented by Cain, on the other hand:

> Therefore the Lord God sent him forth from the garden of Eden, to work the ground from which he was taken. He drove out the man; and at the east of the garden of Eden he placed the cherubim, and a flaming sword which turned every way, to guard the way to the tree of life. Now Adam knew Eve his wife, and she conceived and bore Cain, saying, "I have acquired a man with the Lord." And again, she bore his brother Abel. Now Abel was a keeper of sheep, and Cain a worker of the ground. (3:23-4:2)

Notice that Adam himself is granted to work outside the garden, and Cain continues this mission of working the ground, which was the duty assigned to Adam in the garden.[18] More importantly, however, Cain is "acquired"[19] by Eve "with the Lord," meaning that he is acquired with God's will and blessing.

Cain lives in the earth into which Adam was expelled, at the east of Eden: "He drove out the man; and *at the east of the garden*

---

[17] *ḥawwah* is from the same root as *ḥay*.

[18] This confirms what I said before regarding the punishment of Adam as being a change in condition rather than a geographical relocation.

[19] Both "Cain" and "acquire" are from the same root in Hebrew.

From Adam to Abraham

of Eden he made dwell the cherubim, and a flaming sword which turned every way, to guard the way to the tree of life ... Then Cain went away from the presence of the Lord, and *dwelt* in the earth of Nod, *east of Eden.*" (3:24; 4:16) Besides being a life of hardship, compared with one of enjoyment in the garden,[20] this new life differs in two more aspects: (1) it is a life of wandering and (2) it is away from the tree of life.

The wandering feature lies in the name *Nod* ([earth of] wandering) which is from the same root as *nad* (wanderer):

> When you work the ground, it shall no longer yield to you its strength; you shall be a fugitive and a wanderer (*nad*) on the earth." Cain said to the Lord, "My punishment is greater than I can bear. Behold, thou hast driven me this day away from the ground; and from thy face I shall be hidden; and I shall be a fugitive and a wanderer (*nad*) on the earth, and whoever finds me will slay me. Then the Lord said to him, "Not so! If any one slays Cain, vengeance shall be taken on him sevenfold." And the Lord put a mark on Cain, lest any who came upon him should kill him. Then Cain went away from the presence of the Lord, and dwelt in the earth of *Nod*, east of Eden." (4:12-16)

Notice that Cain's earth of "dwelling" (from the root *shakan*) is the earth of his "wandering" situated "at the east of Eden." This means that he is bound to wander outside the garden at whose entrance God "made dwell (from the same root *shakan*) the cherubim, and a flaming sword which turned every way, to guard the way to the tree of life" (3:24) which "the Lord God

---

[20] Compare 4:11-12 (And now you [Cain] are cursed from the ground ...When you work the ground, it shall no longer yield to you its strength) with 3:17-19 (cursed is the ground because of you [Adam]; in toil you shall eat of it all the days of your life; thorns and thistles it shall bring forth to you; and you shall eat the plants of the field. In the sweat of your face you shall eat bread till you return to the ground).

made to grow in the midst of the garden" (2:9), forever a reminder that the human beings should have been dwelling where the cherubim were made to dwell instead. The divine punishment of expulsion is phrased thus:

> Then the Lord God said, "Behold, the man has become like one of us, knowing good and evil; and now, lest he put forth his hand and take also of the tree of life, and eat, and live for ever"— therefore the Lord God sent him forth from the garden of Eden, to till the ground from which he was taken. He drove out the man; and at the east of the garden of Eden he placed the cherubim, and a flaming sword which turned every way, to guard the way to the tree of life. (3:22-24)

In the garden of Eden, man was forbidden to eat of the fruit of the tree of the knowledge of good and evil, but not of the tree of life. However, eating the fruit of the tree of life would not save man from God's verdict when he disobeyed his commandment, nor would it grant him "life unto eternity." The "life" from this tree does not refer to eternal life; rather it refers to length of days on earth granted forever under God's aegis. Actually, God's verdict imposed the *ceasing* of eating of the fruit of the tree of life, and this divine verdict shortened man's sojourn in the garden.[21] Yet God granted "the man"[22] to continue to live

---

[21] Compare, for instance, the divine commandment: "Honor your father and your mother, that your days may be long in the land which the Lord your God gives you" (Ex 20:12) with the divine verdicts "Whoever strikes his father or his mother shall be put to death" (21:15) and "Whoever curses his father or his mother shall be put to death" (21:17).

[22] In Gen 1-3 there is an interplay between "man" (*'adam*) referring to the individual and functioning as a personal name, and "the man" (*ha'adam*) referring to humankind. Notice for instance Gen 1:27: "So God created *the man* (*ha'adam*) in his own image, in the image of God he created him; *male and female he created them*." The "him" in "in the image of God he created him" is accounted for on the basis that the noun *'adam* in Hebrew is grammatically masculine in the same way as "earth" (*'eretz*) is

outside the garden. And, as we shall see, this same divine verdict that shortened the sojourn of man in the garden will shorten the life of the children of Jacob in the earth God grants to them, whenever they contravene his commandments.

The Post-Adamic Story

The same theme—that God is concerned with his entire creation—is evident in the chapters that deal with Adam's progeny (Gen 4-5) and Noah's story (Gen 6-9). Human beings are singled out only inasmuch as God's commandments are addressed to them. The first Adamic genealogy (Gen 4:17-24) includes the story of Cain (vv.1-16) and depicts the development of human civilization: notice how Cain's first action is to build a city (v.17).[23] However, civilization per se, which is the outcome of the human being's endeavor, is looked upon negatively in the Bible.[24] The story of Cain culminates with Lamech multiplying sevenfold Cain's destructive action by not caring for his fellow human being (vv.23-24).

Another possibility for humanity is suggested in the parallel genealogy via Seth, Cain's brother. It is a short genealogy that starts with Adam and ends with Seth's son, Enosh, in whose time "men began to call upon the name of the Lord:"

> And Adam knew his wife again, and she bore a son and called his name Seth, for she said, "God has appointed for me another child instead of Abel, for Cain slew him." To Seth also a son was born,

---

feminine and "garden" (*gen*) is masculine. Hebrew morphology has only two genders: masculine and feminine.
[23] Both civilization and city are from the same Latin root *civ*— pertaining to life in and around the city.
[24] This motif will be developed further in the story of the tower of Babel (Gen 11) and in the story of Solomon the city and temple "builder" (1 Kg 6:15-7:51).

and he called his name Enosh. At that time men began to call upon the name of the Lord. (4:25-26).

Contrary to Cain's "way," it is this lifestyle that speaks of the human being behaving as he should, according to God's will. Notice the following features of this short passage:

1. Compare Cain, whom Eve "acquired with God," with Seth, whom "God has appointed for me (viz. Eve) [another child]." Although acquired with (the help of) God, Cain is still Eve's realization (she is the subject of the verb "acquired'), whereas Seth is a gift from God to Eve (God is the subject of the verb "appointed").[25] So Seth is "posited" by God according to his will.

2. This Seth—a man according to God's will—produces Enosh, which is another Hebrew word that means "human being" and thus corresponds to Adam. Seth, son of "man," produces another "man" and another genealogy: he is capable of doing so because he was "appointed" by God himself.

3. Whereas Cain is a worker of the ground (Gen 4:3), Seth is appointed in place of Abel (v.25) and thus a shepherd (v.4). Cain is sedentary and a founder of the city and civilization. In doing this, he introduces an element foreign to the earth as created by God. On the other hand, Seth, with his sheep, roams God's earth feeding on it, the way God intended it to be (1:29-30).

---

[25] In Hebrew the wordplay is intended since the Hebrew name *shet* (Seth) is from the same root as the Hebrew verb *shit* meaning "appoint, put, give."

4. Cain, the builder of cities, erects conduits to supply water. Seth, the shepherd, relies on the rain that God alone provides; thus he truly "calls upon the Lord," and his worship is genuine: "Give us this day the bread unto life (which will sustain us until tomorrow)." (Mt 6:11)

These genealogies offer the two possibilities with two very different ways of life: one way is relying on God's earth and thus on God himself; the other way, in contradistinction, is relying on oneself and one's accomplishments. Scripture opts for the former, since the third genealogy that leads to Noah, through whom God's entire creation will continue, is through Seth (Gen 5:4-8). In this third genealogy we find a much clearer indication that complete obedience to God by walking *all the time*[26] with him (5:22, 24)[27] is the true "way" that humanity is to follow in order to vouchsafe the preservation of God's creation. This feat, we are told, was accomplished by Enoch (*ḥanok*). His singularity as the prime example to follow is evidenced in the following:

1. Enoch is in the seventh position in the ten-tiered genealogy. In symbolic numerology, the numeral 10 refers to the fullness of human history, whereas the number 7 reflects the same but carried on under God's aegis.

2. Enoch's life span, though shorter than others, is 365 years (v.23). This corresponds to the fullness that is

---

[26] This is the technical meaning of the Hebrew *hithallek* (walking to and fro; keep walking) when compared to *halak* (walk in a certain direction).
[27] Notice the repetition, a sign of underscoring, at the beginning and end of the passage on Enoch.

needed, just as a year (365 days) reflects the fullness of all seasons and thus the full rotation of time; this, when extended, only becomes repetitive.

3. The name Enoch is from the root *ḥnk* having the connotation of "dedication."[28] Hence, Enoch is someone who is dedicated, that is, someone who dedicates his entire life to God by continually walking with him.

Consequently, Enoch is the corrective counterpart to Adam. His way of life, if followed by human beings, will prove to be the guarantee for the continuation of all life on God's earth. This will soon be confirmed in that Noah, who will survive the flood that threatened all life on earth, is introduced as one who "walked (*hithallek*) with God" (6:9) just as Enoch did. Where Adam failed, Noah succeeded by following in the footsteps of Enoch. Enoch was so perfect that in him is realized the original promise given to Adam namely, that should he abide by God's command, he would not die. Indeed in Genesis 5 all the patriarchs, including Noah (9:29), die at the end of their earthly life. Of Enoch it is simply written: "and he was not, *for* God took (received) him." (5:24) That is to say, because he "walked with God" during his life on God's earth, God did not strike him with the penalty with which he struck Adam and his progeny.

---

[28] *Hanukkah*, which is the Feast of the (Re)dedication of the Temple under the Maccabees, comes from the same root.

Noah

What was said of the entire humanity is now applied to one man's progeny. Noah and his world function as the exemplar[29] that underscores the scriptural thesis namely, that all ill in the realm of God's creation lies in man's disobedience to God's commands. The biblical description of the creation's status in Noah's times and God's reaction to it are depicted in the most vivid and shattering terms:

> The Lord saw that the wickedness of man was great in the earth, and that every imagination of the thoughts of his heart was only evil continually. And the Lord was sorry that he had made man on the earth, and it grieved him to his heart. So the Lord said, "I will blot out man whom I have created from the face of the ground, man and beast and creeping things and birds of the air, for I am sorry that I have made them." (Gen 6:5-7)

However, given that Noah's righteousness and blamelessness in his walking with God (v.8), the Lord, in his gracefulness, decides to give the world and all creation a second and lasting chance. To underscore that this second chance is as willful as his first one when he created Adam, God commits himself one-sidedly through a covenant binding only to him. Indeed the sign of this covenant, the rainbow, is solely in God's hands; human beings have no control over it (9:12-17). What is important in the rendering of this story is that it underscores God's faithfulness: he commits himself through a promise which he upholds. Before the unleashing of the flood, God says:

---

[29] I qualified Noah's as being "the" and not just "an" exemplar because he functions as the only human of his generation, together with his immediate family, to have survived the flood and thus appears to be as another Adam. This handling of the matter was needed in order to make God's covenant and what it entails (see below) binding on all human beings.

> For behold, I will bring a flood of waters upon the earth, to destroy all flesh in which is the breath of life from under heaven; everything that is on the earth shall die. *But I will establish my covenant with you*; and you shall come into the ark, you, your sons, your wife, and your sons' wives with you. And of every living thing of all flesh, you shall bring two of every sort into the ark, to keep them alive with you; they shall be male and female. Of the birds according to their kinds, and of the animals according to their kinds, of every creeping thing of the ground according to its kind, two of every sort shall come in to you, to keep them alive. Also take with you every sort of food that is eaten, and store it up; and it shall serve as food for you and for them. (6:17-21)

And at the termination of the same flood, God establishes the promised covenant:

> Behold, I establish my covenant with you and your descendants after you, and with every living creature that is with you, the birds, the cattle, and every beast of the earth with you, as many as came out of the ark. I establish my covenant with you, that never again shall all flesh be cut off by the waters of a flood, and never again shall there be a flood to destroy the earth. (9:9-11)

What is not to be missed is that here again we see that God is dealing with the entire creation and not just with the human beings.[30] Thus God's covenanted promise and his purview continue to be all-encompassing and not exclusive, just as in Adam's times. The Adamic "creation" sets the tone for God's continuous action of "salvation;" Noah is only a particular case of that broader picture.

Although the covenant is a commitment on God's part to protect his creation, this does not mean that the human being is "off the hook." Indeed, God the "King," who is the sole

---

[30] The sea animals are not included since the flood does not affect them.

proprietor of everything that exists,[31] is also the Judge who will come to requite the human beings who are assigned as custodians of his creation and world. Their accountability will be reflected in obedience to God's commands, just as it was in Adam's case. Obeying God is precisely what Noah is said to have repeatedly done: "Noah did this; he did all that God commanded him." (6:22; see also 7:5, 9, 16) Noah succeeded where his predecessor, Adam, failed. Noah's success, however, was foreshadowed in Enoch's behavior. Both are presented as a challenge for the rest of humanity, but neither can function as an automatic guarantee that the rest of humanity will be favorably judged by God, since each man will be equitably judged according to his behavior:

> Son of man, when an earth sins against me by acting faithlessly, and I stretch out my hand against it, and break its staff of bread and send famine upon it, and cut off from it man and beast, even if these three men, Noah, Daniel, and Job, were in it, they would deliver but their own lives by their righteousness, says the Lord God. If I cause wild beasts to pass through the earth, and they ravage it, and it be made desolate, so that no man may pass through because of the beasts; even if these three men were in it, as I live, says the Lord God, they would deliver neither sons nor daughters; they alone would be delivered, but the earth would be desolate. Or if I bring a sword upon that earth, and say, Let a sword go through the earth; and I cut off from it man and beast; though these three men were in it, as I live, says the Lord God, they would deliver neither sons nor daughters, but they alone would be delivered. Or if I send a pestilence into that earth, and pour out my wrath upon it with blood, to cut off from it man and beast; even if Noah, Daniel, and Job were in it, as I live, says the

---

[31] The Hebrew root *mlk* has the connotation of "ownership, proprietorship, possession."

Lord God, they would deliver neither son nor daughter; they would deliver but their own lives by their righteousness. (Ezek 14:13-20)

Thus Enoch's behavior did not guarantee that his son, Methuselah, his grandson, Lamech, or even that Noah would not die (5:27, 31; 9:29). Indeed, God's earth is put in jeopardy when one of Noah's children contravened what would be shown to be the first divine commandment dealing with the behavior between human beings: respect for one's parents (9:22-27)[32]. The importance of this is that such behavior reflects the same kind of attitude toward God, who is our ultimate parent.

---

[32] "Honor your father and your mother, that your days may be long in the land which the Lord your God gives you" (Ex 20:12); "Honor your father and your mother, as the Lord your God commanded you; that your days may be prolonged, and that it may go well with you, in the land which the Lord your God gives you." (Deut 5:16)

2

The Patriarchal Narratives

Now that the covenant is introduced as binding on God in his gracefulness and on all human beings in their obedience to him, scripture moves in another direction to show how man keeps contravening this expectation of obedience. The story of Jacob, one descendant of Noah, is used as an exemplar of man's continuing disobedience in spite of God's continuing gracefulness. This is so much the case that the readers of the scriptural text are to view themselves as part of the biblical Israel.[1] This is not just a matter of necessary literary fiction; it is imposed by the biblical literature itself since it presents the story of Jacob *along the same lines* as the stories of Adam and Noah. The stories of Adam and Noah shape the presentation of the subsequent expanded biblical story of Jacob and his progeny between Genesis 25:19 and 2 Kings 25:30. So just as the narratives of Adam and Noah contain the entire thesis of scripture, the overarching patriarchal narratives do the same, only in more detail.

The questions that then arise are: Why include stories of Abraham and Isaac and not just those of Jacob? Why the transition to the main character of the biblical story via Abraham and Isaac, or why not via only one of the two? In order to answer these questions, let me begin by pointing out the obvious strong parallelism between Abraham and Jacob, with Isaac functioning

---

[1] In the same way, for example, as the hearer of the Book of Proverbs has to assume that he is the "son" and the "disciple" referred to in that book, and the hearers of Paul's message to the Corinthians have to assume the role of themselves being those Corinthians.

as "bridge" between the other two. In the biblical text, the main bulk of the information connected with Isaac deals with him as the son of Abraham (his birth and potential sacrifice) or as the father of Jacob (the rather lengthy story of his marriage, the blessing of Jacob rather than Esau). The only exception is his dealings with Abimelech, which will be discussed later. As for Abraham and Jacob, their stories are much more "substantial." One can, so to speak, "make a movie" of either without much of a role for Isaac. An "Isaac movie," however, cannot be done without a starring role for either Abraham or Jacob.

It is also important to point out that the stories of all three forefathers, Abraham, Isaac, and Jacob, have one feature in common and that is God's underlying interest in the entire humanity. Just as God had in his purview *all* the descendants of Adam and *all* the descendants of Noah, so also here in the patriarchal narratives he cares for *all* the descendants of Abraham. Just as with Noah where care is taken to account for the genealogy of all three of his children, so also here in the patriarchal narratives we are appraised in detail of the fate of the progeny of Ishmael and Esau. In the same statement in which God speaks of his covenant with the not yet born Isaac, he promises to care for Ishmael by making him a full people of twelve tribes:

> No, but Sarah your wife shall bear you a son, and you shall call his name Isaac. I will establish my covenant with him as an everlasting covenant for his descendants after him. As for Ishmael, I have heard you; behold, *I will bless him and make him fruitful and multiply him exceedingly; he shall be the father of twelve princes, and I will make him a great nation.* But I will establish my covenant with Isaac, whom Sarah shall bear to you at this season next year. (17:19-21)

The Patriarchal Narratives

Not only are Ishmael's descendants accounted for one by one, but we are also told that God allocates for them the earth of Havilah, which is watered by Pishon, one of the four rivers that flowed out of Eden:

> These are the descendants of Ishmael, Abraham's son, whom Hagar the Egyptian, Sarah's maid, bore to Abraham. These are the names of the sons of Ishmael, named in the order of their birth: Nebaioth, the first-born of Ishmael; and Kedar, Adbeel, Mibsam, Mishma, Dumah, Massa, Hadad, Tema, Jetur, Naphish, and Kedemah. *These are the sons of Ishmael and these are their names, by their villages and by their encampments, twelve princes according to their tribes.* (These are the years of the life of Ishmael, a hundred and thirty-seven years; he breathed his last and died, and was gathered to his kindred.) They dwelt from Havilah to Shur, which is opposite Egypt in the direction of Assyria; he settled over against all his people. (25:12-18)

The same goes for Esau, Jacob's brother. Both his progeny and his area of sojourn are accounted for in a full chapter (Gen 31) of 43 verses.

Looking more closely at the stories of the three main characters in the patriarchal narratives, one can see that all three stories actually fuse into one single narrative, if viewed from the perspective of the earth that is promised to them by God. Indeed, the narrative starts with "Now the Lord said to Abram, 'Go from your earth and your kindred and your father's house to the earth that I will show you'" (Gen 12:1) and ends with a reference to that same earth. This is so whether one considers either the conclusion of Genesis (And Joseph said to his brothers, "I am about to die; but God will visit you, and bring you up out of this earth to the earth which he swore to Abraham, to Isaac, and to Jacob"; 50:24) or the conclusion of the entire Pentateuch

(And the Lord said to him [Moses], "This is the earth of which I swore to Abraham, to Isaac, and to Jacob, 'I will give it to your descendants.' I have let you see it with your eyes, but you shall not go over there"; Deut 34:4). The link between the end of Genesis and that of Deuteronomy is that the entire Law, and the statutes and commandments therein, is to be implemented precisely *on that same earth*. And, as with the descendants of Adam and Noah, Abraham's descendants, and more specifically Jacob and his progeny, will show that they did not hearken to God's commands, and consequently they will be thrown out of that earth (end of 2 Kings), the realm that was given them as a chance to prove their loyalty to God.

Looking closely at the three patriarchs, one notices that they act differently from the perspective of their sojourn on the earth granted to them by God. Abraham is born outside the earth of Canaan and dies in it. Conversely, Jacob is born in Canaan but dies outside it, in Egypt. Isaac is born in the earth of Canaan, *never leaves it*, and dies in it. It is then this Isaac in whom God's will is realized and only in him. Paul correctly understood this when he referred to him as "the son [who came about] of the free woman [Sarah] through [God's] promise" (Gal 4:23) and said to the Gentile Galatians that, if they are children (of God), then they are so as "children of that (same) promise, after the manner of Isaac" (v.28). Paul, the Jew (son of Israel), and they, the Gentiles, are heirs inasmuch as they are "children" *the way Isaac is*. It is as though Isaac has both what Abraham hopes for and Jacob keeps reminiscing about. Yet when Jacob's descendants are granted again that same earth, after a long exile in Egypt, rather

The Patriarchal Narratives

than behaving as Isaac did, they behave as their father did and end up losing that earth again, and are exiled to another Egypt.[2]

What is the reason behind this special handling of the patriarchal narratives? Before answering, let me recapitulate how scripture dealt with the story concerning humanity in general. The most striking feature of the story of humanity is unmistakably that scripture doubled it into two narratives: the Adamic and the Noachic stories. Man lost the perfect Eden due to his disobedience, yet despite this punishment, he persevered in his unruliness. God granted humanity another chance by restarting it through Noah, the obedient one. God even committed himself to a one-sided covenant. Through this covenant he relegated any full punishment until the end of times. At that time he will judge all humanity together and accept into his eternal "ark" only those who will have shown obedience as Noah did. Then he will establish forever his "new heavens and new earth," where the disobedient rebels will be cast out as in the days of Noah:

> For as the new heavens and the new earth which I will make shall remain before me, says the Lord; so shall your descendants and your name remain. From new moon to new moon, and from sabbath to sabbath, all flesh shall come to worship before me, says the Lord. And they shall go forth and look on the dead bodies of the men that have rebelled against me; for their worm shall not die, their fire shall not be quenched, and they shall be an abhorrence to all flesh. (Is 66:22-24)

---

[2] See, e.g., Hos 9:3 where the exile to Assyria is likened to a return to Egypt: "They shall not remain in the land of the Lord; but Ephraim shall return to Egypt, and they shall eat unclean food in Assyria."

But according to his promise we wait for new heavens and a new earth in which righteousness dwells. Therefore, beloved, since you wait for these, be zealous to be found by him without spot or blemish, and at peace. (2 Pet 3:13-14)

As were the days of Noah, so will be the coming of the Son of man. For as in those days before the flood they were eating and drinking, marrying and giving in marriage, until the day when Noah entered the ark, and they did not know until the flood came and swept them all away, so will be the coming of the Son of man. Then two men will be in the field; one is taken and one is left. Two women will be grinding at the mill; one is taken and one is left. Watch therefore, for you do not know on what day your Lord is coming. (Mt 24:37-42)

For if God did not spare the ancient world, but preserved Noah, a herald of righteousness, with seven other persons, when he brought a flood upon the world of the ungodly ... and if he rescued righteous Lot, greatly distressed by the licentiousness of the wicked ... then the Lord knows how to rescue the godly from trial, and to keep the unrighteous under punishment until the day of judgment. (2 Pet 2:5, 7, 9)

Noah's descendants proved to be as wicked as his predecessors, if not actually worse in that they wanted to counteract God's plan of populating the entire earth. God foils their obstinate sedition in order to implement his original will: "Be fruitful and multiply, and *fill the earth* and subdue it; and *have dominion* over the fish of the sea and over the birds of the air and *over every living thing that moves upon the earth.*" (Gen 1:28) As if to underscore the seriousness as well as the solemnity of his decision, God issues this same command thrice to Noah: "Be fruitful and multiply upon the earth ... Be fruitful and multiply, and fill the earth ... And you, be fruitful and multiply, bring forth abundantly on the earth and multiply in it." (8:17; 9:1, 7) And, once again, after having spread humanity all over the earth

The Patriarchal Narratives

he concentrates on one exemplar in order to show that any human living in any given location would do exactly as the earliest Adamic community did. Thus, ultimately, God will be shown to be "justified in his sentence and blameless in his judgment" (Ps 51:4).

So this explains the extra care given to Israel as the biblical exemplar community, similar to that given to Adam. Just as Adam was set in a garden that was already planted and made fruitful by God, Israel is granted a good earth already "flowing with milk and honey." However, as in the case of Adam, the only condition required of Israel is to heed God's commandments:

> You shall therefore keep all the commandment which I command you this day, that you may be strong, and go in and inherit of the earth which you are going over to inherit, and that you may live long on the ground (*'adamah*) which the Lord swore to your fathers to give to them and to their descendants, an earth flowing with milk and honey. For the earth which you are entering to inherit of it is not like the earth of Egypt, from which you have come, where you sowed your seed and *watered* it with your feet, like a *garden* of vegetables; but the earth which you are going over to inherit is an earth of hills and valleys, which drinks water by the rain from heaven, an earth which the Lord your God cares for; the eyes of the Lord your God are always upon it, from the beginning of the year to the end of the year. And if you will obey my commandments which I command you this day, to love the Lord your God, and to serve him with all your heart and with all your soul, I will *give the rain* for your earth in its season, the early rain and the later rain, that you may gather in your grain and your wine and your oil. And I will give *grass in your fields* for your *beasts*, and you shall eat and be full. Take heed lest your heart be deceived, and you turn aside and serve other gods and worship

them, and the anger of the Lord be kindled against you, and he shut up the heavens, so that there be no rain, and the ground (*'adamah*) yield no fruit, and you perish quickly off the good earth which the Lord gives you. (Deut 11:8-17)

The intended parallelism in phraseology with Genesis 1-2 is unmistakable. The earth granted to Israel is not a possession; it is an inheritance. It is another ground and a garden for man to live on, sharing it with all other beings, human and animal alike. The difference, however, is that the commandment given to Israel, unlike that given to Adam, is within the confines of a covenant:

> And now I am about to go the way of all the earth, and you know in your hearts and souls, all of you, that not one thing has failed of all the good things which the Lord your God promised concerning you; all have come to pass for you, not one of them has failed. But just as all the good things which the Lord your God promised concerning you have been fulfilled for you, so the Lord will bring upon you all the evil things, until he have destroyed you from off this good earth which the Lord your God has given you, if you transgress the covenant of the Lord your God, which he commanded you, and go and serve other gods and bow down to them. Then the anger of the Lord will be kindled against you, and you shall perish quickly from off the good earth which he has given to you. (Josh 23:14-16)

> The word that came to Jeremiah from the Lord: "Hear the words of this covenant, and speak to the men of Judah and the inhabitants of Jerusalem. You shall say to them, Thus says the Lord, the God of Israel: Cursed be the man who does not heed the words of this covenant which I commanded your fathers when I brought them out of the earth of Egypt, from the iron furnace, saying, Listen to my voice, and do all that I command you. So shall you be my people, and I will be your God, that I may perform the oath which I swore to your fathers, to give them an earth flowing with milk and honey, as at this day ... Hear the

The Patriarchal Narratives 53

words of this covenant and do them. For I solemnly warned your fathers when I brought them up out of the earth of Egypt, warning them persistently, even to this day, saying, Obey my voice. Yet they did not obey or incline their ear, but every one walked in the stubbornness of his evil heart. Therefore I brought upon them all the words of this covenant, which I commanded them to do, but they did not." (Jer 11:1-8)

The covenant put Israel in a position similar to that of Noah, meaning that they are given a *second* chance. Indeed, the earth or ground that is granted to them is the same earth or ground in which they were born and yet was deserted by them to go down to Egypt, the earth of their slavery.

Before discussing in detail Genesis 12-50, which forms the introduction to and the basis for the rest of scripture, both Old and New Testaments, let me sum up its most salient features:

1. Unlike any of the other descendants of Adam or Noah, the story of Jacob and his progeny is prefaced with a lengthy story of his origins.

2. This story of origins includes that of the father and also of the grandfather. Moreover, it is the story of the grandfather, rather than that of the father, which is expanded. It is as though Jacob is the child of Abraham via Isaac. This is confirmed in the rest of the biblical story where the father of the "Israelites" is Abraham.

3. The importance of Isaac as the "bridge" between Abraham and Jacob lies in that the story of Abraham looks toward Isaac, and the story of Jacob looks back to him, especially from the perspective of the "earth"

where Jacob sojourns. Put otherwise, Isaac enjoyed fully what Abraham hoped for and what Jacob never fully enjoyed. Jacob and his "children" will always be, as Adam was, in the dilemma of choosing between the divine blessing and the divine curse in conjunction with their doing or neglecting to do God's commandments.

4. The importance of the previous feature can be seen in that, already in this story of the origins, we have, in a nutshell, the predicament of Jacob. Though "blessed" he ends up having to toil outside of his earth of birth in order to secure a progeny. And when he returns to this same earth, he is welcomed by his wronged brother, Esau. Still, Jacob squanders this opportunity by again leaving Canaan to end his days in Egypt, the earth where his progeny will be enslaved for many centuries. Put succinctly, the dust of the "earth" from which he was taken and to which he was supposed to return keeps eluding him.

5. Abraham is indeed the "father" of Jacob in that Abraham's story reflects a life of vacillation similar to that of Jacob. This is important in view of the expanded story of Jacob, at the end of which his descendants land among the Chaldeans, where Abraham started. As we shall see, it is there that the same offer which was made to Abraham is made to Israel. This time around, however, there is a surer hope in the sense that, should Israel follow in the footsteps of Abraham, Isaac will be before, that is, "ahead" of them as a beacon of light they can follow.

3
Abraham

The Abraham story begins with God's invitation to Abraham that he relinquish his "earth" of origin for the "earth" God was going to show him: "Go from your earth and your kindred and your father's house to the earth that I will show you." (Gen 12:1) Since this move is intended to end up with a blessing on "all the families of the ground (*'adamah*)" (v.3) and thus to every man (*'adam*), it stands to reason that Abraham's new earth is, after all, a piece of the same global earth that pertains to God: "The earth is the Lord's and the fullness thereof, the world and those who dwell therein." (Ps 24:1) The intention is clear: Abraham is chosen as a specific exemplar of the children of Adam. Just as Adam was assigned a garden within God's earth in order to live and also be tested as to whether he will abide by God's will, so also Abraham is assigned a location of God's choosing. The similarity between the two cases is that Abraham ends up alone—away from his earth of origin, his kindred and his father's house, and without progeny (Now Sarai was barren; she had no child; Gen 11:30).

Abraham is shown as having failed the test of obedience very early. Instead of counting on God when famine struck, he decided to go down and fetch bread in an earth with a great river similar to his earth of origin. This episode is axial since it not only harkens back to Adam, but also looks to what lies ahead to the time when Jacob and his children will behave in a similar manner.

The rest of Abraham's story is a proverb: whenever one follows God's will, one fares well; whenever one challenges that will, one is put to shame. Let us examine more closely that story.

Abraham the Hebrew

The most basic feature of Abraham is that he is presented as a "Hebrew." It is this characteristic that functions as a compass in his relation to God. The word Hebrew (*'ibri*) is from the same root as the verb *'abar* meaning to journey within a given earth. Thus to be a Hebrew ultimately is to be on the go, similar to a shepherd, with an abode being a tent and not a house of brick or stone. The corollary is that one uses the earth without possessing it. Such a way of life also corresponds to the verb *hithallek*, meaning to walk to and fro. This was the lifestyle of both Enoch and Noah (Gen 5:12, 14; 6:9) who are prime paradigms of what man should be like, and this is precisely what Abraham was asked to do in order to secure for himself and his children life on the area assigned to him:

> The Lord said to Abram, after Lot had separated from him, "Lift up your eyes, and look from the place where you are, northward and southward and eastward and westward; for all the earth which you see I will give to you and to your descendants for ever. I will make your descendants as the dust of the earth; so that if one can count the dust of the earth, your descendants also can be counted. Arise, walk (*hithallek*) through the length and the breadth of the earth, for I will give it to you." (13:14-17)

Notice how the earth that is promised to Abraham is not a defined property. Rather it is the breadth of ground he can see from the place where he is at. From the perspective of a shepherd this means that he would be granted enough pasture for himself and his herd and flock. Indeed, immediately following God's promise we hear: "So Abram *moved his tent*,[1] and came and dwelt by the oaks of Mamre, which are at Hebron; and there he built an altar to the Lord." (v.18) The following passage, where the oaks of Mamre are mentioned, introduces Abraham as "the Hebrew": "Then one who had escaped came, and told Abram the Hebrew, who was living by the oaks of Mamre the Amorite, brother of Eshcol and of Aner; these were allies of Abram." (14:13) Chapter 14 is a very interesting passage. It appears to be self-contained; yet its intent is to assure the reader that God's promise will be fulfilled so long as Abraham accepts God's offer for him to be a "Hebrew" and enjoy the earth as a gift from God without ever possessing it. This is to say that as a Hebrew, a sojourner on the earth, Abraham will have God's protection even against the kings of Mesopotamia. The irony is that later Abraham's descendants will fall prey to the kings of Mesopotamia when they decide to establish their own "kings" instead of relying on God to protect them against their adversaries. Those descendants will not have heeded the statement of their forbears: "Pharaoh said to his [Joseph's] brothers, 'What is your occupation?' And they said to Pharaoh, 'Your servants are shepherds, as our fathers were.'" (47:3)

The Covenant of Trust

The status of Hebrew required full trust in God on Abraham's part. Earlier in the story he faltered by going down to Egypt for bread, instead of trusting in God. After learning that the fruits of the earth are the work of God and not of man (just as was the case in Eden) and that his actual survival is not from the earth

---

[1] This phrase is actually one word in Hebrew, which gives the clear impression that Abram understood God's promise as an order for him to keep moving and he immediately did so.

but from God, Abraham is tested to see whether he truly believes that the blessedness of progeny is also a gift from God and not linked to man's inherent biological energy. This test is elaborated in the story of Ishmael and Isaac. Despite Abraham's original trust in God, which insured that he be considered righteous in God's eyes (15:6), he later counted on his own and his wife's devices to implement the success of God's promise regarding his progeny. That is why although Abraham's son Ishmael is fully included in the divine promise—he is even circumcised (17:23-27)—the true heir will be Isaac, who is "called into life" directly by God through a promise (17:21; 18:10, 14; 21:1-2), just as Abraham was "called into a new life" by the same God in conjunction with a promise (12:1-3). However, Isaac will forever be a "thorn in the flesh" for Abraham and his descendants. In Hebrew *yitzḥaq* means "he laughs." So not only is Isaac's name a reminder that Abraham, the man of trust in God, and his wife laughed at God's promise (17:17; 18:12),[2] but his birth is preceded by the institution of the covenant of circumcision to which Isaac will be bound and which ensures real sonship to Abraham.

The covenant of circumcision in the story of Abraham functions the same way as the covenant with Noah functioned in the story of humanity. In the case of Noah, humanity, which was about to be extinct due to its sin against God's will, was saved until the end of times through a unilateral commitment on God's part. Here also, in spite of Abraham's blunder of going down to Egypt, which almost ended with the loss of Sarah, the "mother" of Isaac, God again commits himself unilaterally to a

---

[2] The story has a pun to it. It is as though God is saying to them: "He who laughs last laughs best." Indeed, the name Isaac in Hebrew assumes that there is a person (he) that is laughing continually!

biblical exemplar of that same humanity. Again, just as the covenant with Noah was encompassing, so also the covenant of circumcision is all encompassing. Indeed, not only is it instituted before Isaac the heir is born, but it is not linked to biological standards:

> And I will establish my covenant between me and you and *your progeny* after you throughout their generations for an everlasting covenant, to be God to you and to *your progeny* after you. And I will give to you, and to *your progeny* after you, *the earth of your sojournings*, all the earth of Canaan, for an everlasting possession; and *I will be their God.* As for you, you shall keep my covenant, you and *your progeny* after you throughout their generations. This is my covenant, which you shall keep, between me and you and *your progeny* after you: Every male among you shall be circumcised. You shall be circumcised in the flesh of your foreskins, and it shall be a sign of the covenant between me and you. *He that is eight days old among you shall be circumcised; every male throughout your generations, whether born in your household, or bought with your money from any foreigner who is not of your offspring, both he that is born in your house and he that is bought with your money, shall be circumcised.* So shall my covenant be in your flesh an everlasting covenant. Any uncircumcised male who is not circumcised in the flesh of his foreskin shall be cut off from his people; he has broken my covenant. (Gen 17:7-14)

The salient features of this covenant are unmistakable:

1. The descendants of the biblical Abraham are not his biological progeny, but rather anyone, even a foreigner or a slave, who is circumcised. In Hebrew, the pun is striking. What is translated as progeny (and sometimes translated as "descendants") is actually the Hebrew *zera'* meaning literally "seed," and it is the

same term applied to the seed of vegetation. In other words, it is essentially biological. However, as Paul correctly understood and explained it in Galatians (3:6-14), the real progeny of the biblical Abraham are not those whom he begets, but rather *all* those who are under God's covenant.

2. Just as in the case with Noah where the covenant was all-inclusive of God's entire creation on earth, so also here circumcision is all-encompassing in the sense that it includes not only Abraham's biological progeny, including Ishmael (Gen 17:25), but also all those who live in Abraham's household, even the outsiders (vv.12-13, 23).

3. The sign of circumcision on the eighth day of age could not be a decision made by the one being circumcised. The intent is to stress divine gracefulness and that to be a member of Abraham's family is a gift from God and not an acquired right through birth.

4. Last and in no way least, the earth granted to the progeny of Abraham is that of their "sojournings." This term is from the same root as the verb "sojourn" that describes the patriarchs' stay in Egypt (12:19; 47:4), the earth of the Philistines (21:34), and Haran (32:4). From the same root we have the noun "sojourner" which is used to speak of Israel's status in Egypt (15:13) as well as that of Abraham in Canaan (23:4). In the latter instance it is used in conjunction with Abraham's having no piece of land to bury Sarah. The lesson is clear: Canaan is no more a possession for Abraham and his progeny than is Egypt

or the earth of the Philistines or Mesopotamia. Canaan is just a place to live in during one's lifetime, together with all the other inhabitants, without any right of ownership. God alone is the "King" who possesses all the earth and grants it to his creatures. Anyone who behaves contrary to this premise breaks the covenant of circumcision and comes under the curse of being "cut off" from the people and the earth. Indeed, as we shall see later, Canaan will prove to be the earth of Israel's testing where they will have to show through their behavior whether they consider the earth theirs or God's. One of the aspects of this test will be how they deal with those who share Canaan with them: "You shall not wrong a sojourner or oppress him, for you were sojourners in the earth of Egypt" (Ex 22:21); "You shall not oppress a sojourner; you know the heart of a sojourner, for you were sojourners in the earth of Egypt." (Ex 23:9)

Earlier Noah's behavior, that is his walking with God, was the reason behind God's committing himself one-sidedly to a covenant. The covenant of circumcision requires similar behavior from Abraham:

> So the Lord said, "I will blot out man whom I have created from the face of the ground, man and beast and creeping things and birds of the air, for I am sorry that I have made them." But *Noah found favor in the eyes of the Lord.* These are the generations of Noah. *Noah was* a righteous man, *blameless* in his generation; Noah *walked with God* ... I will bring a flood of waters upon the earth, to destroy all flesh in which is the breath of life from under heaven; everything that is on the earth shall die. But I will establish my covenant with you. (Gen 6:7-9, 17-18)

When Abram was ninety-nine years old the Lord appeared to Abram, and said to him, "I am God Almighty; *walk before me, and be blameless*. And I will make my covenant between me and you, and will multiply you exceedingly." (Gen 17:1-2)

Abraham will prove to be blameless and will walk with God when he understands that everything on the earth granted him to live on belongs to God and thus is to be shared with others. Two lessons will teach Abraham the way, one is by God and the other is by a "stranger." In the first lesson, Isaac, the heir through whom Abraham is to secure his continual presence on earth, is required from him as an offering to God (Gen 22). This is to remind Abraham that the "security" of his own future remains at all times in God's hands. The other lesson is connected with the earth itself as patrimony. Let me begin with the latter.

Abraham did not have a burial lot on the earth granted to him. Such was offered to him as a gift by Ephron the Hittite, a sojourner on the earth just as Abraham was. Although Abraham ended up by purchasing the gift (23:17-20), the legacy of Ephron's magnanimity and his offer of sharing God's earth remains in the story: "Isaac and Ishmael his sons buried him [Abraham] in the cave of Machpelah, *in the field of Ephron the son of Zohar the Hittite*, east of Mamre, the field which Abraham purchased from the Hittites. There Abraham was buried, with Sarah his wife." (25:9-10) Hearers of the Bible, especially Abraham's progeny, are reminded that their forefather's burial place will remain forever within the field of Ephron the Hittite. Had the latter not been willing to give away or sell the cave, Abraham would not have had a foothold in Canaan.

But, in order to comprehend the fullness of the message of this pivotal story, it is necessary to delve further in the phraseology of the original text. First of all, Ephron's property is referred to as a "field," which is the same term used in Genesis 2-3 to speak of the earth to which vegetation and animals are connected:

> These are the generations of the heavens and the earth when they were created. In the day that the Lord God made the earth and the heavens, when no plant of the field was yet in the earth and no herb of the field had yet sprung up, for the Lord God had not caused it to rain upon the earth, and there was no man to till the ground ... So out of the ground the Lord God formed every beast of the field and every bird of the air, and brought them to the man to see what he would call them; and whatever the man called every living creature, that was its name. The man gave names to all cattle, and to the birds of the air, and to every beast of the field; but for the man there was not found a helper fit for him. (Gen 2:4-5, 19-20)

> Now the serpent was more subtle than all the beasts of the field that the Lord God had made ... The Lord God said to the serpent, "Because you have done this, cursed are you above all cattle, and above all the beasts of the field"[3] ... And to Adam he said, "Because you have listened to the voice of your wife, and have eaten of the tree of which I commanded you, 'You shall not eat of it,' cursed is the ground because of you; in toil you shall eat of it all the days of your life; thorns and thistles it shall bring forth to you; and you shall eat the plants of the field." (Gen 3:1, 14, 17-18)

Between Genesis 2-3 and 23, the word "field" appears only once in the story of Cain and Abel. Cain kills his "brother" while they were in the field (4:8). The hearer of the scriptural text cannot miss the connection. It is in the "field" that Ephron proved to be the true "son of Adam," the true human being. He offered to a

---

[3] The pun intended in the original lies in that "subtle" and "cursed" sound very close in Hebrew, *'arur* and *'arur* respectively.

stranger the field that Cain did not want to share with his own brother.

One should add a corollary aspect to this point. The estranged "brothers," Ishmael and Isaac, whom even Abraham was not able to bring together during his lifetime, end up together in the field transformed by Ephron's action: "Isaac and Ishmael his sons buried him in the cave of Machpelah, in the field of Ephron the son of Zohar the Hittite, east of Mamre, the field which Abraham purchased from the Hittites." (25:9-10) It is as though what Abraham was not able to do, Ephron's "humanity" brought to fruition. The linking of Ishmael and Isaac is further underscored in that at this precise juncture, at the same time and in the same terms, we are introduced to Ishmael's progeny and Isaac's progeny: "These are the descendants of Ishmael, *Abraham's son*" (v.12); "These are the descendants of Isaac, *Abraham's son.*" (v.19)

In Hebrew the name Ephron (*'ephron*) is from the same root as dust (*'aphar*) and the name Zohar (*tzohar*) from a root (*tzhr*) meaning yellowish-red, a color similar to the red alluded to in "ground" (*'adamah*) and in "man" (*'adam*). In Arabic the word *tzahr*, which is from the same root *tzhr*, means rock or a rocky earth. The conclusion is inescapable. The author wanted to convey the powerful message that Ephron's behavior is rooted in his correct conviction, consonant with the scriptural teaching, that as a human being, he is after all "dust from dust," and consequently "dust to dust," just as is Abraham. In other words, there is no difference whatsoever between the two in that both share the same earth, living or dead.

In conjunction with this episode of Ephron the Hittite, one cannot help but recall Paul's assertion: "When Gentiles who have not the law do by nature what the law requires, they are a law to themselves, even though they do not have the law. They show that what the law requires is written on their hearts, while their conscience also bears witness and their conflicting thoughts accuse or perhaps excuse them on that day when, according to my gospel, God judges the secrets of men by Christ Jesus." (Rom 2:14-16)

Abraham's Test

In order to ensure God's blessing to Abraham and through him to all the families of God's earth, Abraham has to pass a demanding test to show that he truly comprehends that his security lies in God's promise and not in his own endeavors and realizations. Abraham's test of obedience, if successful, will counterbalance his earlier disobedient behavior. Practically speaking, such a test has to revolve around Abraham's understanding of Isaac. Is Isaac *his* progeny or is Isaac a gift from God in order that Abraham's progeny be ensured *according to God's will?* In other words, Abraham has to be tested as to whether he truly believes that his future lies in the biblical Isaac, as forever God's gift to him, or whether he perceives Isaac as another Ishmael, the product of his and Sarah's smartness. Such a test is indeed necessary, since in a previous miscalculation on his part, Abraham almost lost Sarah herself (Gen 12:10-20)! Now the only foolproof test is for Abraham to show that he could accept God's request that he offer Isaac to him. This is only logical since he would be rendering to God "His own of His own."

> When they came to the place which God had told him, Abraham built an altar there, and laid the wood in order, and bound Isaac his son, and laid him on the altar upon the wood. Then Abraham

put forth his hand and took the knife to slay his son. But the angel of the Lord called to him from heaven and said ... "Do not lay your hand on the lad or do anything to him; for now I know that you fear God seeing you have not withheld your son, your only son from me." (22:9-10, 12)

This time Abraham succeeded where he earlier failed. And with his obedient trust in God, he secured that God's promise of blessing pass unto Isaac. The promise made earlier to Abraham (and by you all the families of the earth shall bless themselves [shall be blessed]; 12:3) now becomes connected with Isaac: "and by your progeny (seed) shall all the nations of the earth bless themselves (shall be blessed), because you have obeyed my voice." (22:18) In other words, it is because Abraham obeyed that he secured the blessing promised to him, and through him to his progeny and to all nations of the earth where he lived. This stress on obedience betrays the fact that earlier Abraham disobeyed; indeed, this is what he did when he left his place of residence in Bethel, where God granted him to spend his earthly life, and journeyed to Egypt to look for bread (12:10-20). In so doing, Abraham showed his lack of trust in God, which he now recovered. Besides words related to the promise of blessing, the connection between the episode of disobedience and that of obedience is further evidenced in that both are handled similarly, yet in opposition. In both cases, Abraham moves away from his place of sojourn, Bethel in the first instance (12:8; 13:3), Beer-sheba in the second (21:33; 22:19). In the first, however, he goes down to Egypt of his own accord, whereas in the second, he goes to "the place of which God had told him" (22:3, 9).

Can more be said about these two locations in conjunction with the message of the two episodes? Bethel, whose meaning in Hebrew is "the house of God" (Gen 28:16-19) will become the cultic center of the Northern Kingdom of Israel (1 Kg 12:28-33;

13:32; 23:15; Am 7:10-13). Instead of being indeed the place where the people would honor God by caring for their brethren, it will become the expression of their blasphemy of and disobedience to God.[4] In Genesis, one detects a harbinger of things to come in that Bethel is mentioned in conjunction with the enmity between the two brothers Jacob and Esau: "God said to Jacob, 'Arise, go up to Bethel, and dwell there; and make there an altar to the God who appeared to you when you fled from your brother Esau.'" (Gen 35:1)

Beer-sheba, on the other hand, is the place of concord with all who share this same earth. It is the place where Hagar resides with her son Ishmael (21:14). It is also the place where Abraham resides with the Philistines in a covenant of peace under an oath made to God. It is worth quoting the entire pericope:

> At that time Abimelech and Phicol the commander of his army said to Abraham, "God is with you in all that you do; now therefore swear to me here by God that you will not deal falsely with me or with my offspring or with my posterity, but as I have dealt loyally with you, you will deal with me and with the earth where you have sojourned." And Abraham said, "I will swear." When Abraham complained to Abimelech about a well of water which Abimelech's servants had seized, Abimelech said, "I do not know who has done this thing; you did not tell me, and I have not heard of it until today." So Abraham took sheep and oxen and gave them to Abimelech, and the two men made a covenant. Abraham set seven ewe lambs of the flock apart. And Abimelech said to Abraham, "What is the meaning of these seven ewe lambs which you have set apart?" he said, "These seven ewe lambs you will take from my hand, that you may be a witness for me that I dug this well." Therefore that place was called Beer-sheba; because

---

[4] Am 3:14; 4:4; 5:5-6.

there *both of them swore an oath. So they made a covenant at Beer-sheba.* Then Abimelech and Phicol the commander of his army rose up and returned to the earth of the Philistines. Abraham planted a tamarisk tree in Beer-sheba, and called there on the name of the Lord, the Everlasting God. *And Abraham sojourned many days in the earth of the Philistines.* (21:22-34)[5]

The mention of "Everlasting God" in conjunction with a covenant as well as Abraham's true worship is telling. The term "everlasting" (*'olam*) is found elsewhere in Genesis in connection with God's covenant with Noah (9:12, 16), with the covenant linked to circumcision (17:7, 8, 13, 19), and with God's blessing and promise linked to the earth (13:15; 49:26). The only other instance of "Everlasting God" is found in conjunction of his being the creator of the earth in Genesis 1: "The Lord is the everlasting God, the Creator of the ends of the earth." (Is 40:28) Any part of God's earth is, after all, a place of sojourn between birth and death. This is reflected in the name Gerar (from the root *ger*), the place of residence of Abimelech where Abraham settled: "From there Abraham journeyed toward the territory of the Negeb, and dwelt between Kadesh and Shur; and he sojourned in Gerar (*wayyagar bigerar*)." (20:1) The wordplay is evident in that both "sojourn" and "Gerar" are from the same root in Hebrew, thus making Gerar "the place of sojourn" which is to be shared even with our presumed "enemies."

The conclusion is obviously that Abraham's obedience lies in his living up to the oath he took to keep the covenant of peace on God's earth. In order to do this, Abraham is to realize that sharing the earth with others will bring about the necessary protection and peace that are ultimately *gifts* from "the Lord, the

---

[5] Beer-sheba in Hebrew means "the well of (the) oath;" hence the interplay between 'well" and "oath" in the story.

everlasting God, and the Creator of the ends of the earth." And through his obedient trust in God, Abraham secured that God's promise of blessing pass onto Isaac.

4

Isaac

The story of Isaac is intended to function as the *terminus ad quem* of the promise made to Abraham and, consequently, as a permanent challenge to Jacob as the example to follow. Moreover, since the biblical story is one of continuous failure, to be known as "Isaac's son" sounds ironical given that this literally means "the son of one who keeps laughing (at you, his son)"!

In the Bible, Isaac is indeed the full heir since he spends his entire life in the earth secured for him by God, *without ever acting as if it were his possession*! In his life's itinerary he takes an active part in the preparation for his own sacrifice, which is already a sign of what is to ensue in that it is a paradigm of trust and obedience. Notice how Isaac is said to carry the wood (Gen 22:6). The importance of this passage was previously discussed in conjunction with Abraham's test. Another important aspect of Isaac's share in the story of Abraham's progeny can be seen in how Beer-sheba functions in his life, much as it did in Abraham's. In addition, we are told in the lengthy chapter of Genesis 24 that Isaac did not have to toil to acquire a wife to ensure his progeny; he did not even have to leave his residence. His bride was brought to him by Abraham's *servant* (slave). In contradistinction, Isaac's son, Jacob, will have to *serve* (slave) for his brides.

Another lengthy story concerns Isaac's dealings with the same Abimelech, King of the Philistines, with whom Abraham also had dealings. As in the case of Abraham, we are told that Isaac resided with Abimelech in Gerar. However the episode is intentionally more complex in that it links Isaac's sojourn with sojourns of Abraham, both in Egypt and in Gerar:

> Now there was a famine in the earth, besides the former famine that was in the days of Abraham. And Isaac went to Gerar, to Abimelech king of the Philistines. And the Lord appeared to him, and said, "Do not go down to Egypt; dwell in the earth of which I shall tell you. Sojourn (*gur*) in this earth, and I will be with you, and will bless you; for to you and to your descendants I will give all these areas, and I will fulfill the oath which I swore to Abraham your father. I will multiply your descendants as the stars of heaven, and will give to your descendants all these areas; and by your descendants all the nations of the earth shall bless themselves: because Abraham obeyed my voice and kept my charge, my commandments, my statutes, and my laws."(26:1-6)

The incident took place at Gerar, just as was the case with Abraham in Genesis 20:1-18, during a famine, just as was the case in Genesis 12:10 with Abraham, however, Isaac was prevented from going down to Egypt by God himself, and was summoned to dwell as a "sojourner" (resident alien) in the earth of Gerar (26:2-3, 6). In order to keep the blessing and the promise alive, Isaac had no choice but to obey since God's promise was phrased thus: "I will fulfill the oath which I swore to Abraham your father. I will multiply your descendants as the stars of heaven, and will give to your descendants all these areas; and by your descendants all the nations of the earth shall bless themselves: *because Abraham obeyed my voice and kept my charge, my commandments, my statutes, and my laws.*" (26:3-5)

Isaac learned the lesson and thus lived within the realm of the Law and its commandments and statutes governing the earth, and this is what will be conveyed to Israel: "And he (God) humbled you and let you hunger and fed you with manna, which you did not know, nor did your fathers know; that he might make you know that any human being (*ha'adam*) does not live by bread alone, but any human being (*ha'adam*) lives by *everything* that proceeds out of the mouth of the Lord." (Deut 8:3) Better, then, to dwell as a sojourner (that is, without possessing the land) in the location assigned by God's word (of command) and share it with the presumed enemy, rather than end up dying in slavery in a seemingly "friendly" land of plenty.

The remainder of the story of Isaac underscores his resilience in following God's command and remaining *as a sojourner* in the earth of Gerar, in spite of the repeated adversities with Abimelech's men, which Abraham himself did not experience. Just as in the case with Abraham, Isaac's story starts in Gerar (Gen 20:1-2; 26:1, 6, 17, 20) and ends up at Beer-sheba (Gen 21:14, 31-33; 26:23-33), the location of the covenant of peace with the presumed enemies. Again, as in the case with Abraham, it is worth quoting the extensive passage:

> Then Abimelech went to him from Gerar with Ahuzzath his adviser and Phicol the commander of his army. Isaac said to them, "Why have you come to me, seeing that you hate me and have sent me away from you?" They said, "We see plainly that the Lord is with you; so we say, let there be *an oath between you and us*, and let us make *a covenant with you*, that you will do us no harm, just as we have not touched you and have done to you nothing but good and *have sent you away in peace*. You are now the blessed of the Lord." So he made them a feast, and they ate and drank. In the morning they rose early and took oath (*yishshabe'u*) with one another; and Isaac set them on their way, and *they departed from him in peace*. That same day Isaac's servants came and told him about the *well* (*be'er*) which they had dug, and said to him, "*We have found water.*" He called it Shibah (*shib'ah*); therefore the name of the city is Beer-sheba (*be'er sheba'*) to this day. (26:26-33)

Notice throughout the play on the root meaning "take an oath" and how it is intimately connected with the root meaning "well (of water)." Notice also how the life-sustaining water is found only when the covenant of peace with the presumed enemy is consummated. Indeed the message in the story is clear: human beings do not live by bread or water, alone, but of *everything* that proceeds from God's mouth. Furthermore, ultimately it is obedience to God's will and sharing his earth with all others that secures his blessings.

5
Jacob

In the story of Jacob we can see the parallelism with Abraham's behavior in going to Egypt. This is in contrast to Isaac who did not trespass from the Negeb into Egypt under the duress of famine (Gen 26:1-33) as Abraham did: "And Abram journeyed on, still going toward the Negeb. Now there was a famine in the earth. So Abram went down to Egypt to sojourn there, for the famine was severe in the earth ... So Abram went up from Egypt, he and his wife, and all that he had, and Lot with him, into the Negeb." (12:9-10; 13:1) Still, compared to Jacob who died in exile, Abraham ended his days in the earth where God had willed that he spend his life. It is precisely at this point that Abraham resembles Isaac rather than Jacob. So, in a way, he too functions as a paradigm for Jacob.

It is against the background of God's promise having been realized in Isaac that the detailed story of Jacob and his progeny is presented, beginning with Genesis 25:19 and ending in 2 Kings. It is a story of continual disobedience and repeated failure.

The passage relating the birth of Esau and Jacob is introduced before the episode concerning Isaac in Gerar and Beer-sheba. This is done on purpose. The intent is twofold: to introduce, in a nutshell, Jacob's attitude and, concomitantly, to present Jacob with an example of how he is supposed to act, that is, by following in Isaac's footsteps. So early on the Bible introduces the essential discrepancy between Isaac's attitude and that of Jacob. Isaac understood that God's promise of blessing consisted in fully sharing his earth with the original inhabitants and the new sojourner, and Isaac lived accordingly. Jacob and his progeny will not do so.

The birth of Isaac's sons is worth analyzing in detail. The entire story is intended to show how Jacob, unlike Isaac, usurps the right of his brother in a specific part of God's earth. However, let me first point out the difference between Abraham's attitude and that of Isaac regarding progeny. Abraham took in his own hands a solution to his wife's barrenness. "Isaac prayed to the Lord for his wife, because she was barren; and the Lord granted his prayer, and Rebekah his wife conceived" (Gen 25:21). One sees here how Isaac put his entire destiny in God's hands. However, man being man, with the exception of the "perfect" Isaac, trouble was looming ahead even with Isaac's progeny: "The children struggled together within her; and she said, 'If it is thus, why do I live?' So she went to inquire of the Lord. And the Lord said to her, 'Two nations are in your womb, and two peoples, born of you, shall be divided; the one shall be stronger than the other, the elder shall serve the younger.'" (vv.22-23) One's attention is drawn to the fact that this statement on the Lord's part is not necessarily the expression of his will.[1] He is just relaying to Rebekah the truth of the matter.

Actually, Rekekah's predicament is similar to that of Eve with Cain and Abel, which shows, as I indicated before, that the story of Jacob is not so much a special story of a "chosen" people as it is a specific exemplar of the general story of humankind. The name Abel, in Hebrew *hebel*, means "breath, vapor" and thus

---

[1] Point in case, for instance, is the Lord's allowing the people to have a king in Samuel's time although the decision was against his will. In that case, his intention was to show them how wrong they were and, consequently, to show himself just in his indictment and final verdict against them.

something passing. The same noun is translated "vanity" in Ecclesiastes, from the Latin for "emptiness." The connotation is clear. Abel is representative of the human being whose life, however long, is after all like a passing breath: "The years of our life are threescore and ten, or even by reason of strength fourscore; yet their span is but toil and trouble; they are soon gone, and we fly away." (Ps 90:10) In the Jacob story, Esau functions in the same way. His qualities and behavior reflect that he is representative of man in general, the original inhabitant of the earth (of Canaan). We are told that he was both "the first" and "red" (*'admoni*) (Gen 25: 25) from the same Hebrew root as "ground" (*'adamah*). Esau comes from the "field" and asks to calm his hunger with "the red, this red" (*ha'adom ha'adom hazzeh*). Notice the author's comment: "Therefore his name was called Edom." (v.30). The "red" Esau was referring to is nothing other than the product of the "ground" (*'adamah*), bread and lentils (v.34). However, instead of sharing the fruit of God's earth with his twin—the closest possible form of "brotherhood"—Jacob sells it for Esau's birthright (vv.32, 34), which is ultimately God's gift since he alone decides when to grant life.

In Hebrew, the name Jacob is from the root "follow" and means "he comes after," "the one who comes after," and thus a junior. The story that follows in Genesis 26, the sojourn in Gerar, depicts Isaac's opposite behavior and functions as a critique of Jacob's action. Jacob behaves as a usurper. He did not heed his father's lead, but proceeded in his own way to unjustly secure the full blessing, the birthright, for himself alone (Gen 27). For all his apparent success, Jacob's action leads to the curse of centuries-long exile in Egypt for his progeny. Esau, ironically, remains in Canaan.

The Bible tells us that Jacob gets a foretaste of his exile in Egypt while he is in Haran trying to secure a progeny for himself. Here again, one can see the discrepancy between Isaac and his son. Although both were to take a wife from Haran and not from Canaan, Isaac did not have to leave the earth of Canaan, let alone toil for his bride. Jacob had to work as a slave to Laban, the same man who acted graciously toward Isaac. Jacob got himself into this predicament the moment he decided not to share God's blessings and live by the oath of peace with those around him. Indeed, we are told that, in going to Haran, he actually *went out of Beer-sheba* (Gen 28:10). Furthermore, his attitude when leaving is far from one of gratitude. God vows to protect him by promising to be as much his God as he was that of Abraham and Isaac:

> I am the Lord, the God of Abraham your father and the God of Isaac; the earth on which you lie I will give to you and to your descendants; and your descendants shall be like the dust of the earth, and you shall spread abroad to the west and to the east and to the north and to the south; and by you and your descendants shall all the families of the earth bless themselves. Behold, I am with you and will keep you wherever you go, and will bring you back to this land; for I will not leave you until I have done that of which I have spoken to you. (Gen 28:13-15)

Jacob's response is a conditional vow: "*If* God will be with me, and will keep me in this way that I go, and will give me bread to eat and clothing to wear, so that I come again to my father's house in peace, then the Lord shall be my God, and this stone, which I have set up for a pillar, shall be God's house; and of all that thou givest me I will give the tenth to thee." (vv.20-22)

This lack of trust is further depicted in his attitude upon his return from Haran. After having escaped all possible hardships, including a threat on his life, Jacob is still in fear of Esau. This is a double sin: besides the lack of trust in God, he considers Esau to be the same kind of person he is, vengeful. Esau, however, proves to be a true *'adam*, that is, a person who knows that the ground is to be shared with all other human beings, let alone a "twin brother":

> Esau said, "What do you mean by all this company which I met?" Jacob answered, "To find favor in the sight of my lord." But Esau said, "I have enough, my brother; keep what you have for yourself." Jacob said, "No, I pray you, if I have found favor in your sight, then accept my present from my hand; for truly to see your face is like seeing the face of God, with such favor have you received me. Accept, I pray you, my gift that is brought to you, because God has dealt graciously with me, and because I have enough." Thus he urged him, and he took it. Then Esau said, "Let us journey on our way, and I will go before you." But Jacob said to him, "My lord knows that the children are frail, and that the flocks and herds giving suck are a care to me; and if they are overdriven for one day, all the flocks will die. Let my lord pass on before his servant, and I will lead on slowly, according to the pace of the cattle which are before me and according to the pace of the children, until I come to my lord in Seir." So Esau said, "Let me leave with you some of the men who are with me." But he said, "What need is there? Let me find favor in the sight of my lord." So Esau returned that day on his way to Seir. (33:8-16)

Not only does Esau receive Jacob well without asking anything in return, but actually offers to protect him further on the way! And Esau's offer is made to the one who stripped him of his birthright! In the text itself, God's judgment of shame on Jacob is actually done through Esau's magnanimity. Notice how Jacob says: "for truly to see your face is like seeing the face of God, with such favor have you received me."

Just before the encounter with Esau, we have the episode describing the uneasy encounter between God and Jacob, where Jacob sees the face of God: "So Jacob called the name of the place Peniel, saying, 'For I have seen God face to face, and yet my life is preserved.' The sun rose upon him as he passed Penuel, limping because of his thigh." (32:30-31). Seeing God face to face, as Isaiah experienced, means facing him as the judge (Is 6:1-5). Rather than punishment unto destruction, the magnanimous God opts for striking Jacob unto instruction through shame. Jacob will be limping the rest of his life, and he, as well as his progeny, will forever be reminded of the reason behind it: "Therefore to this day the Israelites do not eat the sinew of the hip which is upon the hollow of the thigh, because he touched the hollow of Jacob's thigh on the sinew of the hip." (Gen. 32:32) It is at this precise moment that we are told Jacob was presented with the graceful face of God through that of Esau: "And Jacob lifted up his eyes and looked, and behold, Esau was coming, and four hundred men with him." (33:1) However, the powerful Esau did not strike as God did, and Jacob got the message: he had better fear God rather than his presumed enemies. Indeed, in his recent own words to Laban, he refers to the Lord as the God of Abraham and the Fear of Isaac:

> These twenty years I have been in your house; I served you fourteen years for your two daughters, and six years for your flock, and you have changed my wages ten times. If the God of my father, the God of Abraham and the Fear of Isaac, had not been on my side, surely now you would have sent me away empty-handed. God saw my affliction and the labor of my hands, and rebuked you last night. (31:41-42)

The Continual Desecration of the Earth of Canaan

The rest of the story of Jacob and his progeny in Canaan is a sad saga. The first incident describes the complete elimination of the host residents of Shechem, using circumcision, the sign of God's covenant, as a subterfuge.

Shechem was Abraham's first place of residence upon his arrival from Mesopotamia: "Abram passed through the earth to the place at Shechem, to the oak of Moreh. At that time the Canaanites were in the earth. Then the Lord appeared to Abram, and said, 'To your descendants I will give this earth.' So he built there an altar to the Lord, who had appeared to him." (12:6-7) Shechem is also the first place of Jacob's residence upon his return from the same Mesopotamia: "And Jacob came safely to the city of Shechem, which is in the earth of Canaan, on his way from Paddan-aram; and he camped before the city." (33:18) He pitched his tent (v.19) on a piece of land he purchased for a hundred pieces of money from the Canaanite Hamor and his sons, just as his forebear Abraham bought a burial cave in the field from Ephron the Hittite. Yet, it was here that the unfathomable happened: a personal vendetta was brought against a well-meaning neighbor who wanted to atone in the most honorable way for his mistake. In those times the rule in the Law was: "If a man seduces a virgin who is not betrothed, and lies with her, he shall give the marriage present for her, and make her his wife" (Ex 22:16); "If a man meets a virgin who is not betrothed, and seizes her and lies with her, and they are found, then the man who lay with her shall give to the father of the young woman fifty shekels of silver, and she shall be his wife, because he has violated her; he may not put her away all his days." (Deut 22:28-29) In the story (Gen 34), Shechem, son of Hamor the Hivite, offered marriage to Dinah, the daughter of

Jacob, after he seduced her. Before consenting to the marriage, Simeon and Levi, the sons of Jacob through Leah, insisted upon circumcision for every male of the city. Three days after the males were circumcised Simeon and Levi entered the city, killed all the men, and plundered the city. Even Jacob was aghast and condemned their action, which threatened the very existence of his household: "Then Jacob said to Simeon and Levi, 'You have brought trouble on me by making me odious to the inhabitants of the earth, the Canaanites and the Perizzites; my numbers are few, and if they gather themselves against me and attack me, I shall be destroyed, both I and my household.'" (34:30)

The sin of Simeon and Levi is compounded by who they were: the second and third sons of the "hated" Leah, on whom God had mercy:

> When the Lord saw that Leah was hated, he opened her womb; but Rachel was barren. And Leah conceived and bore a son, and she called his name Reuben; for she said, 'Because the Lord has looked upon my affliction; surely now my husband will love me.' She conceived again and bore a son, and said, 'Because the Lord has heard that I am hated, he has given me this son also'; and she called his name Simeon. Again she conceived and bore a son, and said, 'Now this time my husband will be joined to me, because I have borne him three sons'; therefore his name was called Levi. (29:31-34)

The first of the two perpetrators is Simeon, who is expressly connected to God's mercy through the one who is "hated." Yet, he did not have mercy. The second perpetrator is Levi, through whom is secured the marriage bond between Jacob and Leah; yet he did not give importance to the future of his own family. The name of their sister Dinah is from the Hebrew root *din* meaning "to judge, condemn." Consequently, the episode is ironical:

those who decided to condemn others in the name of God, using his own covenant of circumcision, end up condemned themselves. The ultimate expression of their sin is the use of circumcision, God's covenant of peace, to destroy their neighbors. In doing this they jeopardized their own future.

When God promised Abraham and Isaac to care for all those under the covenant of circumcision, he included Esau in his care, as well as Jacob (35:1-26). And just as Ishmael joined his brother Isaac at their father's burial, and information is given about his progeny (25:7-18), here also Jacob is joined by Esau at the burial of their father (35:27-28), and the Bible gives full consideration to the progeny of Esau (Gen 36).

In contrast to the intolerant behavior of the sons of Jacob, God shows that he is the Merciful as well as Almighty and cares equally for all the inhabitants of Canaan, in spite of their behavior. He is capable, as he showed in Noah's time, of going beyond the revolt of the human beings and caring for them for their own good, as only a true parent can and does.

6

The Joseph Cycle

It is precisely the point of caring for all that is conveyed in the Joseph cycle, which is officially presented as "the generations (subsequent genealogy; subsequent story; *toledot*) of Jacob" (Gen 37:2). This history revolves around two grave sins this "family" committed in the earth of Canaan. The first sin is selling their brother into slavery, which is strictly prohibited in the Law and by the prophets:

> When you buy a Hebrew slave, he shall serve six years, and in the seventh he shall go out free, for nothing. (Ex 21:2)

> And if your brother becomes poor beside you, and sells himself to you, you shall not make him serve as a slave: he shall be with you as a hired servant and as a sojourner. He shall serve with you until the year of the jubilee; then he shall go out from you, he and his children with him, and go back to his own family, and return to the possession of his fathers. For they are my servants, whom I brought forth out of the earth of Egypt; they shall not be sold as slaves. You shall not rule over him with harshness, but shall fear your God. (Lev 25:39-43)

> If your brother, a Hebrew man, or a Hebrew woman, is sold to you, he shall serve you six years, and in the seventh year you shall let him go free from you. And when you let him go free from you, you shall not let him go empty-handed; you shall furnish him liberally out of your flock, out of your threshing floor, and out of your wine press; as the Lord your God has blessed you, you shall give to him. You shall remember that you were a slave in the earth of Egypt, and the Lord your God redeemed you; therefore I command you this today. (Deut 15:12-15)

This sin is again none other than that perpetrated in Israel according to the prophets:

> The word of the Lord came to Jeremiah from the Lord: "Thus says the Lord, the God of Israel: I made a covenant with your fathers when I brought them out of the earth of Egypt, out of the house of bondage, saying, 'At the end of six years each of you must set free the fellow Hebrew who has been sold to you and has served you six years; you must set him free from your service.' But your fathers did not listen to me or incline their ears to me." (Jer 34:12-14)

> Thus says the Lord: "For three transgressions of Israel, and for four, I will not revoke the punishment; because they sell the righteous for silver, and the needy for a pair of shoes." (Am 2:6)

The second sin is seeking bread outside the earth that God considered adequate. Besides lack of trust, such amounted to putting bread on a higher level than the Lord's word of command, which actually assures us our livelihood: "man does not live by bread alone, but that man lives by everything that proceeds out of the mouth of the Lord." (Deut 8:3) At any rate, the children of Jacob had no excuse. They knew that Abraham went down to Egypt due to famine in Canaan and almost lost Sarah, their ancestress, and thus put in jeopardy their own existence. They also knew that Isaac heeded the lesson and refused to go down to Egypt; he remained in Canaan and put up with the scarcity of wells because he trusted in the Lord. With these two examples before them, the children of Jacob still opted to go down to Egypt, and were stuck there for four hundred and thirty years (Ex 12:40). They would have fared better had they accepted the famine as a punishment for the sin of having sold one of their own into slavery.

But again God was faithful to his covenants with Noah and with Abraham and brought about salvation and forgiveness at the hands of the wronged brother, the same way he did through Esau, another wronged brother. Joseph, whose name in Hebrew means "he (the Lord) will add," is the first son of Jacob's beloved wife, Rachel. She was barren and hoped for another son: "she called his name Joseph, saying, 'May the Lord add to me another son!'" (Gen 30:24) In reality, however, Joseph proved to be the one through whom God multiplied the people. As the father of Manasseh and Ephraim, Joseph ended up being represented by the two largest and most powerful tribes of Israel.

Joseph and Abraham

The story of Joseph resembles that of Abraham in that the value of both lies ahead. The promise to Abraham was fulfilled in Isaac, meaning that the ultimate value of Abraham lies in Isaac who came not from the womb, but rather from God's mouth. One notices a similar handling of the Joseph story. At the beginning, Joseph looks like someone with no future, not only in Canaan where, out of envy, he is thrown into a pit, but also in Egypt where, out of evil revenge, he is thrown into another pit, the jail. Yet, in both cases it is the intervention of divine providence that saves him, and he emerges as a blessing for Egypt as well as for his own people. One cannot help but recall God's promise to Abraham: "And I will make of you a great nation, and I will bless you, and make your name great, so that you will be a blessing. I will bless those who bless you, and him who curses you I will curse; and by you all the families of the earth shall bless themselves." (Gen 12:2-3) Also, as in the case of Abraham, Joseph's future is not so much linked to his biological progeny, but to what comes out of God's mouth. Of all the twelve sons of Jacob, Joseph will be the most blessed both by his father (Gen 49) and by Moses (Deut 33):

> Joseph is a fruitful bough, a fruitful bough by a spring; his branches run over the wall. The archers fiercely attacked him, shot at him, and harassed him sorely; yet his bow remained unmoved, his arms were made agile by the hands of the Mighty One of Jacob (by the name of the Shepherd, the Rock of Israel), by the God of your father who will help you, by God Almighty who will *bless* you with *blessings* of heaven above, *blessings* of the deep that couches beneath, *blessings* of the breasts and of the womb. The *blessings* of your father are mighty beyond the *blessings* of the eternal mountains, the bounties of the everlasting (*'olam*) hills; may they be on the head of Joseph, and on the brow of him who was separate from his brothers. (Gen 49:22-26)

> And of Joseph he said, "Blessed by the Lord be his earth, with the choicest gifts of heaven above, and of the deep that couches beneath, with the choicest fruits of the sun, and the rich yield of the months, with the finest produce of the ancient mountains, and the abundance of the everlasting (*'olam*) hills, with the best gifts of the earth and its fullness, and the favor of him that dwelt in the bush. Let these come upon the head of Joseph, and upon the crown of the head of him that is prince among his brothers. His firstling bull has majesty, and his horns are the horns of a wild ox; with them he shall push the peoples, all of them, to the ends of the earth; such are the ten thousands of Ephraim, and such are the thousands of Manasseh." (Deut 33:13-17)

If one looks closer at these two passages, one can more readily see the importance and centrality of Joseph:

1. Although the testament of Jacob is one of blessing (All these are the twelve tribes of Israel; and this is what their father said to them as he *blessed* them, *blessing* each with the *blessing* suitable to him; Gen

49:28), the term "blessings" is found only and profusely in the prediction concerning Joseph.

2. In the same text we encounter the Hebrew *'olam* (everlasting) which is usually connected throughout Genesis with the covenants and the blessings of the promise. The importance of this is further corroborated in that the phrase "the eternal mountains, the bounties of the everlasting (*'olam*) hills" uttered by Jacob has a close counterpart in Moses' blessing: "the finest produce of the ancient mountains, and the abundance of the everlasting (*'olam*) hills." This indicates that God's will is ultimately carried through Joseph, not only at the end of Genesis but also at the end of the entire Torah (the Pentateuch).

3. In Moses' blessings, we can clearly see that Joseph, through his sons, Manasseh and Ephraim, will form the heart of Israel, both numerically and in matter of importance. This will be later seen especially in the Book of Judges. Besides, both Joshua and Samuel were Ephraimites (Josh 24:29-30; Judg 2:8-9; 1 Sam 1:1-2, 20).

Yet, practically speaking, Joseph will "disappear" from the picture and his two sons will supplant him as part of the "twelve tribes." Jacob will adopt Manasseh and Ephraim as his own (And Jacob said to Joseph ... "And now your two sons, who were born to you in the earth of Egypt before I came to you in Egypt, are mine; Ephraim and Manasseh shall be mine, as Reuben and Simeon are"; Gen 48:3, 5) and consequently, the Joseph tribe will receive double allotment, one for Manasseh and one for Ephraim:

> For Moses had given an inheritance to the two and one-half tribes beyond the Jordan; but to the Levites he gave no inheritance among them. For the people of Joseph were two tribes, Manasseh and Ephraim; and no portion was given to the Levites in the earth, but only cities to dwell in, with their pasture lands for their cattle and their substance. (Josh 14:3-4)

> The people of Joseph, Manasseh and Ephraim, received their inheritance ... Then allotment was made to the tribe of Manasseh, for he was the first-born of Joseph ... Then Joshua said to the house of Joseph, to Ephraim and Manasseh, "You are a numerous people, and have great power; you shall not have one lot only." (16:4; 17:1, 17)[1]

Just as Abraham's legacy was linked to God's promise that produced Isaac, the true heir promised by God, so here also Joseph "remained" without progeny to carry on his legacy, since his children were adopted by Jacob. The bones of Joseph were preserved for four hundred years and carried out of Egypt and set to repose—only he of all the brothers—in the earth of Canaan which he left unwillingly, being forced to do so by his own brothers:

> And Joseph said to his brothers, "I am about to die; but God will visit you, and bring you up out of this earth to the earth which he swore to Abraham, to Isaac, and to Jacob." Then Joseph took an oath of the sons of Israel, saying, "God will visit you, and you shall carry up my bones from here." So Joseph died, being a hundred and ten years old; and they embalmed him, and he was put in a coffin in Egypt. (Gen 50:24-26)

---

[1] See also Num 1:32-35; 2:18-21; 10:22-23; 13:8 and 11; 26:28-37.

The Joseph Cycle

And Moses took the bones of Joseph with him; for Joseph had solemnly sworn the people of Israel, saying, "God will visit you; then you must carry my bones with you from here." (Ex 13:19)

The bones of Joseph which the people of Israel brought up from Egypt were buried at Shechem, in the portion of ground which Jacob bought from the sons of Hamor the father of Shechem for a hundred pieces of money; it became an inheritance of the descendants of Joseph. (Josh 24:32)

Joseph's meteoric "success," through God's providence, is presented as being indeed "complete." He is presented as having, in spite of his death, survived the plan of Pharaoh to obliterate his memory as well as his family. This is to say, Joseph's story does not end in Genesis but continues through the exodus—through the trek in the wilderness where virtually all his "brethren" were relegated into oblivion by God himself and where Moses himself found his end—until finally his bones are brought to rest in the earth of the promise made to Abraham. Thus, if Isaac functions as the true heir of Abraham, Joseph functions as the true Abrahamide, the one who is of the kind of Abraham. Whereas even Isaac himself has a human generation (descendants, *toledot*; Gen 25:19) which included Jacob whose life is replete with sins against God's will, Joseph's story, like only that of the forefather Abraham, is not introduced in scripture as a *toledot*, a human story controlled by begetting.[2] The intention is clear: in both cases, the "continual" presence of the person is not through "human begetting" but rather through God's intervention.

---

[2] The Hebrew *toledot* is from the verbal root *yalad* (bear, bring forth, beget) the way all mammals do.

In the case of Abraham, we have a clear cut situation. Isaac was born through God's promise and not through Abraham's seed, as Paul pointed out magisterially:

> For it is written that Abraham had two sons, one by a slave and one by a free woman. But the son of the slave was born according to the flesh, the son of the free woman was through promise. (Gal 4:22-23)[3]

The case of Joseph is handled in a different way. Though he himself begat two children, Manasseh and Ephraim (Gen 41:50-52), these were adopted by Jacob (Gen 48) and became two of his sons during the allotment of the earth (Josh 14:1-4). That is why, early on in the Books of Judges, "the house of Joseph" is split into Manasseh and Ephraim, both of whom we hear about extensively throughout that book.

Consequently, Abraham's and Joseph's biblical stories are presented as hanging by God's word rather than by actions of human endeavor. Abraham's story culminates with Isaac who fully inherits the earth of God's promise. Joseph's story, on the other hand, does not follow the same path. However, the story line is complete. It starts with a forced exile into Egypt and continues there with a full success when everyone expected complete failure. Moreover, this success is painted as a realization of the promise to Abraham (Gen 12:1-3): Joseph, who was taken away from "his country and his kindred and his father's house" proves to be a blessing for Egypt as well as for his own people. Then, after his sons are adopted by Jacob and thus after he was, as it were, disinherited of his human *toledot*, he—in his bones—finds final rest in the earth of promise (Josh 24:32) before that earth was brought under God's curse (Judg 2:11-15). Thus,

---

[3] See *Gal* 238-242.

Joseph's story, like Isaac's, is a story of full success from beginning to end *in spite of all adversities*. Joseph combines in his person the personalities of both Abraham and Isaac.

Judah and Tamar

The inclusion of an episode in the life of Judah (Gen 38) *within* the framework of the larger unit dealing with the cycle of Joseph (Gen 36-50) has consistently puzzled scholars and interpreters. Why does it not appear earlier with the episode concerning the behavior of Simeon and Levi toward the inhabitants of Shechem (Gen 34)? Why does it "interrupt" the Joseph cycle? Clearly it is intended to contrast Joseph with Judah, the father of the tribe whence originated the Davidic dynasty that wrought havoc and brought about disaster, destruction, and exile upon Jerusalem and its kingdom. This episode is introduced here to connect Judah's failures with Joseph's success in having secured the survival of his people in Egypt for more than 400 years. The story of Judah and Tamar predicts in a way that of David's house. Suffice it to point out here that the woman whose predicament was connected to her being the wife of two sons of Judah bears the name Tamar, the same as David's daughter whose predicament was related to two of his sons (2 Sam 13) and started the internecine fights within David's house. In both cases, the apparently decent houses of Judah and David hid a mound of self-righteousness. Consequently, scripture's intention in including the episode of Judah and Tamar *within* the cycle of Joseph, and early on for that matter, is to turn the hearers away from Judah and invite them to zero in on Joseph as being the central character of the cycle that introduces both the long sojourn in Egypt and the exodus. Although rejected, Joseph alone is the one through whom and in whom God fulfills his promise. In this sense, Joseph functions, as Isaac did before him, as a figure of the suffering servant of Isaiah whom God will raise to show the way to salvation for those exiled in Babylon due to the sins of the Davidic dynasty, the kings of Judah.

Part II

The Law and the Prophets

7

The Mosaic Law

The Law of God's Earth

The most striking feature of God's law found in the books of Exodus, Leviticus, Numbers, and Deuteronomy is what we would call today "the law of the land," yet it is *fully* delivered in the wilderness before the entrance into Canaan. The instant the people set foot in Canaan, they are reminded of that Law and are judged by it, and all subsequent criticisms refer back to it. Several reasons lie behind this oddity. First and foremost, it is a constant reminder that Israel was brought into Canaan in the same way as Abraham: from the earth of Egypt, a place they had gotten used to and had become their "home," into Canaan, a new territory that they had never seen. Notice how the people not only resisted the exodus from Egypt (Ex 14:10-12), but also wanted to return there after they left (16:1-3). Just as Abraham had to obey, the real test for Israel was not so much observing the minutia of the Law, but obedience to God's will. This is what Jeremiah vividly ascertained:

> Thus says the Lord of hosts, the God of Israel: "Add your burnt offerings to your sacrifices, and eat the flesh. For in the day that I brought them out of the earth of Egypt, I did not speak to your fathers or command them concerning burnt offerings and sacrifices. But this command I gave them, 'Obey my voice, and I will be your God, and you shall be my people; and walk in all the way that I command you, that it may be well with you.' But they did not obey or incline their ear, but walked in their own counsels and the stubbornness of their evil hearts, and went backward and not forward. From the day that your fathers came out of the earth

of Egypt to this day, I have persistently sent all my servants the prophets to them, day after day; yet they did not listen to me, or incline their ear, but stiffened their neck. They did worse than their fathers. So you shall speak all these words to them, but they will not listen to you. You shall call to them, but they will not answer you. And you shall say to them, 'This is the nation that did not obey the voice of the Lord their God, and did not accept discipline; truth has perished; it is cut off from their lips.'" (Jer 7:21-28)

This is corroborated in that the entire generation of those who left Egypt was punished in the wilderness. They were punished for having revolted against God's will, and this is precisely what we find in the Pentateuch. This punishment in the wilderness, effective against anyone who disobeys God, explains why the Prophet Ezekiel will be harsh in his indictment against people who were already being punished with exile for the sins they committed while they were in Jerusalem. Even in the earth of their exile, the children of Jacob will be accountable for every disobedience toward God, since "the earth—any and every earth—is the Lord's and the fullness thereof, the world and those who dwell therein" (Ps 24:1). Consequently, the issuance of the Law in the wilderness has a wide-ranging value that covers the entire scripture.[1] All the aforementioned, in turn, will make the new generation, which arose in the wilderness after the demise of the first one and was about to enter the earth of Canaan, take in utmost earnest the threat of curse in case of disobedience to any commandment of the Law:

> Behold, I set before you this day a blessing and a curse: the blessing, if you obey the commandments of the Lord your God, which I command you this day, and the curse, if you do not obey the commandments of the Lord your God, but turn aside from the

---

[1] Later, I shall discuss the value of such in the mission to the nations.

way which I command you this day, to go after other gods which you have not known. (Deut 11:26-28)[2]

And when all these things come upon you, the blessing and the curse, which I have set before you, and you call them to mind among all the nations where the Lord your God has driven you ... I call heaven and earth to witness against you this day, that I have set before you life and death, blessing and curse; therefore choose life, that you and your descendants may live. (30:1, 19)

The hearers of Scripture cannot help but recall the similar situation of Adam in Eden. It is not the ground (*'adamah*), which is, after all, a gift from God, that will protect the human being (*ha'adam*) by ensuring him life as a mother (earth) would; rather it is abiding by God's will. Indeed, earlier in Deuteronomy, Moses stated: "... that he [God] might make you know that the human being (*ha'adam*) does not live by bread alone, but that the human being (*ha'adam*) lives by everything that proceeds out of the mouth of the Lord." (Deut 8:3) And what proceeded from the Lord's mouth in Deuteronomy are words of commandments.

So ultimately it does not matter who one is, which generation we are dealing with, or where one happens to be residing, God's law is issued for all generations as promised in his covenant with Noah, that is to say, until the end of times:

Only take heed, and keep your soul diligently, lest you forget the things which your eyes have seen, and lest they depart from your heart all the days of your life; make them known to your children and your children's children—how on the day that you stood before the Lord your God at Horeb, the Lord said to me, "Gather the people to me, that I may let them hear my words, so that they

---

[2] See also Deut 28:1-2, 15, 45.

may learn to fear me all the days that they live upon the earth, and that they may teach their children so" … When you beget children and children's children, and have grown old in the earth, if you act corruptly by making a graven image in the form of anything, and by doing what is evil in the sight of the Lord your God, so as to provoke him to anger, I call heaven and earth to witness against you this day, that you will soon utterly perish from the earth which you are going over the Jordan to possess; you will not live long upon it, but will be utterly destroyed … Therefore you shall keep his statutes and his commandments, which I command you this day, that it may go well with you, and with your children after you, and that you may prolong your days in the land which the Lord your God gives you for ever. (Deut 4:9-10, 25-26, 40)

This generalization of the Law is actually a tenet of the rest of the Pentateuch (Exodus through Deuteronomy). It reflects the inclusiveness of all humankind in the purview of scripture as was the case with the Book of Genesis. In other words, the interest of the four scriptural books dealing with the legislation handed down through Moses is not addressed exclusively to Israel. As Paul will say correctly, scripture was not given to the Jews, nor is the New Testament the property of the followers of the apostles, to do with as they please. It is only put in their trust: "Then what advantage has the Jew? Or what is the value of circumcision? Much in every way. To begin with, the Jews are entrusted with the oracles of God." (Rom 3:1-2) Moses himself, the lawgiver, married the daughter of Jethro, a Midianite priest (Ex 2:16-22).[3] Though an "outsider," Jethro proved to be

---

[3] Moses even married a Kushite, that is, not even a Semite as Jethro's daughter, but a descendant of Ham. This prompted the ire of the people, including his siblings Miriam and Aaron, against him. However, God sided with Moses, underscoring thus the openness toward all outsiders who are ultimately—whether through Shem, Ham, or Japheth—"children of Noah and Adam."

instrumental in counseling Moses to assign judges to carry on his duty and administer the Law to the children of Jacob (18:13-27). In a way, Jethro acted as God himself later will, that is, according to the Book of Judges, by taking care of Israel through the intermediacy of judges for nearly 500 years! Later, Moses' choice to be Joshua's companion in leading Israel into Canaan was Caleb, a Kenizzite, that is, a descendant of Kenaz (Num 32:12), whose father Eliphaz was the son of Esau and Adah, the Hittite. Moreover, Caleb's patrimony is none other than Hebron, the resting place of Abraham and his progeny (Josh 14:13-14). Since this city is within the area of Judah, Caleb, the outsider, ends up as part of the tribe of Judah, one of the twelve sons of Israel. His case, more than Jethro's, speaks for the fact that the Law is ultimately addressed to all human beings, as we actually hear in Deuteronomy:

> You shall not abhor an Edomite, for he is your brother; you shall not abhor an Egyptian, because you were a *sojourner* (*ger*) in his earth. The children of the third generation that are born to them may enter the assembly of the Lord. (23:7-8)

> And Moses commanded them, "At the end of every seven years, at the set time of the year of release, at the feast of booths, when all Israel comes to appear before the Lord your God at the place which he will choose, you shall read this law before all Israel in their hearing. Assemble the people, men, women, and little ones, and the *sojourner* (*ger*) within your towns, that they may hear and learn to fear the Lord your God, and be careful to do all the words of this law, and that their children, who have not known it, may hear and learn to fear the Lord your God, as long as you live in the earth which you are going over the Jordan to possess." (31:10-13)

The Three Major Feasts

In God's law, the centrality of the earth and its produce can be seen in that the three major feasts require a pilgrimage (*hag*), where the entire people go to meet God at the place he will have assigned to them.

> Three times a year all your males shall appear before the Lord your God at the place which he will choose: at the feast of unleavened bread, at the feast of weeks, and at the feast of booths. They shall not appear before the Lord empty-handed; every man shall give as he is able, according to the blessing of the Lord your God which he has given you. (Deut 16:16-17)

The feast of weeks is that of the first-fruits of wheat harvest (Ex 34:22); the feast of booths is the ingathering of the fruits, mainly the grapes (Deut 16:13). What is interesting in this compendium is that it harkens back to the creation narrative, where the earth is presented as a feeding mother, and we are to be thankful to God who has made it so: "And God said, 'Let the earth put forth vegetation, plants yielding seed, and fruit trees bearing fruit in which is their seed, each according to its kind, upon the earth.' And it was so. The earth brought forth vegetation, plants yielding seed according to their own kinds, and trees bearing fruit in which is their seed, each according to its kind. And God saw that it was good." (Gen 1:11-12) Thus, we are to acknowledge that such a view of the earth (the reality that the earth is not our possession) is the avenue for ensuring God's "blessing" that will enable us to multiply and fill that same earth that feeds us:

> So God created man in his own image, in the image of God he created him; male and female he created them. And God blessed them, and God said to them, "Be fruitful and multiply, and fill the earth and subdue it; and have dominion over the fish of the sea

The Mosaic Law

and over the birds of the air and over every living thing that moves upon the earth." And God said, "Behold, I have given you every plant yielding seed which is upon the face of all the earth, and every tree with seed in its fruit; you shall have them for food. And to every beast of the earth, and to every bird of the air, and to everything that creeps on the earth, everything that has the breath of life, I have given every green plant for food." And it was so. (Gen 1:27-30)

One is to render to God according to what one receives as a blessing from him. This is clear from what we hear in the statutes concerning the feasts of weeks and booths:

> Then you shall keep the feast of weeks to the Lord your God with the tribute of a freewill offering from your hand, which you shall give as the Lord your God *blesses* you ... For seven days you shall keep the feast to the Lord your God at the place which the Lord will choose; because the Lord your God will *bless* you in all your produce and in all the work of your hands, so that you will be altogether joyful. (Deut 16:10, 15)

Two extra features of these feasts underscore that ultimately (1) God's care is not just for a given number of chosen individuals, and (2) the fruitful earth is not the possession of those offering the thanksgiving. The first element, that God's care encompasses all those living on that earth, is reflected in the intentional repetition of this statement in the passages dealing with the feasts of weeks and booths:

> ... and you shall rejoice before the Lord your God, you and your son and your daughter, your manservant and your maidservant, the Levite who is within your towns, the sojourner (*ger*), the fatherless, and the widow who are among you, at the place which the Lord your God will choose, to make his name dwell there ... you shall rejoice in your feast, you and your son and your

daughter, your man-slave and your maid-slave, the Levite, the sojourner (*ger*), the fatherless, and the widow who are within your towns. (Deut 16:11, 14)

The reason given for this total inclusiveness is that the children of Jacob were themselves "slaves"—that is, socially speaking, below the level of the majority—when God poured his mercy upon them: "You shall remember that you were a slave in Egypt; and you shall be careful to observe these statutes." (v.12) This is the reason behind the mention of the slaves (manservant and maidservant) before the sojourner, the fatherless, and the widow, and even the Levite.

The second point is that the sustaining earth is not the possession of those who live off it. This can be seen in that these earth feasts are to be pilgrimages. Usually, earth feasts are celebrated in the locale of the harvest. However, these scriptural feasts are to be done away from that locale, as a perpetual reminder that it is indeed God who feeds not so much the owners of the earth, since he alone is the King who owns all the earth, but rather feeds those who are *in need*. This is the reason why the feast of passover, during which the exodus from Egypt is reminisced, has been linked to the earth feast of the unleavened bread. These two feasts which were originally separate, as indicated in Leviticus 23:5-6 and Numbers 28:16-17, were coalesced in Deuteronomy 16:1-8. Still, even the original setup is reflective of the intentional linkage of passover with the first earth feast of the year: the passover is celebrated a day before the beginning of the seven days of unleavened bread. At any rate, it is this linkage that was instrumental in transforming earth feasts from localized events into pilgrimages.

The first time one encounters the root *hag* (pilgrimage) in scripture is in conjunction with the exodus. At the outset, where the events leading to the exodus are set in motion we hear: "Afterward Moses and Aaron went to Pharaoh and said, Thus says the Lord, the God of Israel, 'Let my people go, that they may *hold a feas*t (*yahoggu*; from the verb *hagag*) to me in the wilderness.'" (Ex 5:1) At the end of the showdown between Moses and Pharaoh (10:8), once more we are reminded of the initial reason for the exodus: "And Moses said, 'We will go with our young and our old; we will go with our sons and daughters and with our flocks and herds, for it is a feast (*hag*) to the Lord for us.'" (v.9) Later in a forceful statement combining both the verb and the noun, the people are reminded that the celebration of this feast is an ordinance to be kept throughout the generations: "This day shall be for you a memorial day, and you shall keep (*haggotem*; celebrate as a pilgrimage) it as a feast (*hag*; pilgrimage feast) to the Lord; throughout your generations you shall observe it (*tehagguhu*; celebrate it as a pilgrimage) as an ordinance for ever." (12:14) The ordinance immediately following in v.15 introduces the feast of unleavened bread: "Seven days you shall eat unleavened bread."

The hearers of scripture cannot miss the point that three of their major yearly feasts are to be celebrated as pilgrimages. This is to remind them that they are to live on the earth granted them as though they are always on the move out of their earth and into the wilderness where God grants true life through his Law which, in all its aspects, boils down to caring for anyone who is needy.

The Day of Atonement

Another major yearly feast is the Day of Atonement. In contrast to all other festivities, the Day of Atonement is one of solemnity during which *the entire earth* is purified of all the sins committed by the human beings living on it, especially the children of Israel: "And this shall be an everlasting statute for you, that atonement may be made for the children of Israel once in the year because of all their sins." (Lev 16:34) Such solemnity is linked to the curse that would strike the earth for the sins of its inhabitants, a matter with which the Book of Leviticus concludes (26:14-45). God's interest in the earth cannot escape the notice of anyone who hears the words with which the exile is handled: "I walked contrary to them and brought them into the earth of their enemies; if then their uncircumcised heart is humbled and they make amends for their iniquity ... And the earth shall be left by them, and shall *enjoy its sabbaths* while it lies desolate without them [that is, having been rid of them]; and they shall make amends for their iniquity, because they spurned my ordinances, and their soul abhorred my statutes." (26:41, 43) In other words, the earth will fare well under the "good riddance" status. It is as though God instituted the Day of Atonement for the sake of the future generations in order to preserve the earth from the calamity imposed upon it by "this generation." This reminds us of the curse issued against the earth *because* of Adam's disobedience. Moreover, just as the earth of Eden was preserved from the consequences of the sin of the only one privy to the knowledge of God's will—there was no other human besides Adam when the commandment was issued in Eden—so here also the earth is to be purified preeminently of the sins of those to whom God's law was entrusted. In God's eyes, they are the culprits when it comes to the curse that would befall the earth on which they are living.

The sins of those who are privy to God's commandments are not only calamitous but also disastrous to God's earth, his creation, and thus to his realm. So the action that takes the lion's share in the purification process is the atonement of God's abode itself: the sanctuary, the tent of meeting, and the altar! Not only that, but the altar is to be atoned from the sins of the people:

> Then he shall go out to the altar which is before the Lord and *make atonement for it,* and shall take some of the blood of the bull and of the blood of the goat, and put it on the horns of the altar round about. And he shall sprinkle some of the blood upon it with his finger seven times, and *cleanse it and hallow it from the uncleannesses of the people of Israel.* (Lev 16:18-19)

If the earth, including and predominantly God's abode, is not cleansed of the impurity brought upon it by the people's sins, God himself, the Holy One, will end up leaving the earth. And if that happens, then the following generations of its inhabitants will not have a chance to be in his life-granting presence. Thus, the real aim of the Day of Atonement is to remind the inhabitants living anywhere on the earth that unless they abide by God's law, there is no future for them on the earth.

The Sabbatical and Jubilee Years

This precedence of the earth over Israel can be seen at its best in two major divine directives that deal with events that are not annual: the sabbatical year and the jubilee year. These directives actually protect the earth from the children of Israel along the same lines as those pertaining to the Day of Atonement. The concentration on the earth per se during the sabbatical year is not so much to protect it from the human beings' sins as it is to protect it from being overworked by them. This "liberation" of the earth from those who assume that they own it allows it to be a "mother" for the vegetation, animals, and human beings that live on it:

> Say to the people of Israel, When you come into the earth which I give you, the earth shall keep a sabbath to the Lord. Six years you

shall sow your field, and six years you shall prune your vineyard, and gather in its fruits; but in the seventh year there shall be a sabbath of solemn rest for the earth, a sabbath to the Lord; you shall not sow your field or prune your vineyard. What grows of itself in your harvest you shall not reap, and the grapes of your undressed vine you shall not gather; it shall be a year of solemn rest for the earth. The sabbath of the earth shall provide food for you, for yourself and for your male and female slaves and for your hired servant and the sojourner who lives with you; for your cattle also and for the beasts that are in your earth all its yield shall be for food. (Lev 25:2-7)

The care for the needy takes the prime place in rules governing the jubilee (50th) year. Over time some human beings were subjugated to need and thus became slaves. This was because others did not heed God's design that, yes, each one is one's brother's keeper (Gen 4:9). So, besides giving rest to the earth (Lev 25:11-12) as in the sabbatical year, the jubilee year is specifically a time of total liberation for the earth and its inhabitants. Slaves are to be liberated, and everyone goes back to his patrimony (vv. 13-53). This aspect of the liberation of the individual in conjunction with a piece of the earth where he could function as a true human being is so essential that it was integrated into some of the texts dealing with the sabbatical year (Deut 15:12-18). Every seven years, the sabbatical year, the earth was to return to the state in which God willed it in the garden of Eden, and every seven years God was going to check on this matter. Furthermore, to make sure that the matter would be handled to perfection, in case something was missed here and there along the way, a special year, the fiftieth year—the jubilee year—would be set aside to even the score:

> And you shall count seven weeks of years, seven times seven years, so that the time of the seven weeks of years shall be to you forty-

nine years. Then you shall send abroad the loud trumpet on the tenth day of the seventh month; on the day of atonement you shall send abroad the trumpet throughout all your earth. And you shall hallow the fiftieth year, and proclaim liberty throughout the earth to all its inhabitants; it shall be a jubilee for you, when each of you shall return to his property and each of you shall return to his family. (Lev 25:8-10)

Let us analyze this passage in more detail:

1. The jubilee year doubles up the forty-ninth year, which is itself a sabbatical year. In other words, there are two years in a row, the sabbatical year and the jubilee year, that function as years of liberation, thus not allowing anyone a lame excuse for not implementing God's will.

2. The jubilee year is to be announced on the Day of Atonement, meaning that it is a year when Israel is to show God that confession of their sins is not just a lip service that would fall under God's condemnation: "Behold, the Lord's hand is not shortened, that it cannot save, or his ear dull, that it cannot hear; but your iniquities have made a separation between you and your God, and your sins have hid his face from you so that he does not hear. For your hands are defiled with blood and your fingers with iniquity; your lips have spoken lies, your tongue mutters wickedness." (Is 59:1-3) Earlier, in a similar passage,[4]

---

[4] Is 1:10-20: "Hear the word of the Lord, you rulers of Sodom! Give ear to the teaching of our God, you people of Gomorrah! What to me is the multitude of your sacrifices? says the Lord; I have had enough of burnt offerings of rams and the fat of fed beasts; I do not delight in the blood of bulls, or of lambs, or of he-goats. When you come to appear before me, who requires of you this trampling of my courts? Bring no

Isaiah likens the children of Israel in Jerusalem and Judah to Sodom and Gomorrah, cities that were utterly erased from the earth for having contravened God's will of respect and care for the visiting stranger (Gen 13:10, 13; 19:1-29).

3. The jubilee year is considered a year of liberation (*deror*), a term found elsewhere with this meaning[5] only in two other passages (Jer 34:8-17; Is 61:1-2). It is disobedience to God's request of liberating the slaves which is the reason behind his striking Jerusalem and Judah and exiling the inhabitants of those cities to Babylon (Jer 34:8-22). In Isaiah 61:1-2 God proclaims liberty to these same exiles only after they received "from the Lord's hand double for their sins" (Is 40:2). Consequently, the jubilee year is an opportunity for Israel to implement the meaning of the Day of Atonement: expiate for their sins by liberating all the inhabitants of the earth so that God would not destroy the earth or "liberate" it from the children of Israel by sending them into exile (Lev 26:43). This intention is further corroborated in that the chapter on the sabbatical and jubilee years (Lev 25) stands just before the chapter offering the

---

more vain offerings; incense is an abomination to me. New moon and sabbath and the calling of assemblies—I cannot endure iniquity and solemn assembly. Your new moons and your appointed feasts my soul hates; they have become a burden to me, I am weary of bearing them. When you spread forth your hands, I will hide my eyes from you; even though you make many prayers, I will not listen; your hands are full of blood. Wash yourselves; make yourselves clean; remove the evil of your doings from before my eyes; cease to do evil, learn to do good; seek justice, correct oppression; defend the fatherless, plead for the widow."

[5] The same word means also "swallow (the bird)" (Ps 84:3; Prov 26:2) and "liquid myrrh" (Ex 30:23).

children of Israel two possible paths: the blessing of remaining in the earth or the curse of being expelled from it (Lev 26).

The Sabbath

The two years we have been discussing are related to the institution of the sabbath,[6] which is the weekday when the children of Israel are required to gather, *wherever they happen to be on the face the earth*, to hear God's law in order to implement it wherever they are: "Hear, O Israel, the statutes and the ordinances which I speak in your hearing this day, and you shall learn them and be careful to do them" (Deut 5:1); "Hear therefore, O Israel, and be careful to do them; that it may go well with you" (6:3); "This day the Lord your God commands you to do these statutes and ordinances; you shall therefore be careful to do them with all your heart and with all your soul." (26:16) Otherwise, "if you will not obey the voice of the Lord your God or be careful to do all his commandments and his statutes which I command you this day, then all these curses shall come upon you and overtake you" (28:15)

The first mention of the sabbath, however, appears in conjunction with food for sustenance, the manna from heaven. When the people in the wilderness murmured that they were lacking food, God promised to give them enough dew from heaven for each day; anything that would remain uneaten would rot and would not last overnight. The exception was the sixth day when the people were asked to gather double the amount in order to last them over the following day:

---

[6] Whence the adjective "sabbatical."

On the sixth day they gathered twice as much bread, two omers apiece; and when all the leaders of the congregation came and told Moses, he said to them, "This is what the Lord has commanded: 'Tomorrow is a day of solemn rest, a holy sabbath to the Lord; bake what you will bake and boil what you will boil, and all that is left over lay by to be kept till the morning.'" So they laid it by till the morning, as Moses bade them; and it did not become foul, and there were no worms in it. Moses said, "Eat it today, for today is a sabbath to the Lord; today you will not find it in the field. Six days you shall gather it; but on the seventh day, which is a sabbath, there will be none." On the seventh day some of the people went out to gather, and they found none. And the Lord said to Moses, "How long do you refuse to keep my commandments and my laws? See! The Lord has given you the sabbath, therefore on the sixth day he gives you bread for two days; remain every man of you in his place, let no man go out of his place on the seventh day." (Ex 16:22-29)

Consequently, the sabbatical year and, by extension, the jubilee year are not only connected to the sabbath name wise, but also functionally since the ordinance concerning the law of the sabbath links together the earth with all those that it sustains, animals as well as human beings, including the slaves and the sojourners. This link is made clear in the Book of Exodus:

For six years you shall sow your earth and gather in its yield; but the seventh year you shall let it rest and lie fallow, that the poor of your people may eat; and what they leave the wild beasts may eat. You shall do likewise with your vineyard, and with your olive orchard. Six days you shall do your work, but on the seventh day you shall rest; that your ox and your ass may have rest, and the son of your bondmaid, and the sojourner (*ger*), may be refreshed. (Ex 23:10-12)

The importance of the sabbath ordinance can be gathered from it being one of the Ten Commandments wherein the reason given is that the sabbath is the day of either God's rest or the rest (liberation) of the people from the servitude of Egypt:

> Remember the sabbath day, to keep it holy. Six days you shall labor, and do all your work; but the seventh day is a sabbath to the Lord your God; in it you shall not do any work, you, or your son, or your daughter, your manservant, or your maidservant, or your cattle, or the sojourner (*ger*) who is within your gates; for in six days the Lord made heaven and earth, the sea, and all that is in them, and rested the seventh day; therefore the Lord blessed the sabbath day and hallowed it. (Ex 20:8-11)

> Observe the sabbath day, to keep it holy, as the Lord your God commanded you. Six days you shall labor, and do all your work; but the seventh day is a sabbath to the Lord your God; in it you shall not do any work, you, or your son, or your daughter, or your manservant, or your maidservant, or your ox, or your ass, or any of your cattle, or the sojourner (*ger*) who is within your gates, that your manservant and your maidservant may rest as well as you. You shall remember that you were a slave in the earth of Egypt, and the Lord your God brought you out thence with a mighty hand and an outstretched arm; therefore the Lord your God commanded you to keep the sabbath day. (Deut 5:12-15)

It ensues that the duty to respect and hold in esteem all human beings, especially the needy, is not something to do every seven years, but is incumbent on us every week and, by extension, every day. That this is the intention can be seen from the rules governing the sabbatical year in Deuteronomy:

> At the end of every seven years you shall grant a release ... If there is among you a poor man, one of your brethren, in any of your towns within your earth which the Lord your God gives you, you shall not harden your heart or shut your hand against your poor brother, but you shall open your hand to him, and lend him sufficient for his need, whatever it may be. Take heed lest there be

a base thought in your heart, and you say, "The seventh year, the year of release is near," and your eye be hostile to your poor brother, and you give him nothing, and he cry to the Lord against you, and it be sin in you. You shall give to him freely, and your heart shall not be grudging when you give to him; because for this the Lord your God will bless you in all your work and in all that you undertake. For the poor will never cease out of the earth; therefore I command you, You shall open wide your hand to your brother, to the needy and to the poor, in the earth. (Deut 15:1, 7-11)

The universality of this sabbath ordinance is that it was instituted in the wilderness and was functional there as well. It is meant to be imperative upon the children of Israel wherever they might find themselves. And since they gather on the sabbath to hear God's law and its ordinances, they are continually reminded of what is expected of them. It is no wonder then that the Apostle Paul concluded that the Law and its commandments are summed up, existentially as well as factually, in obedience to God and caring love for the needy neighbor.

8
The Book of Joshua

The crimson thread that binds together the entire biblical story of the sojourn of Israel in Canaan, from their settlement as recounted in the Book of Joshua, up to their destruction and exile out of Canaan as recounted at the end of the Book of 2 Kings, is the continual testing as to whether or not they abide by God's will. In other words, it is an expanded version of the sojourn of Adam in the garden of Eden. As I mentioned earlier, God's will is the written Law delivered once and for all by Moses and which is to be reminisced "day and night," at least by the leaders, especially the kings, so that there would be no doubt as to the reason for God's punishment.

> And when he [the king] sits on the throne of his kingdom, he shall write for himself in a book a copy of this law, from that which is in the charge of the Levitical priests; and it shall be with him, and he shall read in it all the days of his life, that he may learn to fear the Lord his God, by keeping all the words of this law and these statutes, and doing them; that his heart may not be lifted up above his brethren, and that he may not turn aside from the commandment, either to the right hand or to the left; so that he may continue long in his kingdom, he and his children, in Israel. (Deut 17:18-20)

A close look at the Book of Joshua will show that its story is woven in a way that binds it to the patriarchal story as well as to the exodus and the sojourn in the wilderness. Right from the beginning we are told that the leader Joshua (Hebrew for Jesus—"the Lord saves") receives from God conditional assurance for the success of his mission to settle the people in Canaan:

Be strong and of good courage; for you shall cause this people to inherit the earth which I swore to their fathers to give them. Only be strong and of good courage, being careful to do according to all the law which Moses my servant commanded you; turn not from it to the right hand or to the left, that you may have good success wherever you go. This book of the law shall not depart out of your mouth, but you shall muse over its content day and night, that you may be careful to do according to all that is written in it; for then you shall make your way prosperous, and then you shall behave wisely. (Josh 1:6-8)

Thus, even after settlement in Canaan, the children of Israel are in the same boat as their predecessors and, by the same token, God's dealings with them have the same basis, wherever on God's earth they may find themselves, be it Egypt, the wilderness, Canaan, and, eventually, Assyria or Babylon.

Let me start with the rather lengthy story of the entrance into Canaan. First, we hear of spies whose function is supposedly to prepare for the taking of Jericho. Yet their spying visit will prove totally immaterial for the actual entrance, except for the fact that it prepared the eventual sparing of the harlot Rahab and her extended family. This episode with Rahab is strange, to say the least, unless one takes into consideration that the Hebrew name *raḥab*, found only in Joshua (2:1, 3:6:17, 23, 25) in the entire Old Testament, is from a root, *rḥb*, meaning "width, breadth, open area"; "wide, large."[1] Earlier in Genesis this root was encountered in passages related either to the earth of sojourn of

---

[1] The mythical sea monster Rahab is from a different root, the middle letter *h* being a different consonant that the one found in the harlot's name and in the terms connected with "width." The Hebrew language has two different consonants ה (sounding as our "h" as in "home;" this is the second letter of the noun Rahab [the sea monster]) and ח (found in the name Rachel as well as [the harlot] Rahab, and thus often transliterated as "ch").

the Patriarchs or to the rule of hospitality. The only exception is its use in describing the breadth of Noah's ark (Gen 6:15). I am asking my readers' indulgence in my rather extensive handling of this matter since it is precisely therein that lies the misreading of the Book of Joshua, which is mistakenly considered by many as depicting a "conquest."

Actually, the first instance of the root *rḥb* in the story of Noah governs the value of all other instances. An ark with the following dimensions, "three hundred cubits in length, fifty cubits in breadth (*rḥb*), and thirty cubits in height,"[2] (Gen 6:15) can hardly be a place where all the earth animals and birds mentioned would fit (7:2-3, 8-9). So the intention is that the ark, just as the garden in Eden, is to function as God's entire earth, where all his creatures enjoy life in full togetherness.

The next instance of *rḥb* occurs in a divine address to Abram:

> The Lord said to Abram, after Lot had separated from him, "Lift up your eyes, and look from the place where you are, northward and southward and eastward and westward; for all the earth which you see I will give to you and to your descendants for ever. I will make your descendants as the dust of the earth; so that if one can count the dust of the earth, your descendants also can be counted. Arise, walk through the length and the breadth (*rḥb*) of the earth, for I will give it to you." (Gen 13:14-17)

Two points are important in this passage. First, seeing as far as one can see from where one is standing, along with the invitation to walk the length and breadth of that earth, reflects Abraham's

---

[2] A cubit is roughly the length of the human arm.

status as shepherd, and thus someone who sojourns that earth without owning any of it. Secondly, the descendants of Abraham would include the progenies of Ishmael and Esau as well as that of Isaac and Jacob. Here again, we see the inclusiveness of all human beings living on the earth of God's promise. Such inclusiveness is expressed in sharing, that is to say, in hospitality.

The third instance of the word *rḥb* is found in a story that relates the fate of utter destruction visited by God himself upon those living in Sodom and Gomorrah who did not hospitably share God's earth. What saved Lot from among all the inhabitants of Sodom was his hospitality:

> The two angels came to Sodom in the evening; and Lot was sitting in the gate of Sodom. When Lot saw them, he rose to meet them, and bowed himself with his face to the earth, and said, "My lords, turn aside, I pray you, to your servant's house and spend the night, and wash your feet; then you may rise up early and go on your way." They said, "No; we will spend the night in the open (*reḥob*; from the root *rḥb*)." But he urged them strongly; so they turned aside to him and entered his house; and he made them a feast, and baked unleavened bread, and they ate. (Gen 19:1-3)

Indeed, the two angels in question were close companions of the Lord himself and thus representatives of him (Gen 18:1-2). Sodom failed the test of hospitality that both Abraham and Lot passed. What is impressive in this story is that in it we already have the teaching that Matthew presents as the basis for the final judgment, care for the needy other in whatever circumstance: "Truly, I say to you, as you did it to one of the least of these my brethren, you did it to me ... Truly, I say to you, as you did it not to one of the least of these, you did it not to me" (Mt 25:40, 45).

The clearest instance of its all-encompassing inclusiveness is linked to Isaac, the "perfect" being whom we are all invited to emulate. After persevering in his peaceful attitude of not quarrelling with his presumed enemies who kept contending with him about the wells he would dig (Gen 26:19-21), Isaac was finally graced with a well that cemented the peace with the Philistines he was yearning for in the earth granted to him by God: "And he moved from there and dug another well, and over that they did not quarrel; so he called its name *Rehoboth*,[3] saying, 'For now the Lord has made room (*hirḥib*; from the root *rḥb*) for us, and we shall be fruitful in the earth.'" (v.22)

The last instance of *rḥb* in Genesis appears in conjunction with the odious sin committed by the sons of Jacob when they flagrantly used circumcision as a guise to slaughter the inhabitants of Shechem, who welcomed Jacob's family: "These men are friendly with us; let them dwell in the land and trade in it, for behold, the earth is *large enough* [*raḥab*] for them; let us take their daughters in marriage, and let us give them our daughters. Only on this condition will the men agree to dwell with us, to become one people: that every male among us be circumcised as they are circumcised." Gen 34:21-22) The original text is very interesting, since the actual expression translated as "large enough" is *raḥabat-yadayim* (wide the width of both hands). This is clearly a phrase reflecting a full welcome made with both hands (or arms). Consequently, the text means that the inhabitants of Shechem *welcomed with open arms* the children of Jacob to share their earth with them. Yet, Jacob's

---

[3] Hebrew *reḥobot*.

sons used circumcision, the sign of the covenant of all-inclusiveness, to massacre the Shechemites!

The subsequent instance found in Exodus 3:8 is a judgment on the behavior just described: "I have come down to deliver them out of the hand of the Egyptians, and to bring them up out of that earth to a good and broad (*reḥabah*) earth, an earth flowing with milk and honey, to the place of the Canaanites, the Hittites, the Amorites, the Perizzites, the Hivites, and the Jebusites."

All of this digression is to help understand what happened in the Book of Joshua. The entrance was not the "work" of the spies, nor the work of Israel; rather it was exclusively the "work" of God to instruct both the spies and Israel in the ways of Isaac. To use the terminology of Ezekiel, Rahab, the welcoming one, who was a harlot, actually extended a helping hand to the needy. This, subsequently, Israel will not do, and it is this lack of mercy that will be the reason for their demise:

> You [Jerusalem] are the daughter of your mother, who loathed her husband and her children; and you are the sister of your sisters [Samaria and Sodom], who loathed their husbands and their children. Your mother was a Hittite and your father an Amorite. And your elder sister is Samaria, who lived with her daughters to the north of you; and your younger sister, who lived to the south of you, is Sodom with her daughters. Yet you were not content to walk in their ways, or do according to their abominations; within a very little time you were more corrupt than they in all your ways. As I live, says the Lord God, your sister Sodom and her daughters have not done as you and your daughters have done. *Behold, this was the guilt of your sister Sodom: she and her daughters had pride, surfeit of food, and prosperous ease, but did not aid the poor and needy.* They were haughty, and did abominable things before me; therefore I removed them, when I saw it. (Ezek 16:45-50)

Through a shaming example performed, no less, by a "harlot," God sought to impose on Israel sharing the earth with its other inhabitants and even learning hospitality from them! However, the children of Israel, in their turn a "harlot" (Ezek 16 and 23), did not heed the lesson and welcome with open arms the poor and the needy. Thus their end will be that of Sodom, a prime example of lack of hospitality.

Other aspects of the story will corroborate the fact that the Book of Joshua is depicting the "entrance into" rather than the "conquest of" Canaan. Just before the procession into Canaan, God requires Joshua to circumcise the new generation of males, since the previous generation was destroyed by him in the wilderness for not having hearkened to his voice (Josh 5:2-7). The lesson here is twofold. On the one hand, circumcision per se is not a guarantee that one would inherit the earth promised to Abraham. Indeed, the covenant of circumcision is an invitation to be under Abraham's tent where one is bound to the covenant of the Law, that is, to obedience to God's voice. This is what the circumcision performed by Joshua was inviting the new generation to do. It is such obedience that is true circumcision:

> And now, Israel, what does the Lord your God require of you, but to fear the Lord your God, to walk in all his ways, to love him, to serve the Lord your God with all your heart and with all your soul, and to keep the commandments and statutes of the Lord, which I command you this day for your good? Behold, *to the Lord your God belong* heaven and the heaven of heavens, *the earth with all that is in it*; yet the Lord set his heart in love upon your fathers and chose their descendants after them, you above all peoples, as at this day. *Circumcise therefore the foreskin of your heart, and be no longer stubborn.* For the Lord your God is God of gods and Lord of Lords, the great, the mighty, and the terrible God, who is not

partial and takes no bribe. *He executes justice for the fatherless and the widow, and loves the sojourner, giving him food and clothing. Love the sojourner therefore; for you were sojourners in the earth of Egypt.* (Deut 10:12-19)

Later Paul will write along these same lines in Romans (2:25-29).

The other lesson is that the covenant of circumcision is an invitation to recall the earlier and first covenant of God, the one established with the entire earth and its inhabitants, animals as well as human beings. Indeed, the only other mention of circumcision occurs in Deuteronomy after the catalog of blessings and curses and is formulated thus:

> And the Lord your God will circumcise your heart and the heart of your offspring, so that you will love the Lord your God with all your heart and with all your soul, that you may live … And you shall again obey the voice of the Lord, and keep all his commandments which I command you this day. The Lord your God will make you abundantly prosperous in all the work of your hand, *in the fruit of your body, and in the fruit of your cattle, and in the fruit of your ground*; for the Lord will again take delight in prospering you, as he took delight in your fathers, if you obey the voice of the Lord your God, to keep his commandments and his statutes which are written in this book of the law, if you turn to the Lord your God with all your heart and with all your soul. (Deut 30:6, 8-10)

The centrality of God's will expressed in the Law is evident since the entrance into Canaan is done around God who is present among the people through his "icon," as it were, the Book of the Law containing his "voice" and preserved in the ark of the covenant:

Early in the morning Joshua rose and set out from Shittim, with all the people of Israel; and they came to the Jordan, and lodged there before they passed over. At the end of three days the officers went through the camp and commanded the people, "When you see the ark of the covenant of the Lord your God being carried by the Levitical priests, then you shall set out from your place and *walk after* it—yet there shall be a space between you and it, a distance of about two thousand cubits; do not come near it—so that you may *know the way you shall go, for you have not walked this way before.*" ... And Joshua said, "Hereby you shall know that the living God is among you and that he will without fail ensure for you an inheritance among the Canaanites, the Hittites, the Hivites, the Perizzites, the Girgashites, the Amorites, and the Jebusites. Behold, the ark of the covenant of the master of all the earth is to pass over before you into the Jordan." (Josh 3:1-4, 10-11)

The hearers of the original Hebrew cannot miss the wordplay in vv.3-4 on the use of the terms "walk" and "way" which, in the terminology of the Law, refer to following the path prescribed by the commandments; hence the distance to be kept between the people and the ark. The ark is not to be touched with the hands. It is touched through hearing, as it were. If the God of the Law has no statue and thus cannot be seen or touched, he is nonetheless living and actually the Master of all the earth, with his presence being felt among the people through his teaching preserved in the ark. It is precisely this covenant of the Law, then, that is to be binding on the children of Israel in the earth of Canaan. If they do not follow it, as they are asked to do here, then before God, the Judge of all, they will not fare any better than the nations around them.

Another aspect of the story is that Joshua is introduced as "Moses' minister" (Josh 1:1), whose mission is to ensure that the people abide by God's law. He is not their military leader, a function reserved only to the "commander of the Lord's army" (5:14-15). In fact the encounter between this commander and Joshua is depicted in the same manner as that between God and Moses: "Then he [the Lord] said, 'Do not come near; put off your shoes from your feet, for the place on which you are standing is holy ground'" (Ex 3:5); "And the commander of the Lord's army said to Joshua, 'Put off your shoes from your feet; for the place where you stand is holy.' And Joshua did so." (Josh 5:15) Similarly, the entrance into Canaan is rendered in the same manner as the exodus from Egypt: direct divine intervention leading the new generation through divided waters. All this militates for an "entrance" rather than a "conquest." Moreover, the passage *through the waters* at the exodus *out of Egypt* is a reminder to the people that they were formed by God just as the earth on which they live was formed *out of the waters* in Genesis 1, yet this did not save the earth from God's wrath that submerged it under those same waters in Noah's time. So the passage through the waters of the Jordan *into the earth of inheritance* is an everlasting reminder to the people that, should they disobey God, they too will suffer his wrath. They are to remember that the earth of Canaan or any other part of the planet earth is God's and only his. Consequently Canaan is an inheritance, a patrimony, a place to carry on one's life, rather than a possession or a piece of real estate registered in one's name.

The stories of the fall of Jericho and Ai illustrate the intention of the Book of Joshua. Rather than falling prey to the army of the people, Jericho falls at the processing ark of the covenant, thus making of it God's city. In those times, the city was declared *ḥerem* (an item devoted or dedicated exclusively to the deity; Josh 6:17; 7:13). What is the meaning of and the intention behind the *ḥerem*, whose unfortunate or willful misunderstanding throughout the centuries has produced unheard of as well as uncalled for atrocities in the name of the living and loving God? The result as well as the intention of war is the spoil, since it would, normally speaking, be silly to wage a war and come out of it "empty handed." By declaring Jericho, the first city in Canaan to fall, a *ḥerem* (Josh 6:17), Joshua was reminding the people that all that lives or is found on the earth they were entering was God's property. It can never become theirs to do with as they please. In other words, they were not to take advantage of that earth or anything that lives on it and is found in it. That earth is under God's aegis and protection. A clear indication of this intention can be seen in that Joshua's command regarding the *ḥerem* excluded Rahab and her relatives. Furthermore, the slightest disobedience to this command, including the preservation of Rahab, will make the people themselves subject to penalty linked to that *ḥerem*:

> And at the seventh time, when the priests had blown the trumpets, Joshua said to the people, "Shout; for the Lord has given you the city. And the city and all that is within it shall be devoted (*ḥerem*) to the Lord for destruction; only Rahab the harlot and all who are with her in her house shall live, because she hid the messengers that we sent. But you, keep yourselves from the things devoted to God (*ḥerem*), lest when you have devoted (*teḥarimu*; from the same root as *ḥerem*) them you take any of the devoted things (*ḥerem*) and make the camp of Israel a thing for destruction (*ḥerem*), and bring trouble upon it. But all silver and gold, and vessels of bronze and iron, are sacred to the Lord; they shall go into the treasury of the Lord." (Josh 6:16-19)

This command was not fully followed: "But the people of Israel broke faith in regard to the devoted things (*herem*); for Achan the son of Carmi, son of Zabdi, son of Zerah, of the tribe of Judah, took some of the devoted things (*herem*); and the anger of the Lord burned against the people of Israel." (7:1) What was taken is immaterial. The real matter is *that* something was taken in direct opposition to God's command. By acting so, Israel considered Jericho their possession and, if so, unless God intervenes, they might consider the inhabitants of that earth their property as well. This is precisely what will happen, as we shall see, with the advent of the kings (*melakim*), that is, kings who will act as owners and possessors of the earth and its inhabitants.[4]

The story that follows, recounting the fall of Ai, is meant to show that God was serious about his express instruction: he and only he disposes of the earth and its inhabitants. If the people want to have it their way, then let it be so, but they will pay the consequences. Notice how from the start this story is totally different than that of Jericho where everything was orchestrated around the processing ark of the covenant under the leadership of "the commander of the army of the Lord" (5:13-15) This time the arrogance of the scouts takes over in their report to Joshua: "Let not all the people go up, but let about two or three thousand men go up and attack Ai; do not make the whole people toil up there, for they are but few." (7:3) The result is disastrous:

---

[4] As a reminder, the Hebrew root *mlk* has the connotation of "ownership, proprietorship, possession."

So about three thousand went up there from the people; and they fled before the men of Ai, and the men of Ai killed about thirty-six men of them, and chased them before the gate as far as Shebarim, and slew them at the descent. And the hearts of the people melted, and became as water. (vv.4-5)

And to Joshua's complaining inquiry as to the reason of the utter failure, God's response was:

> Arise, why have you thus fallen upon your face? Israel has sinned; they have transgressed my covenant which I commanded them; they have taken some of the devoted things (*ḥerem*); they have stolen, and lied, and put them among their own stuff. Therefore the people of Israel cannot stand before their enemies; they turn their backs before their enemies, because they have become a thing for destruction. I will be with you no more, unless you destroy the devoted things (*ḥerem*) from among you. Up, sanctify the people, and say, "Sanctify yourselves for tomorrow; for thus says the Lord, God of Israel, 'There are devoted things (*ḥerem*) in the midst of you, O Israel; you cannot stand before your enemies, until you take away the devoted things from among you.'" (vv.10-13)

The situation could not be redressed until the perpetrators themselves were struck with the penalty linked to the *ḥerem*:

> And Achan answered Joshua, "Of a truth I have sinned against the Lord God of Israel, and this is what I did: when I saw among the spoil a beautiful mantle from Shinar, and two hundred shekels of silver, and a bar of gold weighing fifty shekels, then I coveted them, and took them; and behold, they are hidden in the earth inside my tent, with the silver underneath." So Joshua sent messengers, and they ran to the tent; and behold, it was hidden in his tent with the silver underneath. And they took them out of the tent and brought them to Joshua and all the people of Israel; and they laid them down before the Lord. And Joshua and all Israel

with him took Achan the son of Zerah, and the silver and the mantle and the bar of gold, and his sons and daughters, and his oxen and asses and sheep, and his tent, and all that he had; and they brought them up to the Valley of Achor. And Joshua said, "Why did you bring trouble on us? The Lord brings trouble on you today." And all Israel stoned him with stones; they burned them with fire, and stoned them with stones. And they raised over him a great heap of stones that remains to this day; then the Lord turned from his burning anger. Therefore to this day the name of that place is called the Valley of Achor.[5] (vv.20-26)

In order to set the record "in stone" for the ages to come, an official reading of the Law took place, after the taking of Ai, in the same manner as done in Deuteronomy, with the hearers divided between the two mounts of Gerizim and Ebal, so that everyone could hear the rules of blessing and curse that would be governing all the inhabitants of the earth of Canaan:

> Then Joshua built an altar in Mount Ebal to the Lord, the God of Israel, as Moses the servant of the Lord had commanded the people of Israel, as it is written in the book of the law of Moses, "an altar of unhewn stones, upon which no man has lifted an iron tool"; and they offered on it burnt offerings to the Lord, and sacrificed peace offerings. And there, in the presence of the people of Israel, he wrote upon the stones a copy of the law of Moses, which he had written. And all Israel, *sojourner (ger) as well as homeborn*, with their elders and officers and their judges, stood on opposite sides of the ark before the Levitical priests who carried the ark of the covenant of the Lord, half of them in front of Mount Gerizim and half of them in front of Mount Ebal, as Moses the servant of the Lord had commanded at the first, that they should bless the people of Israel. And afterward he read all the words of the law, the blessing and the curse, according to all that is written in the book of the law. There was not a word of all that

---

[5] The Hebrew root of this word means "trouble."

Moses commanded which Joshua did not read before all the assembly of Israel, and the women, and the little ones, and the sojourners (*ger*) who lived among them. (8:30-35)

Notice how, in this pivotal passage, God is presented as the God of all the peoples of Canaan and not just the children of Israel.

If the case of the taking of Jericho and Ai showed that the curse can reach both cities, the story of the Gibeonites (Josh 9-10) makes it clear that, conversely, the blessing also can. Once a covenant of peace is sworn before God, as was done with the Gibeonites, it cannot be broken, lest one risk God's ire. So, regardless of the reason behind the covenant of peace between Israel and the inhabitants of Gibeon, it could not be broken. In fact, Israel is bound to help the Gibeonites against any danger. We see in the story of the Gibeonites an intended repeat of the story of Abraham with Lot. Even after their "separation," Abraham and Lot still shared the same earth, just as did Israel and the Gibeonites, which bound Abraham to come to Lot's rescue. The importance of the story of the Gibeonites is that it continues later in the times of Saul and David; though they were *kings*, they were nonetheless bound by that covenant of peace sworn before God:

> Now there was a famine in the days of David for three years, year after year; and David sought the face of the Lord. And the Lord said, "There is bloodguilt on Saul and on his house, because he put the Gibeonites to death." So the king called the Gibeonites. Now the Gibeonites were not of the people of Israel, but of the remnant of the Amorites; although the people of Israel had sworn to spare them, Saul had sought to slay them in his zeal for the people of Israel and Judah. And David said to the Gibeonites, "What shall I do for you? *And how shall I make expiation, that you may bless the heritage of the Lord?*" (2 Sam 21:1-3)

Notice a striking feature in this passage, namely, that not only is Israel to atone for its sin, but also that the Lord's forgiveness for the latter is to be communicated through the Gibeonites! This underscores that the blessing originates in God and in him alone, and is not, so to speak, "bound" to Abraham, let alone to any of his descendants. Rather it is God who is bound to his inclusive promise, expressed for the first time in the covenant with Noah, to take care of his entire creation living on his earth.

It is with this in mind that the twelve tribes of Israel receive the allotment of the earth of Canaan (Josh 14-21). It is, indeed, an assigning of the tribes to certain parts of that earth, and not an allocation of land to each of the tribes as though each would become the owner. As we shall see in Ezekiel, the children of Israel are the flock of God and as such graze (live) in a certain area which they are accustomed to, but they do not own the earth in any way. The intention of the assignment of the tribes throughout Canaan is to show the realization of the promise made to Abraham, then to Isaac, then to Jacob, that their progeny would find a living space in Canaan. However, the promise of blessing proffered upon Abraham and through him upon "all the families of Israel" is inclusive of all other "families of the earth" (Gen 12:3). It is co-habitation with the "presumed" enemy that is the realization of God's promise. So what Cain failed to do, his descendants are time and again invited to do because it is their only way of salvation. God's assigned leader Joshua—whose name in Hebrew means "the Lord saves"—realizes this and actually forces the children of Israel to cohabitate the earth of Canaan with its other sojourners. To confirm this, let us examine the data. First we have the case of the Gibeonites, which was discussed earlier. It is not, however, an isolated case, but rather a typical one, that is, it functions as a paradigm.

Indeed, in spite of the impression that Joshua exterminated all the populations of Canaan, this "impression" is actually false. At the end of the description of what is falsely referred to as the "conquest" of Canaan (Josh 6-8; 10-11) we read:

> Now Joshua was old and advanced in years; and the Lord said to him, "You are old and advanced in years, and there remains yet very much earth to be possessed. This is the earth that yet remains: all the regions of the Philistines, and all those of the Geshurites (from the Shihor, which is east of Egypt, northward to the boundary of Ekron, it is reckoned as Canaanite; there are five rulers of the Philistines, those of Gaza, Ashdod, Ashkelon, Gath, and Ekron), and those of the Avvim, in the south, all the earth of the Canaanites, and Mearah which belongs to the Sidonians, to Aphek, to the boundary of the Amorites, and the earth of the Gebalites, and all Lebanon, toward the sunrising, from Baalgad below Mount Hermon to the entrance of Hamath, all the inhabitants of the hill country from Lebanon to Misrephothmaim, even all the Sidonians. I will myself drive them out from before the people of Israel; only allot the earth to Israel for an inheritance, as I have commanded you." ... Yet the people of Israel did not drive out the Geshurites or the Maacathites; but Geshur and Maacath dwell in the midst of Israel *to this day*. (13:1-6, 13)

Later we read: "But the Jebusites, the inhabitants of Jerusalem, the people of Judah could not drive out; so the Jebusites dwell with the people of Judah at Jerusalem *to this day*" (15:63); "However they [the Ephraimites did not drive out the Canaanites that dwelt in Gezer: so the Canaanites have dwelt in the midst of Ephraim *to this day*." (16:10) And even later, at the beginning of the Book of Judges: "But the people of Benjamin did not drive out the Jebusites who dwelt in Jerusalem; so the Jebusites have dwelt with the people of Benjamin in Jerusalem *to this day*." (Judg 1:21) The same phrase "to this day" is found in conjunction with the Gibeonites (Josh 9:27) with whom Joshua made a covenant of peace that would ensure their sojourning in the earth alongside the children of Israel. This phrase is also used to speak of Rahab: "But Rahab the harlot, and her father's household, and all who belonged to her, Joshua saved alive; and she dwelt in Israel *to this day*, because she hid the messengers whom Joshua sent to spy out Jericho" (6:25).

How is one to understand this phrase and its function? The hearers having scripture read to them have no choice but to understand it as applying to their time, or at least the time of the writer, which is beyond the period of the original event. The conclusion is that the sharing of the earth as an inheritance from God remains a continuing challenge as well as lesson for the ages. Let me mention once again that the phraseology of scripture underscores that the earth is not the property of any human, it is always God's and his alone. Just as other populations dwell in the midst of or with the children of Israel, so the converse is true:

> Manasseh did not drive out the inhabitants of Bethshean and its villages, or Taanach and its villages, or the inhabitants of Dor and its villages, or the inhabitants of Ibleam and its villages, or the inhabitants of Megiddo and its villages; but the Canaanites persisted in dwelling in that earth. When Israel grew strong, they put the Canaanites to forced labor, but did not utterly drive them out. And Ephraim did not drive out the Canaanites who dwelt in Gezer; but the Canaanites dwelt in Gezer among them. Zebulun did not drive out the inhabitants of Kitron, or the inhabitants of Nahalol; but the Canaanites dwelt among them, and became subject to forced labor. Asher did not drive out the inhabitants of Acco, or the inhabitants of Sidon, or of Ahlab, or of Achzib, or of

Helbah, or of Aphik, or of Rehob; but *the Asherites dwelt among the Canaanites, the inhabitants of the earth*; for they did not drive them out. *Naphtali* did not drive out the inhabitants of Bethshemesh, or the inhabitants of Beth-anath, but *dwelt among the Canaanites, the inhabitants of the earth*; nevertheless the inhabitants of Bethshemesh and of Beth-anath became subject to forced labor for them. (Judg 1:27-33)

Still, there is something more to the matter. Just as Israel is presented as an exemplar for the entire humanity, so the earth of Canaan is an exemplar for the rest of God's earth. It is a place where God tests the people, just as the garden of Eden was in the story of Adam, and the earth outside Eden was in the story of Cain. In the wilderness, God tested the people's attitude toward him, that is to say, tested their willingness to obey his command at any cost. Biblically, this period in the wilderness corresponds to that of Adam in the garden of Eden: in both cases God's command was issued. In Canaan, the test continues, however this time it is in conjunction with God's command concerning the neighboring sojourner. This corresponds to the test spelled out in the Book of Judges:

> So the anger of the Lord was kindled against Israel; and he said, "Because this people have transgressed my covenant which I commanded their fathers, and have not obeyed my voice, I will not henceforth drive out before them any of the nations that Joshua left when he died, that by them I may test Israel, whether they will take care to walk in the way of the Lord as their fathers did, or not." So the Lord left those nations, not driving them out at once, and he did not give them into the power of Joshua. (Judg 2:20-23)

The test lies in whether the children of Israel would follow God's will to share the earth with "the Canaanites, the inhabitants of the earth" (Judg 1:32 and 33) or they would follow the path of Cain.

9
The Book of Judges

In the Book of Judges, as was the case in the Book of Joshua, the fate of the children of Israel remains in God's hands and not in their own valor or power. The point of reference for God's action remains full obedience or, conversely, utter disobedience to his will. Actually, the people were consistently disobedient:

> And the people of Israel did what was evil in the sight of the Lord and served the Baals; and they forsook the Lord, the God of their fathers, who had brought them out of the earth of Egypt; they went after other gods, from among the gods of the peoples who were round about them, and bowed down to them; and they provoked the Lord to anger. They forsook the Lord, and served the Baals and the Ashtaroth. So the anger of the Lord was kindled against Israel, and he gave them over to plunderers, who plundered them; and he sold them into the power of their enemies round about, so that they could no longer withstand their enemies. Whenever they marched out, the hand of the Lord was against them for evil, as the Lord had warned, and as the Lord had sworn to them; and they were in sore straits. Then the Lord raised up judges, who saved them out of the power of those who plundered them. And yet they did not listen to their judges; for they played the harlot after other gods and bowed down to them; they soon turned aside from the way in which their fathers had walked, who had obeyed the commandments of the Lord, and they did not do so. Whenever the Lord raised up judges for them, the Lord was with the judge, and he saved them from the hand of their enemies all the days of the judge; for the Lord was moved to pity by their groaning because of those who afflicted and oppressed them. But whenever the judge died, they turned back and behaved worse

than their fathers, going after other gods, serving them and bowing down to them; they did not drop any of their practices or their stubborn ways. (Judg 2:11-19)

An analysis of the Book of Judges will corroborate that disobedience to God's law threatens life on his earth. The overall narrative within Judges spans a period of 480 years, which is equivalent to that of the sojourn in Egypt (430 years). The delay in the settlement announced in Joshua is due to disobedience to God, as the above quoted passage underscores. God punished the progeny of Israel by prolonging their exile in Egypt away from the earth of Canaan. Out of mercy, God decided to give them another chance in Canaan. However, this time they disobeyed even more. In Egypt, they were given one savior, Joseph, and, although in exile, they prospered to the extent that their number threatened Egypt (Ex 1:7, 9, 12). In Canaan, on the other hand, they were given twelve chances, and yet they failed time and again. These twelve chances correspond to the number of the children of Jacob, meaning that God gave attention to each of the tribes in its own area, and thus that he tried to take care of each of them individually. This aspect is stressed in view of what Solomon will eventually do: abuse the tribes for his own glory within the "city of David," which he considered his own personal property.

The six detailed narratives in the book bear out the thesis of the entire work. The first story of Deborah and Barak (Judg 4-5) is undoubtedly the most impressive in that it both encapsulates the entire message of the book and sets the tone for the rest of the stories. When heard in the original it is clear that it is God in the power of his teaching, and not the people through the prowess of their earthly leader, who ensures life. Barak, whose name means "lightning," is a mighty general. Deborah, a mere woman in those patriarchal times, is the prophetess who speaks on God's behalf. This last element is underscored in that the name Deborah is from the same root as the Hebrew term for "word" (*dabar*). An extra pun, linked to the name Deborah, is that this noun both is morphologically the feminine of *dabar*[1] and means "bee" in Hebrew. Thus, the story tells us that Deborah put Barak to shame with her "stinging words."

The second and lengthiest story of the judge Gideon is clearly an anti-kingly one that sets the tone for the showdown between God's prophet Samuel and the people concerning the absolute kingship of God. And here again, in order to remind the hearers of the primacy of divine teaching, the story is put under the aegis of God's prophetic word:

> When the people of Israel cried to the Lord on account of the Midianites, the Lord sent a prophet to the people of Israel; and he said to them, "Thus says the Lord, the God of Israel: I led you up from Egypt, and brought you out of the house of bondage; and I delivered you from the hand of the Egyptians, and from the hand of all who oppressed you, and drove them out before you, and gave you their earth; and I said to you, 'I am the Lord your God; you shall not pay reverence to the gods of the Amorites, in whose earth you dwell.' But you have not given heed to my voice." (Judg 6:7-10)

Yet and in spite of the Samuel-like stand that Gideon took ("I will not rule over you, and my son will not rule over you; the Lord will rule over you." 8:23), his son, Abimelech, becomes a king whose end proves to be pathetic (Judg 9).

---

[1] In the same way as *'adamah* is the feminine of *'adam*.

Jephthah's story recounted in Judges 10-12 reminds us of the Iliad: the cost of victory is the sacrifice of the leader's daughter (11:29-40) and an internecine feud between the children of the same people (12:1-6). The parallelism is intended with an additional twist of irony. Instead of beginning with a brotherly tension as in the case of Agamemnon and Achilles, it ends with a bloody battle between "brothers." Jephthah's victory is only superficial. Jephthah is not the one who puts an end to the ills of the children of Israel in Canaan; he needs to be followed by four other "judges."

Samson's story, a prelude to the narratives concerning the Philistines in 1 and 2 Samuel, makes it clear that the Philistines are only the "presumed" enemy and, as was the case with the Egyptians (Ex 12:12), it is their deity that is the real enemy. Indeed, Samson, God's elect in the same way as Samuel will be—both were born to barren mothers[2]—married a Philistine woman (Judg 14:1-11), yet was still God's chosen judge (15:20). The real and ultimate showdown in the story is between the deity Dagon and Samson, or rather between Dagon and the Lord, who is the true agent behind Samson and to whom Samson calls for help:

> Now the lords of the Philistines gathered to offer a great sacrifice to Dagon their god, and to rejoice; for they said, "Our god has given Samson our enemy into our hand." And when the people saw him, they praised their god; for they said, "Our god has given our enemy into our hand, the ravager of our country, who has slain many of us." And when their hearts were merry, they said, "Call Samson, that he may make sport for us." So they called Samson out of the prison, and he made sport before them. They made him stand between the pillars ... And Samson grasped the

---

[2] Judg 13:1-7; 1 Sam 1:1-18.

two middle pillars upon which the house rested, and he leaned his weight upon them, his right hand on the one and his left hand on the other. And Samson said, "Let me die with the Philistines." Then he bowed with all his might; and the house fell upon the lords and upon all the people that were in it. So the dead whom he slew at his death were more than those whom he had slain during his life. (16:23-25, 29-30)

The two additional stories relating to Dan (Judg 17-18) and Benjamin (Judg 19-21) form a hinge between the Book of Judges and the following Books of Samuel. The first story closes the former and the second story prepares for the latter. The tribe of Dan has to "relocate" from the heartland of Canaan to the utmost northeast, practically outside the original limits, despite the fact that the original assignment was made under the directive of God himself. That this relocation is specifically associated with the tribe of Dan has to do with the meaning of the name, "to judge." Thus, it is an ever reminder to all the tribes that the "inheritance" is not a possession, but merely a "living space" where the people are always dependent on God's judgment over them. At any time, any one of the tribes can fall into the fate of Dan, which is precisely underscored in the following story.

The story of Benjamin serves two purposes. The first one is to bring the message of the previous story to an extreme. Whereas the tribe of Dan was forced to relocate, the tribe of Benjamin, Jacob's beloved son, was almost brought to extinction (Judg 21). The second message is related to the name Benjamin, whose meaning, "son of the right (hand)," refers to the one seated at the place of honor the way a king is at God's right hand: "The Lord says to my lord: 'Sit at my right hand, till I make your enemies your footstool.'" (Ps 110:1) Benjamin was the warrior tribe

("Benjamin is a ravenous wolf, in the morning devouring the prey, and at even dividing the spoil." Gen 49:27) whence will rise King Saul. This story at the end of Judges is ever a reminder that any such belligerent stand, contrary to the will of the God whose emissary brings about peace,[3] will doom its proponent, whoever he might be, even a king anointed by God himself as both Saul and David will be.

---

[3] "For to us a child is born, to us a son is given; and the government will be upon his shoulder, and his name will be called 'Wonderful Counselor, Mighty God, Everlasting Father, Prince of Peace.' Of the increase of his government and of peace there will be no end, upon the throne of David, and over his kingdom, to establish it, and to uphold it with justice and with righteousness from this time forth and for evermore. The zeal of the Lord of hosts will do this." (Is 9:6-7)

10
1 & 2 Samuel

The thesis expounded in the Book of Judges is further probed in the Books of Samuel and Kings, especially in conjunction with the establishment of kingship and its hold on the progeny of Israel. Man being king is the epitome of disobedience because it challenges God's kingship, that is, his sole proprietorship of the earth and all that lives on it. Thus it is the king, per se, who is the real source of all troubles. This can be seen in the Books of Samuel, which deal specifically with the rise of kingship, and in the Books of Kings, which showcase the sins of the kings over a 400 year period.

A caveat is in order here. One is not to understand that the office of king is the harbinger of evil. In those times kingship was the common form of leadership and the governmental oversight of the life-producing and life-sustaining earth around a given city. The entire government was encapsulated in the person of the king, who acted as the representative of the city's deity. Since the king was the locum tenens of the deity and answered solely to that deity, he functioned as the owner of the entire city property, which gave him, de facto, free rein if he so chose. In the biblical stories, although the earthly king functioned as the owner of the city property, he himself was not owner and ultimately was accountable to God, as a son to father. The king was the "son of God" by anointment, so the king's dynasty always remained in God's hands both properly and figuratively:

> When your days are fulfilled and you lie down with your fathers, I will raise up your offspring after you, who shall come forth from your body, and I will establish his kingdom. He shall build a house for my name, and I will establish the throne of his kingdom for ever. I will be his father, and he shall be my son. When he commits iniquity, I will chasten him with the rod of men, with the stripes of the sons of men. (2 Sam 7:12-14)

Kingship is always according to God's law, which the king is supposed to uphold:

> And when he [the king] sits on the throne of his kingdom, he shall write for himself in a book a copy of this law, from that which is in the charge of the Levitical priests; and it shall be with him, and he shall read in it all the days of his life, that he may learn to fear the Lord his God, by keeping all the words of this law and these statutes, and doing them; that his heart may not be lifted up above his brethren, and that he may not turn aside from the commandment, either to the right hand or to the left; so that he may continue long in his kingdom, he and his children, in Israel. (Deut 17:18-20)

Actually, the king is intimately bound to fulfill God's law because he is seated on a divine throne: "My heart overflows with a goodly theme; I address my verses to the king; my tongue is like the pen of a ready scribe ... Your divine throne endures for ever and ever." (Ps 45:1, 6a) Consequently, he is to act as God would: "In your majesty ride forth victoriously for the cause of truth and to defend the right; let your right hand teach you dread deeds! ... Your royal scepter is a scepter of equity; you love righteousness and hate wickedness. Therefore God, your God, has anointed you with the oil of gladness above your fellows." (vv.4, 6b-7) That is why, as the Law repeatedly underscored, the king is to act "divinely" by serving not necessarily everyone, but more specifically, by serving those who are in need:

> Give the king thy justice, O God, and thy righteousness to the royal son! May he judge *thy people* with righteousness, and *thy poor* with justice! Let the mountains bear prosperity for the people, and the hills, in righteousness! May he defend the cause of the *poor* of the people, give deliverance to the *needy*, and crush the oppressor! ... May all kings fall down before him, all nations serve him! For he delivers the *needy* when he calls, the *poor* and *him who has no helper*. He has pity on the *weak* and the *needy*, and saves the lives of the *needy*. From oppression and violence he redeems their life; and *precious is their blood in his sight*. (Ps 72:1-4, 11-14)

In caring for those in need, the king would follow in God's footsteps:

> For the Lord your God is God of gods and Lord of lords, the great, the mighty, and the terrible God, who is not partial and takes no bribe. He executes justice for the fatherless and the widow, and loves the sojourner, giving him food and clothing. Love the sojourner therefore; for you were sojourners in the earth of Egypt. (Deut 10:17-19)

All of the preceding explains the story line of 1 and 2 Samuel. The main personality is neither Saul nor David, but Samuel, the "prophet" (1 Sam 3:20). He was the first judge of "all Israel" (1 Sam 3:20; 4:1; 7:5; 12:1), and was indeed God's full representative, as his name indicates: in Hebrew Samuel means "his name is God" or "God is his name." Consequently, with a prophet acting in God's name, matters were under control, and there was no need for a king. Yet, this is what the people requested and for no less than the blasphemous reason of wanting to be "like all the nations" (1 Sam 7:5, 20)! The blasphemy in all this is that they made out of their God one of many gods, and this is specifically forbidden in the scriptural teaching. What is even more important is that those other gods do not even do what is required of God's appointee, that is, care for the needy:

> God has taken his place in the divine council; in the midst of the gods he holds judgment: "How long will you judge unjustly and show partiality to the wicked? Give justice to the weak and the fatherless; maintain the right of the afflicted and the destitute. Rescue the weak and the needy; deliver them from the hand of the wicked." They have neither knowledge nor understanding, they walk about in darkness; all the foundations of the earth are shaken. I say, "You are gods, sons of the Most High, all of you; nevertheless, you shall die like men, and fall like any prince." Arise, O God, judge the earth; for to thee belong all the nations! (Ps 82:1-8)

The other facet of the blasphemy is that it jeopardizes the will of the true God, whose special feature is mercy. This double blasphemy is played out in the sequence of events describing the kingships of Saul and David. As I mentioned, the people use the presumed threat by the Philistines to request a king to save them from an enemy they create in their own minds. In this case, instead of sharing the one earth of God with the Philistines (as Amos will eventually stress: "Are you not like the Ethiopians to me, O people of Israel?" says the Lord. "Did I not bring up Israel from the earth of Egypt, and the Philistines from Caphtor and the Syrians from Kir?" [9:7]), they use the Philistines as a pretext to implement their own will. Saul—the king whom they "asked for"[1]—proves to be a disaster to the extent that "the Spirit of the Lord departed from Saul, and an evil spirit from the Lord tormented him" (1 Sam 16:14).

---

[1] The Hebrew *sha'ul* (Saul) is the passive participle of the verb *sha'al* (ask [for]).

The second choice of king proves to be no better, if not worse than, the first. Although both shepherd and beloved[2] by God, David ends up betraying both these assets that were supposed to uphold his kingship. In other words, in spite of being endowed with the necessary attributes for kingship, he made a complete masquerade of God's choice and anointment. He used the power granted to him to act neither as a shepherd caring for his flock, nor as a beloved bestowing love upon others.

The story of David's actions with Uriah and Bathsheba, and Nathan's ensuing incriminating parable, show his sinfulness in acting as a "proprietor" king. The centrality of the story is that Bathsheba ends up being the mother of Solomon, David's dynast, who will plant the seed of destruction in both Samaria and Jerusalem which will result in the exile of their inhabitants.

It is important to note the symbolic meaning of the names of those involved in this story. Bathsheba means "the daughter of the oath," and Uriah "the light of the Lord" or "the Lord is my light." David, blinded by his power, never saw "the light" and acted as though both Bathsheba and Uriah were his property to handle as he pleased. God reacted to this by sending his prophet Nathan, whose name means "[he] put forth, posited, asserted, declared," who "put forth" the following parable:

> There were two men in a certain city, the one rich and the other poor. The rich man had very many flocks and herds; but the poor man had nothing but one little ewe lamb, which he had bought. And he brought it up, and it grew up with him and with his children; it used to eat of his morsel, and drink from his cup, and

---

[2] The Hebrew *dwd/dod* (translated as David) actually means "beloved" as we hear in the oft repeated *dody* (my beloved) in the Book of Song of Songs.

lie in his bosom, and it was like a daughter to him. Now there came a traveler to the rich man, and he was unwilling to take one of his own flock or herd to prepare for the wayfarer who had come to him, but he took the poor man's lamb, and prepared it for the man who had come to him. (2 Sam 12:1-4)

When he heard this parable, David the "shepherd" was shaken to the marrow of his bones and expressed his ire, not realizing he was the rich man of the parable: "As the Lord lives, the man who has done this deserves to die; and he shall restore the lamb fourfold, because he did this thing, and because he had no pity." (vv.5-6) Then God "declared" his verdict through Nathan:

Thus says the Lord, the God of Israel, "I anointed you king over Israel, and I delivered you out of the hand of Saul; and I gave you your master's house, and your master's wives into your bosom, and gave you the house of Israel and of Judah; and if this were too little, I would add to you as much more. Why have you despised the word of the Lord, to do what is evil in his sight? You have smitten Uriah the Hittite with the sword, and have taken his wife to be your wife, and have slain him with the sword of the Ammonites. Now therefore the sword shall never depart from your house, because you have despised me, and have taken the wife of Uriah the Hittite to be your wife." Thus says the Lord, "Behold, I will raise up evil against you out of your own house; and I will take your wives before your eyes, and give them to your neighbor, and he shall lie with your wives in the sight of this sun. For you did it secretly; but I will do this thing before all Israel, and before the sun." (vv.7-12)

Despising God, the sole King of Israel, proved costly to David. Not only was his son born of Bathsheba doomed to death (v.14), but his son Absalom "will lie with David's wives" to gain power to the throne. The fullness of irony lies in that Absalom commits his adulterous action on the same roof from which David spotted Bathsheba (2 Sam 16:22).

So, in spite of all the wars that David had won, he proved to be much worse than Saul. His life is replete with actions that confirm that he considered his realm his own personal property: the abuse of the Philistines' goodwill toward him, the capture of the Jebusite Jerusalem, the plan to build a temple, and the census he ordered taken are telling examples of this. Consider the following:

1. David cunningly uses the goodness of the Philistines when he needed a refuge from his "brother" Saul, only to later stab them in the back (1 Sam 27). Worse: he commits blasphemy by using the *ḥerem*, a divine prerogative, for his personal gain (vv.9-11).

2. As we saw earlier, according to the Books of Joshua and Judges, the Jebusites remained in Jerusalem, alongside the Benjaminites (Josh 15:63; Judg 1:21). Yet, David decided to break this long-standing co-existence by storming the city (2 Sam 5:6-12). In so doing he broke a de facto agreement similar to the covenant Joshua made with the Gibeonites. Even more: since Jerusalem was in the lot of Benjamin (Josh 18:21-28; Judg 1:21), David actually trespassed the brotherly covenant among the children of Jacob. His obvious intention was to eradicate any influence of the tribe of Saul, his predecessor, as is evident from the earlier elimination of Saul's son and heir Ishbosheth (2 Sam 4) as well as Saul's commander Abner (3:22-39). Further: in order to secure that the law of the jubilee year would never apply to Jerusalem he declared the city fortress, Zion, his personal property, "the city of David" (5:7, 9). He doubly

contravened God's law by declaring a part of God's earth his property and by using someone else's patrimony to do so.

3. An action closely related to the preceding one was the "imprisonment" of the ark of the covenant in David's city (2 Sam 6), so that the allegiance of the tribes would become a de facto allegiance to David. His plan was to use God to establish his hold on the other tribes, as he did earlier with Benjamin. David's plan was thwarted by God himself through the prophet Nathan (7:1-17): God does not live in man-made buildings, but in a tent as shepherds do. David's double handedness is further evident in that he eliminated the Canaanite Jebusites and conquered their city presumably to destroy its Canaanite palace and temple. He then made a deal with the Canaanite Tyrians to built for himself a presumably Canaanite style palace in that same city (5:11)! That his intention was to have the same Tyrians build for God a Canaanite style temple is corroborated in that it is the same King Hiram, with whom David dealt, who will build the temple commissioned by Solomon (1 Kg 5:1-12).

4. Finally, David ordered a census of the people in spite of the objection of Joab and the other commanders of the army (2 Sam 24:2-4). Actually the intention behind the census was to measure the military power of Judah and Israel. Such was the prerogative of God who alone is "the Lord of the armies" (*yahweh tzebaoth*), as was made clear to Joshua upon the entrance of Canaan (Josh 5:13-15). In other words,

God is the King, and not David. David acknowledged his sin, but the punishment was severe in order to give an unforgettable lesson to him and to his dynasty after him: "So the Lord sent a pestilence upon Israel from the morning until the appointed time; and there died of the people from Dan to Beer-sheba seventy thousand men" (2 Sam 24:15), that is, over the tenth of the warriors counted. So, after God's sword struck David's household, it struck at the heart of his kingly power. Indeed, the story of the census and the ensuing punishment is related immediately after the lengthy passage that proudly enumerates the names and feats of David's "thirty mighty ones" (the elite of his commanders) and "three mighty ones" (the super-elite) (23:8-39). This passage is meant to be a portent of the upcoming disaster since it ends ironically with the name of none other than Uriah the Hittite (v.39) whom David sentenced to death in order to exercise his kingly "ownership" over those who belong solely to God the King.

11
1 & 2 Kings

The seed of destruction that was planted by David's attitude to kingship pervades the reign of Solomon, his heir. His accession to the throne was done through the medium of an internecine family struggle (1 Kg 1-2) indicating that David's family is under a curse of brotherly bloodshed. Solomon begins his reign by ironically killing his brother Adonijah, whose name in Hebrew means "my lord is the Lord (*yahweh*)" (1 Kg 2:21-24). It is as though with this action Solomon eliminated God's lordship over the Davidic reign. Consequently, as in the case of his father David, whose kingship was doomed in spite of his military successes, so also Solomon's kingship is doomed in spite of all the wisdom he has been granted to govern God's people (1 Kg 3). Indeed, his consonantal name in Hebrew *shlmh* means "her [the city's][1] peace," yet he is the one who leads Jerusalem down the path of destruction.

Let us go over his story. Solomon builds the temple, which God did not need, for his own personal glory. He uses the wisdom granted to him by God for the same purpose. Notice how, within the description of the building of the temple (1 Kg 6:1-36; 7:13-51) that took seven years (6:37-38) there is mention of his royal palace (7:2-12) that took eleven years to build (7:1), and the erection in Jerusalem of places of worship for the gods of his many wives, beginning with the daughter of Pharaoh (3:1; 11:7-9). Solomon used the money offering bestowed on him due to the wisdom graced upon him by God (10:1-13) to build his wealth (vv.14-25) and to fund an

---

[1] The noun "city" in Hebrew is grammatically feminine.

unnecessary but very costly army (vv.26-29). He even went so far as to resort to subjugating sojourners as well as his own people (5:13) into "forced labor" (9:15-21). All the aforementioned is strictly forbidden in the Law, a copy of which Solomon was supposed to keep at his side (Deut 17:14-20). Thus, the clock was already ticking the countdown to the destruction of Solomonic Jerusalem and the Babylonian exile. The man who was supposed to bring God's peace to Canaan and all its inhabitants actually, due to his greed and vain glory, planted the seed of their calamity, if not catastrophe.

Upon Solomon's death a portent of the future took place: a division within the one brotherhood of the twelve tribes that God brought out of Egypt to live in peace with the inhabitants of Canaan. The split takes place due to the lack of wisdom of King Rehoboam. Instead of following in the path of wisdom granted by God to Solomon that kept the kingdom united, Rehoboam opts for foolish arrogance:

> Then King Rehoboam took counsel with the old men, who had stood before Solomon his father while he was yet alive, saying, "How do you advise me to answer this people?" And they said to him, "If you will be a servant to this people today and serve them, and speak good words to them when you answer them, then they will be your servants for ever." But he forsook the counsel which the old men gave him, and took counsel with the young men who had grown up with him and stood before him. And he said to them, "What do you advise that we answer this people who have said to me, 'Lighten the yoke that your father put upon us'?" And the young men who had grown up with him said to him, "Thus shall you speak to this people who said to you, 'Your father made our yoke heavy, but do you lighten it for us'; thus shall you say to them, 'My little finger is thicker than my father's loins. And now, whereas my father laid upon you a heavy yoke, I will add to your

yoke. My father chastised you with whips, but I will chastise you with scorpions.'" (1 Kg 12:6-11)

As in the case of Solomon, the name of Rehoboam (meaning "the people expands, is enlarged") proved to be a misnomer. His kingdom shrank, and he ended up with the smaller part: Judah and Benjamin. The larger part of the tribes will follow Jeroboam (the name meaning "the people will multiply").[2]

But the seed of disobedience to God's law had taken root and nothing can protect the kingdom of Israel, with its capital Samaria, or the kingdom of Judah, with its capital Jerusalem, from the curse issued in that Law against those who would contravene it. The former will end up in exile in Assyria and the latter in Babylonia. It is indeed neglecting God's law that brought about disaster on both kingdoms. This is highlighted in the ironical stories of the kings of Judah under whom there was a semblance of abiding by God's law, which had been neglected by previous kings, in order to prepare the readers for God's righteous punishment. Note the case of Hezekiah:

> He removed the high places, and broke the pillars, and cut down the Asherah. And he broke in pieces the bronze serpent that Moses had made, *for until those days the people of Israel had burned incense to it; it was called Nehushtan*. He trusted in the Lord the God of Israel; so that there was none like him among all the kings of Judah after him, nor among those who were before him. For he held fast to the Lord; he did not depart from following him, but kept the commandments which the Lord commanded Moses. (2 Kg 18:4-6).

One would expect that this would be an occasion for a turnabout that would secure the future of the kingdom of Judah.

---

[2] 1 Kg 11:31-32.

But, in the following verses, the author prepares for the actual future by referring to the cause of the fall of Samaria and the kingdom of Israel:

> In the fourth year of King Hezekiah, which was the seventh year of Hoshea son of Elah, king of Israel, Shalmaneser king of Assyria came up against Samaria and besieged it and at the end of three years he took it. In the sixth year of Hezekiah, which was the ninth year of Hoshea king of Israel, Samaria was taken. The king of Assyria carried the Israelites away to Assyria, and put them in Halah, and on the Habor, the river of Gozan, and in the cities of the Medes, *because they did not obey the voice of the Lord their God but transgressed his covenant, even all that Moses the servant of the Lord commanded; they neither listened nor obeyed*. (vv.9-12)

The next story reports that Manasseh, Hezekiah's son, will renege on his father's path and thus put the kingdom of Judah under jeopardy (2 Kg 21:1-16).

The situation under King Josiah is similar to that under Hezekiah, which underscores that in the period between the two kings, spanning roughly one century, the Law remained unheeded. Even more, we are told the Book of the Law was discovered not only inadvertently but also buried, instead of enshrined, in the temple (2 Kg 22:3-10). But it is too late for Josiah's penance ("And when the king heard the words of the book of the law, he rent his clothes"; v.11) since by the king's own confession "great is the wrath of the Lord that is kindled against us, *because our fathers have not obeyed the words of this book*, to do according to all that is written concerning us" (v.13). Indeed, the just verdict is issued: "Thus says the Lord, Behold, I will bring evil upon this place and upon its inhabitants, all the words of the book which the king of Judah has read. Because they have forsaken me and have burned incense to other gods, that they might provoke me to anger with all the work of their hands, therefore my wrath will be kindled against this place, and it will not be quenched." (vv.16-17) Josiah will try to redress the situation by dismantling the altars dedicated to the other gods in Judah (23:1-14) and in Israel (vv.15-20), and by reinstating the celebration of a passover (vv.21-23) that "had not been kept since the days of the judges who judged Israel, or during all the days of the kings of Israel or of the kings of Judah" (v.22). But God's verdict is irreversible:

> Still the Lord did not turn from the fierceness of his great wrath, by which his anger was kindled against Judah, because of all the provocations with which Manasseh had provoked him. And the Lord said, "I will remove Judah also out of my sight, as I have removed Israel, and I will cast off this city which I have chosen, Jerusalem, and the house of which I said, My name shall be there." (vv.26-27)

Josiah will be just spared from seeing "the desolation and the curse" that will hit Judah: "Because your heart was penitent, and you humbled yourself before the Lord... I will gather you to your fathers, and you shall be gathered to your grave in peace, and your eyes shall not see *all the evil which I will bring upon this place.*" (22:19-20)

12

The Prophets

The Books of Joshua, Judges, Samuel and Kings are referred to in scholarly circles as "the Deuteronomic or Deuteronomistic History" because they flesh out through their narratives the teaching of Deuteronomy: in the earth given us to live on, we are under God's blessing or curse depending on whether we follow his law or not. Our fate does not depend on our military strength or weakness; it depends solely on our obedience or disobedience to God. These books from the beginning were considered as a unit, and were referred to in the Jewish tradition as "The Prior or Early Prophets." This title shows that they were perceived as instructional rather than "historical" (in our modern sense) material. It is the prophets (Deborah, Samuel, Nathan, Gad, Elijah, Elisha, Isaiah), rather than the kings, who have the lion's share in the narratives, since they are, at least, on God's side; the kings are shown to continually contravene his will. The content and titles of the books known as "Prior Prophets" are linked to the prophetic literature in the Books of Isaiah, Jeremiah, Ezekiel, and the scroll of the Twelve Prophets, known as "The Latter or Later Prophets," so consequently and expectedly, when one reads these Latter Prophets one will notice that their narratives and instructions also flesh out the teaching of Deuteronomy. However, these books have a special feature: part of their teaching looks ahead, pointing in hope to a time when God will graciously grant the people being punished another last chance to attain a "blessed" future by living according to God's will. To demonstrate this I shall concentrate on the Book of Ezekiel since it deals with our topic, "Land and Covenant," in a more direct way than any of the other prophetic books. Ezekiel seems to be the prophet par excellence, and he functions as such totally outside Canaan.

In contrast to the Books of Isaiah and Jeremiah, Ezekiel's contemporaries who preached in Jerusalem, the Book of Ezekiel stresses two preliminary facts: (1) the king of Jerusalem is in exile, devoid of any power (Ezek 1:2) and (2) the priest Ezekiel is in Babylon, devoid of any priestly prerogative, yet empowered by God as a prophet (v.3). The God who speaks is doing so from outside Jerusalem, its palace and its temple. Actually, the God that Ezekiel speaks for abhors temples, buildings, mountains, heights, and especially kings. This is the order God gives Ezekiel regarding his "new earth and city":

> Son of man, this is the place of my throne and the place of the soles of my feet, where I will dwell in the midst of the people of Israel for ever. And the house of Israel shall no more defile my holy name, neither they, nor their kings, by their harlotry, and by the dead bodies of their kings, by setting their threshold by my threshold and their doorposts beside my doorposts, with only a wall between me and them. They have defiled my holy name by their abominations which they have committed, so I have consumed them in my anger. Now let them put away their idolatry and the dead bodies of their kings far from me, and I will dwell in their midst for ever. (Ezek 43:7-9)

So right from the start, Jerusalem, as witnessed in Ezekiel 16 and 23, is totally eliminated as a point of reference. More importantly, God is speaking from an unprotected small piece of open land. The Hebrew noun for this is usually translated into either "plain" or "valley." Let me elaborate on this term since it is central to Ezekiel's teaching for at least two reasons:

1. The apparition of God in the *biqʻah,* "open spot," is the referential one for Ezekiel. Whenever God appears to him, he recognizes him as the One who appeared in the "open spot": "The Spirit lifted me up between earth and heaven, and brought me in visions of God to Jerusalem, to the entrance of the gateway of the inner court that faces north, where was the seat of the image of jealousy, which provokes to jealousy. And behold, the glory of the God of Israel was there, *like the vision that I saw in the plain (biqʻah).*" (Ezek 8:3-4)

2. It is in this same "open spot," *biqʻah,* that God, through the prophetic word of Ezekiel, will give his breath of life to the dry bones, thus raising the people he had previously punished (37:1-14) to a new life which will be in an "open land" (Ezek 48), as in the times of Joshua before the institution of kingship and the rise of "harlot" Jerusalem.

In other words, God's saving action in Ezekiel begins in an "open space," stays there, and ends there. It is as though Ezekiel's message of hope lies in giving the punished people, now in exile, a last chance to follow in the footsteps of Abraham, the shepherd who ended his life in the "open space" of Canaan, sharing that earth with the other inhabitants, never considering it a possession but rather a granted inheritance to enjoy while he lives. This is corroborated by the importance given to the imagery of flock and pasture in Ezekiel 34, which is the parallel passage to Ezekiel 37. Indeed, both end on the same note where we find the only references to David in the entire book:

> And I will set up over them one shepherd, my servant David, and he shall feed them: he shall feed them and be their shepherd. And

I, the Lord, will be their God, and my servant David shall be prince among them; I, the Lord, have spoken. (34:23-24)

My servant David shall rule over them; and they shall all have one shepherd. They shall follow my ordinances and be careful to observe my statutes. They shall dwell in the earth where your fathers dwelt that I gave to my servant Jacob; they and their children and their children's children shall dwell there for ever; and my servant David shall be prince among them. (37:24-25)

The close link between the two passages is unmistakably intentional. The only reference to shepherd in Ezekiel outside of chapter 34 is found in 37:24, as though to remind the people that, unlike the first David of 1 and 2 Samuel, the true representative of God must rule as a shepherd in order to "mirror" God and indeed be the "son of God." This explains why the recurrent tiles of the new David in both chapters are shepherd and *prince*. Actually, "prince" is tribal leadership terminology. Unlike the king, who as *melek* is an owner and possessor, the prince is just a leader, someone who is put at the head of a community, the "principal" person. Indeed it is on this tone that both statements end: "my servant David shall be prince among them." That the new David would rule as a prince, and not a king, is imperative in view of the situation in God's "new earth and city" where kings are not allowed (Ezek 43) and only "the prince" will be ruling (Ezek 44-48).

The "open space" referred to in Ezekiel 48 corresponds to the allotment of God's earth to the twelve tribes under Joshua:

This is the earth which you shall allot as an inheritance among the tribes of Israel, and these are their several portions, says the Lord God. These shall be the exits of the city: On the north side, which is to be four thousand five hundred cubits by measure, three gates, the gate of Reuben, the gate of Judah, and the gate of Levi, the gates of the city being named after the tribes of Israel. On the east side, which is to be four thousand five hundred cubits, three gates, the gate of Joseph, the gate of Benjamin, and the gate of Dan. On the south side, which is to be four thousand five hundred cubits by measure, three gates, the gate of Simeon, the gate of Issachar, and the gate of Zebulun. On the west side, which is to be four thousand five hundred cubits, three gates, the gate of Gad, the gate of Asher, and the gate of Naphtali. The circumference of the city shall be eighteen thousand cubits. And the name of the city henceforth shall be, The Lord is there. (Ezek 48:29-35)

The city that will be the focus of the life for the tribes is named "The Lord is there." This is obviously metaphorical and corresponds to other metaphorical names in Isaiah: "Afterward you shall be called the city of righteousness, the faithful city" (1:26). Such is clearly meant to offset the city's previous status: "How the faithful city has become a harlot, she that was full of justice! Righteousness lodged in her, but now murderers." (v.21) As in Isaiah, so also in Ezekiel, the city that was destroyed by God is reinstated. And, just as in Isaiah, so also in Ezekiel the city is bound to the implementation of God's law:

> Therefore say, "Thus says the Lord God: I will gather you from the peoples, and assemble you out of the countries where you have been scattered, and I will give you the earth of Israel." And when they come there, they will remove from it all its detestable things and all its abominations. And I will give them one heart, and put a new spirit within them; I will take the stony heart out of their flesh and give them a heart of flesh, *that they may walk in my statutes and keep my ordinances and obey them*; and *they shall be my people, and I will be their God*. But as for those whose heart goes after their detestable things and their abominations, I will requite their deeds upon their own heads, says the Lord God. (Ezek 11:17-21)

Cast away from you all the transgressions which you have committed against me, and get yourselves a new heart and a new spirit! *Why will you die, O house of Israel?* For I have no pleasure in the death of any one, says the Lord God; *so turn, and live.* (18:31-32)

A new heart I will give you, and a new spirit I will put within you; and I will take out of your flesh the heart of stone and give you a heart of flesh. And I will put my spirit within you, and *cause you to walk in my statutes and be careful to observe my ordinances.* You shall dwell in the earth which I gave to your fathers; and *you shall be my people, and I will be your God.* (36:26-28)

It is only to the extent to which the people implement God's will that they are *his* people and he is *their* God. This is precisely why, earlier in Ezekiel, *all* went forth out of the earth of exile through God's intervention with the express intention to undergo judgment, and *only* those who will have been found faithful to his law while they were in the exile will enter the earth:

As I live, says the Lord God, surely with a mighty hand and an outstretched arm, and with wrath poured out, I will be king over you. I will bring you out from the peoples and gather you out of the countries where you are scattered, with a mighty hand and an outstretched arm, and with wrath poured out; and I will bring you into *the wilderness of the peoples*, and there I will enter into judgment with you face to face. As I entered into judgment with your fathers in the wilderness of the earth of Egypt, so I will enter into judgment with you, says the Lord God. I will make you pass under the rod, and I will let you go in by number. *I will purge out the rebels from among you, and those who transgress against me; I will bring them out of the earth where they sojourn, but they shall not enter the earth of Israel.* Then you will know that I am the Lord. (20:33-38)

This centrality of God's will expressed in his law forces us to revisit the narrative of the exodus and realize anew that God did not get Israel out of Egypt in order to settle them in Canaan, but to give them the Law that would protect them during their sojourning there: "But I will be with you; and *this shall be the sign for you, that I have sent you: when you have brought forth the people out of Egypt, you shall serve God upon this mountain.*" (Ex 3:12) Moses' request to Pharaoh was in accordance with God's command: "Thus says the Lord, the God of Israel, 'Let my people go, that they may hold a feast to me in the wilderness'" (5:1), and more specifically "Let my people go, that they may *serve me* in the wilderness" (7:16). Later, and repeatedly, the stress of the exodus is on service to the Lord: "Let my people go, that they may serve me." (8:1, 20; 9:1, 13; 10:3) The Hebrew root for "serve" and "service" has the connotation of "slavery," which implies unconditional obedience. The period of the wilderness is one of testing *on the way to* the earth granted to them as a place to sojourn until they die. God's people are supposed to live there in unconditional obedience to God. Disobedience to God would *shorten* their stay there. In other words, both the giving of the Law and the testing in the wilderness happened *before* the access to the earth *because* in that earth the people, *through their behavior*, will have to choose between the way to life and the way to death:

> I call heaven and earth to witness against you this day, that I have set before you life and death, blessing and curse; therefore choose life, that you and your descendants may live, loving the Lord your God, obeying his voice, and cleaving to him; for that means life to you and length of days, that you may dwell in the earth which the Lord swore to your fathers, to Abraham, to Isaac, and to Jacob, to give them. (Deut 30:19-20)

The parallelism in terminology as well as intention between Ezekiel and the Pentateuch is telling. In both, the earth is granted as a place of inheritance to live in, but not to possess. In both, the preparatory test and eventual judgment take place while the people are living among the nations. Notice how Ezekiel specifically calls the wilderness, which is the place of test for the exiles, "wilderness of the peoples" and uses it in parallel with the "wilderness of Egypt" where their fathers were tested: "I will bring you into the wilderness of the peoples, and there I will enter into judgment with you face to face. As I entered into judgment with your fathers in the wilderness of the earth of Egypt, so I will enter into judgment with you, says the Lord God." (20:35-36) In both, the condition for length of sojourn in that earth is dependent on whether or not one implements God's will. Indeed in both texts, the addressees are called to serve, that is, to unconditionally obey the Lord and abide by his statutes in order for them to be his people. The hearers of scripture have no excuse since they have before them the examples of their predecessors. This point is repeatedly stressed in Ezekiel 16 and 20 where Jerusalem, the city of those exiled in Babylon, is presented as the younger sister who should have heeded the experience of Samaria, her older sister. This second chance may well be the last chance, as is underscored at the end of Malachi, the last prophetic book, and thus in the last words of the prophetic literature:

> For behold, the day comes, burning like an oven, when all the arrogant and all evildoers will be stubble; the day that comes shall burn them up, says the Lord of hosts, so that it will leave them neither root nor branch. But for you who fear my name the sun of righteousness shall rise, with healing in its wings. You shall go forth leaping like calves from the stall. And you shall tread down the wicked, for they will be ashes under the soles of your feet, on

the day when I act, says the Lord of hosts. Remember the law of my servant Moses, the statutes and ordinances that I commanded him at Horeb for all Israel. Behold, I will send you Elijah the prophet before the great and terrible day of the Lord comes. And he will turn the hearts of fathers to their children and the hearts of children to their fathers, lest I come and smite the earth with a curse. (Mal 4:1-6)

The conclusion is inescapable. Whether the hearers of scripture are in Canaan or somewhere else on God's earth, the requirement is the same: abide by God's will expressed in his Law. The new city of God—and its temple—is not built by the hand of man. It is any given earth where God's will is done. God, after all, does not abide in a human construction: "Thus says the Lord: 'Heaven is my throne and the earth is my footstool; what is the house which you would build for me, and what is the place of my rest? All these things my hand has made, and so all these things are mine, says the Lord. But this is the man to whom I will look, *he that is humble and contrite in spirit*, and trembles at my word.'" (Is 66:1-2) The "ground of Israel" is thus any ground (*'adamah*) where "any man (*'adam*) does not live by bread alone, but by everything that proceeds out of the mouth of the Lord" (Deut 8:3). It is then no coincidence that Ezekiel refers repeatedly to the restored Canaan as the "ground (*'adamah*) of Israel" rather than the "earth of Israel."[1] This, in turn, explains why the name of God's true city— not the one subjugated by David for his own personal gain and purposes—is "the Lord is there" or "the city of righteousness," "the faithful

---

[1] Seventeen occurrences of the former (Ezek 7:2; 11:17; 12:19, 22; 13:9; 18:2; 20:38, 42; 21:2, 3; 25:3, 6; 33:24; 36:6; 37:12; 38:18, 19) versus only 3 for the latter (27:17; 47:18; 40:2). RSV, in this regard, is confusing, if not outright misleading, since it translates both as "land of Israel."

city," that is, the city where the Lord rules through obedience to his righteous commandments.

Judaism's followers understood that entering this kind of Canaan, "the ground of Israel" whose capital city is "The Lord is there," is treading on a ground (*'adamah*) where God rules supremely in his law and grants his blessing on every man (*'adam*) living there. Throughout the subsequent centuries they understood the message and took it very seriously. The alternative was the curse of disaster and death. So, the majority of the followers of Judaism remained where they were, on their ground, congregating on the sabbath in and as a synagogue (congregation) around God's law and "giving heed to the statutes and the ordinances which I teach you, and do them; that you may live, and go in and inherit of the earth which the Lord, the God of your fathers, gives you" (Deut 4:1). This was the situation in the first century B.C. and the first century A.D. and explains the high number of Jews living in the cities of Mesopotamia as well as in cities of the Roman Empire. Alexandria is a striking example, not only because the Jewish community there constituted a high percentage of the total population, but also because it was in Egypt, the earth of Pharaoh, *where those to whom the Law was handed were under strict orders not to return.* Even more: it is most probably there that the translation of scripture from Hebrew into Greek took place, the aim of which was to invite the Jews throughout the Roman empire to remain where they were, and try, to the best of their ability, to abide by the Law's requirements:

> When I came to Egypt in the thirty-eighth year of the reign of Euergetes and stayed for some time, I found opportunity for no little instruction. It seemed highly necessary that I should myself devote some pains and labor to the translation of the following

book, using in that period of time great watchfulness and skill in order to complete and publish the book *for those living abroad who wished to gain learning, being prepared in character to live according to the law.* (Prologue to the translation of the Book of Sirach)

Ezekiel proved to be the "father of Judaism." His hearers understood fully and correctly his teaching and abided by it. It is beyond comprehension to imagine that adherents of modern political Zionism use that same book to come up with an opposite conclusion!

Love for Any Needy Neighbor

If the teaching of the Prophets parallels that of the Pentateuch regarding the centrality of the Law as the first and last rule of behavior on God's earth, then one should expect that their view of that Law would also parallel what we find in the Pentateuch. And indeed, this is precisely what we find. In their criticism of the (mis)behavior that brought down the kingdoms of Israel and Judah, the Prophets are unanimous in pointing out repeatedly the lack of justice and care toward *all* the needy of Canaan. That this was their main interest can be seen in their frequent use of all possible terms extant in the language, as though they were covering all possible bases and not allowing any excuse in a court of law: "For three transgressions of Israel, and for four, I will not revoke the punishment; because they sell the *righteous* for silver, and the *needy* for a pair of shoes—they that trample the head of the *poor* into the dust of the earth, and turn aside the way of the *afflicted*." (Am 2:6-7) This intention is most evident in their singling out two cases of life and death in the society of the times, those of the widow and the orphan. Given that there were no social or health care programs as we have today, the widow and the orphan were condemned to sure death if they were not taken care of. Their primary caretaker was the god of the community where they lived. This is clear in Psalm 82, where God takes to task all other deities:

> God has taken his place in the divine council; in the midst of the gods he holds judgment: "How long will you judge unjustly and show partiality to the wicked? Give justice to the weak and the fatherless; maintain the right of the afflicted and the destitute. Rescue the weak and the needy; deliver them from the hand of the wicked." (Ps 82:1-4)

What God finds wanting in the other deities are the qualifications that define him as a just judge:

> Thou dost see; yea, thou dost note trouble and vexation, that thou mayest take it into thy hands; the hapless commits himself to thee; thou hast been the helper of the fatherless. Break thou the arm of the wicked and evildoer; seek out his wickedness till thou find none. The Lord is king for ever and ever; the nations shall perish from his earth. O Lord, thou wilt hear the desire of the meek; thou wilt strengthen their heart, thou wilt incline thy ear to do justice to the fatherless and the oppressed, so that man who is of the earth may strike terror no more. (Ps 10:14-18)

> Sing to God, sing praises to his name; lift up a song to him who rides upon the clouds; his name is the Lord, exult before him! Father of the fatherless and protector of widows is God in his holy habitation. God gives the desolate a home to dwell in; he leads out the prisoners to prosperity; but the rebellious dwell in a parched land. (68:4-6)

Conversely, to stress the seriousness of the matter, the divine curse wished on the wicked is formulated thus:

> May his days be few; may another seize his goods! May his children be fatherless, and his wife a widow! May his children wander about and beg; may they be driven out of the ruins they

inhabit! May the creditor seize all that he has; may strangers plunder the fruits of his toil! Let there be none to extend kindness to him, nor any to pity his fatherless children! May his posterity be cut off; may his name be blotted out in the second generation! (109:8-13)

If the justice of God the King is ultimately revealed and tested in his care for those who cannot repay him (since he possesses everything), the same then applies to the earthly king, God's representative, who owns the treasury of the earth allocated to him:

> Give the king thy justice, O God, and thy righteousness to the royal son! May he judge thy people with righteousness, and thy poor with justice! Let the mountains bear prosperity for the people, and the hills, in righteousness! May he defend the cause of the poor of the people, give deliverance to the needy, and crush the oppressor! ... May all kings fall down before him, all nations serve him! For he delivers the needy when he calls, the poor and him who has no helper. He has pity on the weak and the needy, and saves the lives of the needy. From oppression and violence he redeems their life; and precious is their blood in his sight. (Ps 72:1-4, 11-14)

This essential feature of those who speak and act in God's name is the justice they are bound to uphold. This is not just a matter of doing something "out of the goodness of one's own heart." Justice is a "must," not an option. It is required of God's elect, the new David:

> There shall come forth a shoot from the stump of Jesse, and a branch shall grow out of his roots. And the Spirit of the Lord shall rest upon him, the spirit of wisdom and understanding, the spirit of counsel and might, the spirit of knowledge and the fear of the Lord. And his delight shall be in the fear of the Lord. He shall not

judge by what his eyes see, or decide by what his ears hear; but with righteousness he shall judge the poor, and decide with equity for the meek of the earth; and he shall smite the earth with the rod of his mouth, and with the breath of his lips he shall slay the wicked. Righteousness shall be the girdle of his waist, and faithfulness the girdle of his loins. (Is 11:1-5)

However, as is clear from the above passage, this justice emanates from God and is bestowed by him to the assignee who is accountable for its execution. That is why the divine assignee's "delight is in the fear of the Lord," which is an expression linked to doing submissively God's will as is expressed in his law. Furthermore, given that God's law is specifically issued to be implemented in the earth of Canaan, where the children of Israel are allocated to live—and, as we saw in Ezekiel, by extension to any earth where they will eventually be exiled to live—they are bound to make sure that that Law is applied to all who live on that earth. Hence, the scriptural interest in the oppressed, that is, the ones unjustly treated by those in power, on the one hand, and in the sojourner (*ger*), that is, the one unrelated to us, who shares the same earth, on the other hand. The divine verdict against oppression and violence lies in that the perpetrator assumes a right of ownership which is reserved only to God, and it is an accusation not only leveled against the king, but also against the rich:

> Proclaim to the strongholds in Assyria, and to the strongholds in the earth of Egypt, and say, "Assemble yourselves upon the mountains of Samaria, and see the great tumults within her, and the oppressions in her midst." "They do not know how to do right," says the Lord, "those who store up violence and robbery in their strongholds" ... "Hear, and testify against the house of Jacob," says the Lord God, the God of hosts, "that on the day I punish Israel for his transgressions, I will punish the altars of

The Prophets

> Bethel, and the horns of the altar shall be cut off and fall to the ground. I will smite the winter house with the summer house; and the houses of ivory shall perish, and the great houses shall come to an end," says the Lord. "Hear this word, you cows of Bashan, who are in the mountain of Samaria, who oppress the poor, who crush the needy, who say to their husbands, 'Bring, that we may drink!'" (Am 3:9-10, 13-15; 4:1)

> For wicked men are found among my people; they lurk like fowlers lying in wait. They set a trap; they catch men. Like a basket full of birds, their houses are full of treachery; therefore they have become great and rich, they have grown fat and sleek. They know no bounds in deeds of wickedness; they judge not with justice the cause of the fatherless, to make it prosper, and they do not defend the rights of the needy. (Jer 5:26-28)[2]

The motive behind this indictment of the rich, if for no other reason, lies in that there would be no rich if the rule of the jubilee year were heeded.

Besides the oppressed, the other special case in God's indictment against the people and their kings is the sojourner, the co-inhabitant who shares the earth with us without being of our "stock" (Jer 7:6; 22:3; Ezek 47:23). In Psalm 94, the sojourner is mentioned alongside the widow and the orphan as someone who functions as a test to see if those in charge truly take care of the needy:

> O Lord, thou God of vengeance, thou God of vengeance, shine forth! Rise up, O judge of the earth; render to the proud their deserts! O Lord, how long shall the wicked, how long shall the wicked exult? They pour out their arrogant words, they boast, all the evildoers. *They crush thy people, O Lord, and afflict thy heritage.*

---

[2] See also Jer 9:23-24.

They slay the widow and the sojourner, and murder the fatherless; and they say, "The Lord does not see; the God of Jacob does not perceive." Understand, O dullest of the people! Fools, when will you be wise? (vv.1-8)

Here we have an appeal to God, as the God of vengeance—a title which is repeated, to underscore the seriousness of the matter—asking him, the just judge, to avenge the wicked who crush his people that have none save him as their helper. What is impressive in this passage is that the sojourner, co-inhabitant (*ger*), is considered as a member of God's people and heritage (inheritance; *naḥalah*). This should make it clear, once and for all, that in scripture, God's people and heritage is not a matter of membership in a social group, let alone nationhood, but rather applies to anyone who is in need. God the King, and thus owner of all the earth, is bound to care for all those living on that earth. Were it not so, then God as judge would show partiality toward those whom he has predilection for and, consequently, would no longer be a just judge. Since the rich by definition are taken care of and thus do not have any need from others in order to live, God's main concern as King, as we have heard in the Psalms, is to care for those in need, and these are his people and heritage.

In reviewing the biblical narratives from this perspective, we shall readily see that the community of Israel is intended as an exemplar to uphold the thesis that God is concerned with those who are in need because and whenever they are not provided for by those who are supposed to care for them. Abraham's itinerary is the prime example for Israel to follow (Gen 11:28, 31; 15:7). He is asked to leave all that sustains his livelihood and life—earth, kindred, father's house—for an insecure future and for no other reason than obedience to God's command (12:1). As a stranger to the earth of Canaan, he is given a lesson in co-dwelling through the generosity of another, who at least originally was a stranger to that same earth (Gen. 23:7-20). Another powerful lesson is in the story of Sodom, a city of Canaan, which is destroyed because of lack of openheartedness toward a visitor. In vain, Abraham tried to defend the city against divine wrath by appealing to the eventual righteousness of some of the inhabitants. God's lesson is that righteousness lies in obeying his will which culminates in the care for the needy neighbor who happens to be sharing the same earth. In other words, Abraham and his progeny are promised length of days in Canaan *so long as* they make of that earth and its cities an abode of no less than divine justice and righteousness (Is 1:18-28).

The promise is also a challenge, namely that one must and can actually abide by God's will if one chooses. To illustrate this we have the story of Isaac, "the son of the promise" of that same God, as a paradigm for all subsequent generations, including those of Ishmael and Esau as well as Israel. Isaac both comes out of God's promise and realizes it by sharing the earth peacefully with the Philistine Abimelech and his people. Isaac understood that the earth is after all God's and remains his as "the earth of *Gerar*," where all the inhabitants are *gerim* (co-dwelling sojourners). That is why Isaac was never "punished" by having to leave the earth even to procure a wife to ensure his progeny. His peaceful and sharing dealings with the Philistines secured him God's blessing. Whenever the children of Israel follow his example, they secure for themselves the same blessing (2 Sam 21:1-9).

Put simply, from the exemplar biblical stories we learn lessons for all human beings. God took care of the children of Israel when they were either needy or co-inhabitants (*gerim*)—which they were in Egypt—on the one hand, or righteous, that is, doing his will which is expressed essentially in taking care of the needy and co-inhabitant, on the other hand. When they acted arrogantly taking for granted God's care for them, they were threatened with famine or siege or outright destruction and exile, and the promise of blessing that ensured length of days in peace was nullified.

The biblical story *in Canaan* begins in Genesis 12 and ends in 2 Kings 25. It is presented as a parable for the edification of the hearers, as we learn from its three shorter versions in Ezekiel 16, 20, and 23, which are also referred to as parables.[3] The lengthiest of these parables is found in Ezekiel 16. It is most enlightening in that:

1. Canaan is referred to as the earth of Jerusalem, and by extension of the kingdom of Judah's origin and birth (16:3; see also 21:30). Jerusalem was a Jebusite city that David took by force and made his personal property. Still Canaan remained an earth that was shared by the two sisters, Samaria and Jerusalem, representing the children of Israel, who lived side by side with their third sister Sodom (16:46-57).

2. Just as was done in the list of the nations in Genesis 10, the children of Israel, represented by Jerusalem and Samaria, are ultimately Amorites and Hittites: "Thus says the Lord God to Jerusalem: Your origin and your birth are of the earth of the Canaanites; your father was an Amorite, and your mother a Hittite … Your mother was a Hittite and your father

---

[3] See also Hosea 12:10: "I spoke to the prophets; it was I who multiplied visions, and through the prophets gave parables."

an Amorite. And your elder sister is Samaria." (Ezek 16:3; 45-46)

3. Although the entire chapter, together with chapter 23, revolves around the sin of disobedience as a harlotry against God, at one point the same sin is phrased in the terminology that reflects the lack of love and care for the needy neighbor: "As I live, says the Lord God, your sister Sodom and her daughters have not done as you and your daughters have done. Behold, this was the guilt of your sister Sodom: she and her daughters had pride, surfeit of food, and prosperous ease, but did not aid the poor and needy. They were haughty, and did abominable things before me; therefore I removed them, when I saw it. Samaria has not committed half your sins; you have committed more abominations than they, and have made your sisters appear righteous by all the abominations which you have committed." (vv.48-51) Notice how the same sin is further cast in the terms of arrogance and haughtiness, and presented as the reason behind the demise of the children of Israel as sojourners in Canaan.

The lesson is unmistakable and is intended for all the descendants of Noah who populate God's earth and share it with others. And all the children of Noah fall under the same divine verdict, as we hear in Jeremiah:

Thus says the Lord: "Let not the wise man glory in his wisdom, let not the mighty man glory in his might, let not the rich man glory in his riches; but let him who glories glory in this, that he understands and knows me, that I am the Lord who *practice kindness, justice, and righteousness* in the earth; for in these things I delight, says the Lord. Behold, the days are coming, says the Lord, when I will punish all those who are circumcised but yet uncircumcised—Egypt, Judah, Edom, the sons of Ammon, Moab, and all who dwell in the desert that cut the corners of their hair; for all these nations are uncircumcised, and all the house of Israel is uncircumcised in heart." (9:23-26)

Indeed, doing God's will is to practice kindness, justice, and righteousness in the earth. This is the word that comes out of the Lord's mouth and applies to every "man": "He has showed you, O man (*'adam*), what is good; and what does the Lord require of you but to *practice justice*, and to *love kindness*, and *to walk humbly* with your God?" (Micah 6:8) Every man is required to act righteously and to do so humbly without arrogance or haughtiness, since majesty and grandeur only befit God. This is where, scripture tells us, everyone seems to fail, starting with the first child of Adam, Cain, who killed his twin brother for no apparent reason other than his unwillingness to share God's earth with him. If only we would understand that the earth is God's and not our property!

God's People

The preceding established that God's people are a not a defined entity that could be segregated, as it were, as though the rest of humanity were not God's people. God's people are those who are related to him in a special way. Primarily, God's people are those in need of him *because* they have no helper but him. Secondarily, God's people are those who are similar to him in that they do his work, which is primarily taking care of his people, the needy and poor; put otherwise, God's people are those who "represent" him by caring for those in need. God's care for his creation is clear from the stories of Adam who works

God's garden, Moses who leads the children of Israel out of Egypt, Joshua who leads them into Canaan, and the earthly kings, the princes, judges, the priests, and the wise men who are supposed to be godly in their duties. Anyone who is in a position of responsibility is supposed to do God's work.

Still, as is clear from the requirements of the Law and the teachings of the Prophets, every single person is ultimately accountable, and it is our attitude toward those who are in need, which will decide our membership in the Lord's family:

> As for you, my flock, thus says the Lord God: Behold, I judge between sheep and sheep, rams and he-goats. Is it not enough for you to feed on the good pasture, that you must tread down with your feet the rest of your pasture; and to drink of clear water, that you must foul the rest with your feet? And must my sheep eat what you have trodden with your feet, and drink what you have fouled with your feet? Therefore, thus says the Lord God to them: Behold, I, I myself will judge between the fat sheep and the lean sheep. Because you push with side and shoulder, and thrust at all the weak with your horns, till you have scattered them abroad, I will save my flock, they shall no longer be a prey; and I will judge between sheep and sheep. And I will set up over them one shepherd, my servant David, and he shall feed them: he shall feed them and be their shepherd. (Ezek 34:17-23)

It is inasmuch that we care for the needy that we become part of God's community:

> Therefore I will judge you, O house of Israel, every one according to his ways, says the Lord God. Repent and turn from all your transgressions, lest iniquity be your ruin. Cast away from you all the transgressions which you have committed against me, and get yourselves a new heart and a new spirit! Why will you die, O

house of Israel? For I have no pleasure in the death of any one, says the Lord God; so turn, and live. (Ezek 18:30-32)

That is why the constituency of the membership in God's people is not only conditional, but also it will not be revealed until the end, when God will judge all:

> Therefore say, "Thus says the Lord God: 'I will gather you from the peoples, and assemble you out of the areas where you have been scattered, and I will give you the *ground* of Israel. And when they come there, they will remove from it all its detestable things and all its abominations. And I will give them one heart, and put a new spirit within them; I will take the stony heart out of their flesh and give them a heart of flesh, *that they may walk in my statutes and keep my ordinances and obey them; and they shall be my people, and I will be their God.*'" (Ezek 11:17-20)

> For I will take you from the nations, and gather you from all the areas, and bring you into your *ground* (*'adamah*). I will sprinkle clean water upon you, and you shall be clean from all your uncleannesses, and from all your idols I will cleanse you. A new heart I will give you, and a new spirit I will put within you; and I will take out of your flesh the heart of stone and give you a heart of flesh. *And I will put my spirit within you, and cause you to walk in my statutes and be careful to observe my ordinances.* You shall dwell in the earth which I gave to your fathers; and you shall be my people, and I will be your God. (Ezek 36:24-28)

From these just quoted passages of Ezekiel one concludes the following:

1. God's people are not a defined static entity; rather they are those who heed his call to become his people by repenting and amending their ways.

2. Repentance does not only mean acknowledgement of previous sins, but also entails obeying God's statutes

and ordinances. Only those who do so "shall be God's people" and "he shall be their God."

3. Most importantly, the earth where God's people live is not a possession, but rather an open "ground" (*'adamah*), where every "man" (*'adam*) is invited to dwell with all others under God's rule of brotherhood and care for the needy.

This openness of God's ultimate earth of inheritance is corroborated in Ezekiel 34:30-31 where "God's people" are tantamount to the "sheep of his pasture:" "And they shall know that I, the Lord their God, am with them, and that they, the house of Israel, are my people, says the Lord God. And you are my sheep, the sheep of my pasture, and I am your God, says the Lord God." The new earth of God is so open it will include even the wilderness: "I will make with them a covenant of peace and banish wild beasts from the earth, so that they may dwell securely in the wilderness and sleep in the woods." (34:25) It is an earth that recalls the world of Adam in Genesis 1-2:

> And I will make them and the places round about my hill a *blessing*; and I will send down the showers in their season; they shall be showers of *blessing*. And *the trees of the field shall yield their fruit*, and the earth shall yield its increase, and they shall be secure in their *ground*; and they shall know that I am the Lord, when I break the bars of their yoke, and deliver them from the hand of those who enslaved them. They shall no more be a spoil to the nations, nor shall the *beasts of the earth* devour them; they shall dwell securely, and none shall make them afraid. (Ezek 34:26-28)

It is no wonder then that this wide openness of God's earth goes hand in hand with an all-inclusiveness concerning his people. Given that the ending of Ezekiel 34 and 37 are corresponding, it stands to reason that the "house of Israel" of 34:30 is the same one that is the subject of chapter 37. There, we are told that it is "all (the entirety of) the house of Israel" (*kol yisra'el*; the whole house of Israel) whose bones shall be raised (v.11). In Ezekiel 20:33-44 we learned that such would be a complete house purged of the wicked, meaning that its totality would be all those who have heeded God's call for repentance and renewal, that is, all those who have accepted that their heart be renewed according to God's spirit. This "whole house of Israel" is inclusive in that it encompasses not only the remnant of the kingdom of Judah, but also that of the long forgotten kingdom of Israel:

> Son of man, take a stick and write on it, "For Judah, and the children of Israel associated with him"; then take another stick and write upon it, "For Joseph (the stick of Ephraim) and all the house of Israel associated with him"; and join them together into one stick, that they may become one in your hand. And when your people say to you, "Will you not show us what you mean by these?" say to them, Thus says the Lord God: Behold, I am about to take the stick of Joseph (which is in the hand of Ephraim) and the tribes of Israel associated with him; and I will join with it the stick of Judah, and make them one stick, that they may be one in my hand. When the sticks on which you write are in your hand before their eyes, then say to them, Thus says the Lord God: Behold, I will take the people of Israel from the nations among which they have gone, and will gather them from all sides, and bring them to their ground; and I will make them one nation in the earth, upon the mountains of Israel; and one king shall be king over them all; and they shall be no longer two nations, and no longer divided into two kingdoms. (Ezek 37:16-22)

As part of biblical Israel, those who pertain to Judah are considered "children of Israel," and not "children of Judah." Although the individual child of Israel is called an "Israelite," the

The Prophets

more common designation is that of Jew, that is, Judahite (Hebrew *yehudi*; Greek *Ioudaios*), someone who pertains to Judah. This is because scripture arose among the exiles of Judah. This also explains why the metaphoric future heavenly city of God, which the exiled and scattered Judahites constantly yearn for, is given the name of Zion (Is 66:8) or Jerusalem (vv.10, 13, 20). Still, the Jew is always reminded that it is inasmuch as he is a "child of Israel" that he will accede to that city and its surrounding earth (Ezek 48). Indeed, as Judahite, son of Judah, the Jew is to become Israelite, son of (his grandfather Jacob) Israel, and, as such, he is to realize that (his father) Judah is only one of the twelve "sons of Israel" with whom he shares the promise. Thus, membership in God's people, Israel, is not an entitlement. It is a call to be pursued.

Besides forcing the Jew to be ready to share God's heritage, the salvation of the Jew (Judahite) *as* Israelite is shaming since the sharing is specifically with Joseph, the brother whom Judah and his siblings sold into slavery and yet who proved to be their savior! Jerusalem, the capital of Judah, in and to her shame, will have to share God's heritage not only with Samaria, the capital of the kingdom championed by the tribe of Ephraim, Joseph's son, but also with Sodom, her other "sister":

> I will restore their fortunes, both the fortunes of Sodom and her daughters, and the fortunes of Samaria and her daughters, and I will restore your own fortunes in the midst of them, that you may bear your disgrace and be ashamed of all that you have done, becoming a consolation to them. (Ezek 16:53-54)

Actually, this inclusiveness encompasses all nations who will share in God's heritage around his city. Just as Sodom is Jerusalem's sister, those who will be gathered from among the nations will be full "brethren," even to the extent that some of them will serve as priests and Levites (Is 66:18-21).

This ending to the Book of Isaiah goes hand in hand with the prophet's message throughout the entire book:

> They shall not hurt or destroy in all my holy mountain; for the earth shall be full of the knowledge of the Lord as the waters cover the sea. In that day the root of Jesse shall stand as an ensign to the peoples; him shall the nations seek, and his dwellings shall be glorious. (Is 11:9-10)

> Behold my servant, whom I uphold, my chosen, in whom my soul delights; I have put my Spirit upon him, he will bring forth justice to the nations. He will not cry or lift up his voice, or make it heard in the street; a bruised reed he will not break, and a dimly burning wick he will not quench; he will faithfully bring forth justice. He will not fail or be discouraged till he has established justice in the earth; and the coastlands wait for his law. (42:1-4)

> It is too light a thing that you should be my servant to raise up the tribes of Jacob and to restore the preserved of Israel; I will give you as a light to the nations, that my salvation may reach to the end of the earth. (49:6)

> Hearken to me, you who pursue deliverance, you who seek the Lord; look to the rock from which you were hewn, and to the quarry from which you were digged. Look to Abraham your father and to Sarah who bore you; for when he was but one I called him, and I blessed him and made him many. For the Lord will comfort Zion; he will comfort all her waste places, and will make her wilderness like Eden, her desert like the garden of the Lord; joy and gladness will be found in her, thanksgiving and the voice of song. Listen to me, my people, and give ear to me, my nation; for a law will go forth from me, and my justice for a light to the peoples. My deliverance draws near speedily, my salvation has

gone forth, and my arms will rule the peoples; the coastlands wait for me, and for my arm they hope. (51:1-5)

Such inclusiveness should not be cause for astonishment or puzzlement since it fits with God's plan from the beginning, as is made clear from the reference to Eden and Abraham. Not only did the promise to Abraham include the blessing upon all nations, but it was actually sealed in the covenant of circumcision that is all inclusive. However, circumcision is not a magic act that ensures entitlement to God's promise of blessing, but rather entails obedience to God. In the covenant of circumcision, Canaan is referred to as the earth of Abraham's sojourning (Gen 17:8), that is, an earth where he was a stranger, co-inhabitant (*ger*). Actually, he almost lost it when he went down to Egypt. That is why, on their way out of this same Egypt toward Canaan, the children of Israel were granted the Law with its eventual curse of being thrown out of Canaan should they not hearken to God's commandments. They could not be in a better position than Abraham himself:

> And the Lord appeared to him [Isaac], and said, "Do not go down to Egypt; dwell in the earth of which I shall tell you. Sojourn in this earth, and I will be with you, and will bless you; for to you and to your descendants I will give all these areas, and I will fulfill the oath which I swore to Abraham your father. I will multiply your descendants as the stars of heaven, and will give to your descendants all these areas; and by your descendants all the nations of the earth shall bless themselves (be blessed) because Abraham obeyed my voice and kept my charge, my commandments, my statutes, and my laws." (Gen 26:2-5)

Hence God's indictment of the arrogant exiles through Ezekiel in these terms:

Son of man, the inhabitants of these waste places on the ground of Israel keep saying, "Abraham was only one man, yet he inherited the earth; but we are many; the earth is surely given us to inherit." Therefore say to them, Thus says the Lord God: You eat flesh with the blood, and lift up your eyes to your idols, and shed blood; shall you then inherit the earth? You resort to the sword, you commit abominations and each of you defiles his neighbor's wife; shall you then inherit the earth? Say this to them, Thus says the Lord God: As I live, surely those who are in the waste places shall fall by the sword; and him that is in the open field I will give to the beasts to be devoured; and those who are in strongholds and in caves shall die by pestilence. And I will make the earth a desolation and a waste; and her proud might shall come to an end; and the mountains of Israel shall be so desolate that none will pass through. Then they will know that I am the Lord, when I have made the earth a desolation and a waste because of all their abominations which they have committed. (Ezek 33:24-29)

The exiles should have remembered that, since the Abrahamic covenant is a matter of obedience, circumcision is not a matter of being marked in the flesh; rather it is a matter of mindset.[4] Thus circumcision is a matter of attitude reflected in actions, as Paul will clarify:

> For, as it is written, "The name of God is blasphemed among the Gentiles because of you." Circumcision indeed is of value if you obey the law; but if you break the law, your circumcision becomes uncircumcision. So, if a man who is uncircumcised keeps the precepts of the law, will not his uncircumcision be regarded as

---

[4]The Hebrew *leb*, which is usually translated as heart, actually means "core, center" (the "heart of the matter," as it were). Consequently, it indicates the "mind" as the center of decision and action, rather than the "heart" as the center of feelings.

circumcision? Then those who are physically uncircumcised but keep the law will condemn you who have the written code and circumcision but break the law. For he is not a real Jew who is one outwardly, nor is true circumcision something external and physical. He is a Jew who is one inwardly, and real circumcision is a matter of the heart, spiritual and not literal. His praise is not from men but from God. (Rom 2:24-29)

In this regard, Paul is not an innovator. He is merely referring to the Old Testament scripture as is evident from his opening remark "as it is written."

Indeed, Moses and the Prophets repeatedly pointed out the true meaning of circumcision. Let us hear Jeremiah's appeal:

Circumcise yourselves to the Lord, remove the foreskin of your hearts, O men of Judah and inhabitants of Jerusalem; lest my wrath go forth like fire, and burn with none to quench it, because of the evil of your doings. (Jer 4:4)

Otherwise, the children of Israel would be no different than the surrounding nations *who are circumcised themselves*:

Behold, the days are coming, says the Lord, when I will punish all those who are circumcised but yet uncircumcised—Egypt, Judah, Edom, the sons of Ammon, Moab, and all who dwell in the desert that cut the corners of their hair; for all these nations are uncircumcised, and all the house of Israel is uncircumcised in heart. (Jer 9:25-26)

But it is already Moses—before the entrance into Canaan and before Joshua circumcised the new-born generation who was to dwell in Canaan—who summed up circumcision in these most clear terms:

> Circumcise therefore the foreskin of your heart, and be no longer stubborn. For the Lord your God is God of gods and Lord of lords, the great, the mighty, and the terrible God, who is not partial and takes no bribe. He executes justice for the fatherless and the widow, and loves the sojourner, giving him food and clothing. Love the sojourner therefore; for you were sojourners in the earth of Egypt. (Deut 10:16-19)

Part III

The Wisdom Literature

13

The Writings *(Ketubim)*

Wisdom Writings

Since the same requirement is made of every man, one can understand how scripture was bound to have a third set of writings besides the Law and the Prophets. The Book (of the Wisdom) of Sirach, from whose prologue I quoted earlier, is among the third part of scripture, after the Law and the Prophets. This last part includes the Book of Psalms and other books commonly known as Wisdom literature. This literature was developed in keeping with Ezekiel's teaching: those entrusted with the Law are to live on God's wide earth together with the other descendants of Adam and Noah, just as they did in Canaan. While sojourning in Canaan, those entrusted with the Law did not heed it and ended up exiled out of that ground. Now, they should know that God can punish them on any ground should they not heed his law. Given that their scripture does not allow them to have any other deity, then their only God is both their judge as well as their instructor. Conversely, if they follow his law they will be blessed. This blessing was promised to Abraham in the following words: "by you all the families of the earth shall bless themselves (be blessed)." (Gen 12:3) Isaac, as I explained earlier, is the only seed through whom the blessing is secured, and we are told that there is a specific reason for this:

> I will multiply your descendants as the stars of heaven, and will give to your descendants all these areas; and by your descendants all the nations of the earth shall bless themselves (be blessed) *because Abraham obeyed my voice and kept my charge, my commandments, my statutes, and my laws.* (Gen 26:4-5)

Thus, the children of the promise made to Abraham "according to (the way of) Isaac" (Gal 4:28) are not only to follow that Law, but also share it so that others may receive the blessing (3:14) by following that Law (5:13-14; 6:2). The "others" among whom the Jews lived were mainly the inhabitants of the Roman empire who were taught in the wisdom of the Hellenes. Scriptural Wisdom literature was produced to proposition them with the following: true wisdom is to be found in God's law, and not in the teachings of Hellenic philosophy. Wisdom is not something to be acquired, but rather a gift from God.

The Solomon Literature

As was established in Ezekiel and Isaiah, those who form the nucleus of the true Israel are the repentant (returning, in Hebrew) Israel, and all those who "return, turn back" to God from among the nations. The king, as the shepherd of that people, is to be a repentant leader who teaches the Law as the only true wisdom to both his people and to the nations. That is why the patron of the large part of Wisdom literature—Proverbs, Ecclesiastes, Song of Songs, Wisdom of Solomon—is said to be Solomon. The repentance of Solomon is at its clearest in the Book of Ecclesiastes: (the) Preacher, the son of David, king in Jerusalem, realizes that all is vanity (1:1-2) unless one submits to the commandments of God who will judge everyone:

> He who obeys a command will meet no harm, and the mind of a wise man will know the time and way. (8:5)

> Though a sinner does evil a hundred times and prolongs his life, yet I know that it will be well with those who fear God, because they fear before him; but it will not be well with the wicked, neither will he prolong his days like a shadow, because he does not fear before God. (8:12-13)

The Writings (Ketubim)

The end of the matter; all has been heard. Fear God, and keep his commandments; for this is the whole duty of man. For God will bring every deed into judgment, with every secret thing, whether good or evil. (12:13-14)

The proper name given the son of David, (the) Preacher, in Hebrew, *Qohelet*, is of import. *Qohelet* means the "congregator," the one who calls God's people to meet as a *qahal* (congregation) in order for them to be taught God's will. The Septuagint translates the term *qahal* into the Greek *ekklēsia* (church); hence the Hebrew Book of *Qohelet* is rendered as the Book of Ecclesiastes (*Ekklēsiastēs*) in the Septuagint. Paul will follow suit, as we shall see, when he teaches the Corinthian church (*ekklēsia*), made up of Jews as well as Gentiles, the true wisdom embedded in God's commandments: "For neither circumcision counts for anything nor uncircumcision, but keeping the commandments of God." (1 Cor 7:19)

The conquests of Alexander the Great at the end of the fourth century B.C. spread the use of the Hellenic or Greek language throughout the area where the Jews resided, nowadays known as the Middle East. That is why in the later scriptural literature, instead of the more common Hebrew *goyim* translated as *ethnē* (ethnies, nations) in the Septuagint, we encounter the Hebrew *yawan* (Javan), *bene yawan* (children of Javan) or *yawanim* (Javanites), being translated as *Hellēnes* (Hellenes, Greeks).[1] This explains the phenomenon found in the New Testament where "nations" and "Greeks" are used as fully equivalent terms. This move from "nations" to "Greeks," however, was not haphazard, since it was prepared for in scripture. Javan appears at the "beginning" of the human story and then again at its "end"

---

[1] See, e.g., Is 66:19; Ezek 27:13; Dan 8:21; 10:20; 11:2; Zech 9:13.

when God will gather the nations together with Israel in his heavenly Jerusalem, where both parties will be on an equal footing:

> The sons of Japheth: Gomer, Magog, Madai, Javan, Tubal, Meshech, and Tiras. The sons of Gomer: Ashkenaz, Riphath, and Togarmah. The sons of *Javan*: Elishah, Tarshish, Kittim, and Dodanim. From these the *coastland peoples* spread. These are the sons of Japheth in their areas, each with his own language, by their families, in their nations. (Gen 10:2-5)

> For I know their works and their thoughts, and I am coming to gather all nations and tongues; and they shall come and shall see my glory, and I will set a sign among them. And from them I will send survivors to the nations, to Tarshish, Put, and Lud, who draw the bow, to Tubal and *Javan*, to the *coastlands* afar off, that have not heard my fame or seen my glory; and they shall declare my glory among the nations. And they shall bring all your brethren from all the nations as an offering to the Lord, upon horses, and in chariots, and in litters, and upon mules, and upon dromedaries, to my holy mountain Jerusalem, says the Lord, just as the Israelites bring their cereal offering in a clean vessel to the house of the Lord. And some of them also I will take for priests and for Levites, says the Lord. (Is 66:18-21)

Thus, from the perspective of the inhabitants of Canaan and Mesopotamia, Javan is part of the "the coastland nations," the nations inhabiting the islands of the Mediterranean, that is, the Greeks.

The treasure most valued by the Greeks was "wisdom," which they sought after and thought separated them from the "barbarians." To quote Paul: "For Jews demand signs and Greeks seek wisdom" (1 Cor 1: 23); "I am under obligation both to Greeks and to barbarians, both to the wise and to the foolish." (Rom 1:14) Yet, according to Isaiah, it is to those Greeks that

God's final emissary will be sent to offer them God's teaching in his law as the ultimate wisdom they were seeking:

> Behold my servant, whom I uphold, my chosen, in whom my soul delights; I have put my Spirit upon him, he will bring forth justice to the nations. He will not cry or lift up his voice, or make it heard in the street; dimly burning wick he will not quench; he will faithfully bring forth justice. He will not fail or be discouraged till he has established justice in the earth; and the coastlands wait for his law. Thus says God, the Lord, who created the heavens and stretched them out, who spread forth the earth and what comes from it, who gives breath to the people upon it and spirit to those who walk in it. I am the Lord, I have called you in righteousness, I have taken you by the hand and kept you; I have given you as a covenant to the people, a light to the nations, to open the eyes that are blind, to bring out the prisoners from the dungeon, from the prison those who sit in darkness. (Is 42:1-7)[2]

The Law, however, was given in the wilderness, that is, away from all cities where Greek wisdom had developed. It was given from God's mountain where only Moses, the lawgiver, ascended and whence he was able to behold God's heavenly house (temple). It was from that temple beyond the clouds that God delivered his *torah* (Law), the vessel of true wisdom. That is why, the "repentant" Solomon speaks in his Proverbs of "lady wisdom" being endowed with divine features, residing in a house that is a temple where offerings are made, teaching her ways:

---

[2] See also Is 49:1, 5-6 (Listen to me, O coastlands, and hearken, you peoples from afar. The Lord called me from the womb, from the body of my mother he named my name ... And now the Lord says, who formed me from the womb to be his servant, to bring Jacob back to him, and that Israel might be gathered to him, for I am honored in the eyes of the Lord, and my God has become my strength—he says: "It is too light a thing that you should be my servant to raise up the tribes of Jacob and to restore the preserved of Israel; I will give you as a light to the nations, that my salvation may reach to the end of the earth.").

I, wisdom, dwell in prudence, and I find knowledge and discretion ... The Lord created me at the beginning of his work, the first of his acts of old. Ages ago I was set up, at the first, before the beginning of the earth. When there were no depths I was brought forth, when there were no springs abounding with water. Before the mountains had been shaped, before the hills, I was brought forth; before he had made the earth with its fields, or the first of the dust of the world. When he established the heavens, I was there, when he drew a circle on the face of the deep, when he made firm the skies above, when he established the fountains of the deep, when he assigned to the sea its limit, so that the waters might not transgress his command, when he marked out the foundations of the earth, then I was beside him, like a master workman; and I was daily his delight, rejoicing before him always, rejoicing in his inhabited world and delighting in the sons of men. And now, my sons, listen to me: happy are those who keep my ways. Hear instruction and be wise, and do not neglect it. (Prov 8:12, 22-33)

Wisdom has built her house, she has set up her seven pillars. She has slaughtered her beasts, she has mixed her wine, she has also set her table. (9:1-2)

Psalms

The itinerary to repentance, which applied to Solomon, applied equally to David as one can see in the Book of Psalms. The psalms taken in the order in which they appear actually trace the Davidic story beginning with the sin of the first David and his people, and culminating in the yearning for the true heavenly Jerusalem and its temple, which will be inaugurated by the new David.[3] Compared to the first David who thought in his arrogance that he could build a temple to God, the new David

---

[3] For more detail see *OTI*$_3$ 99-104.

The Writings (Ketubim)

expects it from God himself since "unless the Lord builds the house, those who build it labor in vain. Unless the Lord watches over the city, the watchman stays awake in vain" (Ps 127:1). The condition for the building of God's city and its temple is David's repentance of his double sin against Uriah the Hittite:

> A Psalm of David, when Nathan the prophet came to him, after he had gone in to Bathsheba. Have mercy on me, O God, according to thy steadfast love; according to thy abundant mercy blot out my transgressions. Wash me thoroughly from my iniquity, and cleanse me from my sin! For I know my transgressions, and my sin is ever before me. Against thee, thee only, have I sinned, and done that which is evil in thy sight, so that thou art justified in thy sentence and blameless in thy judgment. Behold, I was brought forth in iniquity, and in sin did my mother conceive me ... Deliver me from bloodguiltiness, O God, thou God of my salvation, and my tongue will sing aloud of thy deliverance. O Lord, open thou my lips, and my mouth shall show forth thy praise. For thou hast no delight in sacrifice; were I to give a burnt offering, thou wouldst not be pleased. The sacrifice acceptable to God is a broken spirit; a broken and contrite heart, O God, thou wilt not despise. Do good to Zion in thy good pleasure; rebuild the walls of Jerusalem, then wilt thou delight in right sacrifices, in burnt offerings and whole burnt offerings; then bulls will be offered on thy altar. (Ps 51:1-5, 14-19)

That God's true abode is a heavenly one, and thus not made by the hand of man, is corroborated in the concluding psalm: "Praise the Lord! Praise God in his sanctuary; praise him in his mighty *firmament!*" (Ps 150:1) Indeed, the noun "firmament" (*raqia'*) is encountered repeatedly in the creation account in Genesis 1 (nine times) and in the description of the divine apparition to Ezekiel (four times in chapter 1 and once in chapter 10). Elsewhere, we find it only in two more instances, once in Psalm 19:2 (The heavens are telling the glory of God; and the firmament proclaims his handiwork), and another in Daniel 12:3 (And those who are wise shall shine like the brightness of the firmament; and those who turn many to righteousness, like the stars for ever and ever). In all these instances, the firmament is clearly reflective of the heavenly realm, separate from the earthly realm of the human being.

The invitation in Psalm 150 to praise the Lord is inclusive not only of all human beings but also of all creatures, as is clear from the last verse: "Let *any and all breath* (all the breeze; all the breath; *kol hanneshamah*) praise the Lord! Praise the Lord!" (v.6). That the all-inclusiveness of *kol hanneshamah* encompasses not only all creatures, but actually all God's creation can be gathered from Psalm 148 where every part of the creation, inanimate as well as animate, is invited to praise the Lord. Consequently, the reference cannot be to an earthly Jerusalem and its temple, however restored they may be, but rather to "the new heavens and the new earth" of Isaiah 66:22.

A clear indication that the psalms of praise that end the Book, starting with Psalm 135, are to be recited in the heavenly Jerusalem, representing God's "new earth and new heavens," is that they are immediately preceded by fifteen psalms each entitled "song for the ascent (stairs, steps)" (120-134). To assume, as it was done later, that a pilgrimage to the earthly Jerusalem necessarily entailed an ascent, does not stand scrutiny since one does not ascend to Jerusalem when one approaches it from the north. The condition for one to be able to ascend to and then abide in God's heavenly city and kingdom is set out in the lengthy Psalm 119, which precedes the Songs of Ascent. That psalm is a seemingly endless (176 verses) ode to God's words embedded in his law. It is clearly intended as an invitation as well as a reminder that the only "way" to accede to and remain in God's promised earth of peace is to abide by his will. Otherwise, one would end up in the same predicament as the biblical Israel who either perished in the wilderness, that is, on the way to that earth, or was punished and exiled out of that earth.

Job

The same teaching is found in Job, the other major book in the Writings (*ketubim*). This book tells the story of Job, who was tested in his faithfulness to abide by God's commandments inscribed in the Law while he was living away from Jerusalem and the earth surrounding it. The earth of Uz, where Job lived (Job 1:1), is linked to Edom, the earth of Esau, Jacob's twin brother (Gen 36:28). The story starts in Uz and ends there. Job's restoration to his earlier state of blessedness does not translate him to the earth of Judah or Israel. In other words, Job was and remained a Jew, fulfilling God's law, in the place of his sojourn. There is no indication whatsoever that he yearned for Jerusalem and the earth surrounding it. His delight, as Psalm 119 puts it, was in abiding by God's will and fulfilling its commandments: "I find my delight in thy commandments" (vv. 35, 47, 143); "In the way of thy testimonies I delight" (vv.14, 24); "I will delight in thy statutes" (v.16); "thy law is my delight." (vv.70, 77, 92, 174) Thus, Job is presented as the typical Jew of nascent Judaism: it is God's law that is his protector no matter where on earth he happens to be living.

14

The Canon of the Writings *(Ketubim)*

Having covered, for the sake of brevity, the major books of the Writings in order to point out their intent to invite the nations to the true wisdom, God's law, it would behoove us to have a look at the order of the entire literature in the canon.[1] We have seen how the order is of import in the Books of the Law, in the Prior Prophets, and even in the Latter Prophets. The "Writings" are headed with the Book of Psalms which is the hymnal of the heavenly Jerusalem where the biblical story of the earthly sinful Jerusalem is reviewed and the coming heavenly one is promised. It functions thus for the nations as a compendium of the biblical story from its beginning to its promised end. Once the point is made that the length of days on the earth where one lives is not guaranteed unless one abides by God's will, comes the Book of Job. A devout Jew, Job was born and lived all his life outside the earth of Judah and was blessed without ever having been to Jerusalem, let alone returning to it. The reason is that God made him understand that true wisdom lay in God's law, and following it secured the blessing. If that is true of the Jew Job, then it is also true of the nations who, upon hearing the message of God's law brought to them by his emissary, should stay where they are, looking ahead for the new heavenly Jerusalem, which will be the abode of Jews and nations alike. The Book of Proverbs follows, which universalizes the application of the teaching of Job. It is a compendium of behavior based on the premise that "The fear of the Lord is the beginning of knowledge; fools despise wisdom and instruction"

---

[1] I am following the Hebrew Old Testament canon.

(Prov 1:7). As we learn from the Law, one fears God by keeping his commandments. This is the true wisdom that is delivered as instruction to human beings and their leaders by "Lady Wisdom" whose abode is in God's heavenly temple.[2]

The following five short books, Ruth, The Song of Songs, Ecclesiastes, Lamentations, and Esther, known as *megillot* (scrolls) and read at different feasts, underscore the message contained in the previous trilogy. Although Moabite, Ruth ended by being the ancestress of David. In other words, she, the non-Israelite, pertained to God's patrimony even before Solomon was born, let alone issued his call to the nations. Thus, the call to the nations is not to join the ranks of Israel, but to heed the call of Israel's God and, by so doing, inherit his city and earth! The same message is carried in The Song of Songs which is the call of the repentant Solomon to another outsider, the Shulammite (6:13), inviting her and, through her, all the nations, to join him in God's city Jerusalem.[3]

The book of Ecclesiastes is an invitation to congregate in the synagogue—not in the temple made by man—listening to the reading of God's law and the teaching of his prophets in order to be found faithful and become citizens of God's heavenly city.

The fourth book is a series of Lamentations for the unfaithful city of David and Solomon. It is a caveat stressing that it is neither David's city nor Solomon's temple that offers protection to the people, but it is by being obedient to God's will that the nations will be blessed. As Jeremiah preached, "Thus says the Lord of hosts, the God of Israel, amend your ways and your doings, and I will let you dwell in this place. Do not trust in

---

[2] See Prov 8:10-16, 22-23 and 9:1-2 quoted earlier.
[3] For more detail see *OTI₃* 140-141.

The Canon of the Writings (Ketubim)

these deceptive words: 'This is the temple of the Lord, the temple of the Lord, the temple of the Lord'" (7:3-4).

Lastly, the book of Esther confirms the teaching of the entire collection. It is a book telling of God's salvation wrought in the earth of sojourning that underscores the message to remain faithful to God's teaching and he will protect you wherever you are upon the earth. For centuries commentators have pointed out the absence of the noun "God" throughout the book. The intention is to underscore his concealment, but in no way his absence. This is reflected in the name of the heroine, Esther (Esth 2:7), whose Hebrew original *'ester* means "I (shall) hide." Although God is hiding his presence, he still fully rules as "the King of all." This is precisely what he did in his law: unlike the idols, he is fully present in his will, although absent to the sight. It is through his will that he can dispense curse as well as blessing. Thus the Book of Esther reflects to its fullest the teaching of the Law, the Prophets, and the Writings.

The Book of Daniel completes the thesis of the "Writings" and opens the way for the New Testament literature. In it we meet the hero, Daniel, who, like Esther, is saved in a foreign earth. However, his story is cast in the same vein as that of Joseph. From near destruction he rises to fame and, with the divine wisdom bestowed upon him, he helps the ruler in whose hand lies his own fate. Thus, at the close of scripture, the hearers are taken back to the Book of Genesis where, during Joseph's lifetime, the children of Jacob were protected in Egypt where they had ended up because of their sin. Yet, God, through Joseph and his memory, preserved them and they multiplied and prospered, just as the Jews would later do in Alexandria of Egypt. In the same way, the Book of Daniel is inviting its hearers, wherever they may be sojourning, to live in the fear of God who governs beyond the rulers of any kingdom. Earthly kingdoms and empires, however mighty they may appear, will crumble. Above and beyond them, God's coming kingdom will always loom asking us to walk in its light. Still, unlike earthly rulers, God rules not through armies and police. Rather he rules through his teaching and punishes according to it as can be seen from Daniel's prayer:

> O Lord, the great and terrible God, who keepest covenant and steadfast love with those who love him and keep his commandments, we have sinned and done wrong and acted wickedly and rebelled, turning aside from thy commandments and ordinances; we have not listened to thy servants the prophets, who spoke in thy name to our kings, our princes, and our fathers, and to all the people of the earth ... All Israel has transgressed thy law and turned aside, refusing to obey thy voice. And the curse and oath which are written in the law of Moses the servant of God have been poured out upon us, because we have sinned against him. He has confirmed his words, which he spoke against us and against our rulers who ruled us, by bringing upon us a great calamity; for under the whole heaven there has not been done the like of what has been done against Jerusalem. As it is written in the law of Moses, all this calamity has come upon us, yet we have not entreated the favor of the Lord our God, turning from our iniquities and giving heed to thy truth. Therefore the Lord has kept ready the calamity and has brought it upon us; for the Lord our God is righteous in all the works which he has done, and we have not obeyed his voice. (Dan 9:4-6, 11-14)

Such was to be expected since we read earlier:

> Then this Daniel became distinguished above all the other presidents and satraps, because an excellent spirit was in him; and the king planned to set him over the whole kingdom. Then the presidents and the satraps sought to find a ground for complaint

against Daniel with regard to the kingdom; but they could find no ground for complaint or any fault, because he was faithful, and no error or fault was found in him. Then these men said, "We shall not find any ground for complaint against this Daniel unless we find it in connection with the law of his God." (Dan 6:3-5)

The Hebrew Canon of the *Ketubim* ends with the four Books of Ezra, Nehemiah, and 1 and 2 Chronicles, which seem to be the work of the same school of writers, usually referred to as "the Chronicler." What is immediately eye-catching is that their order is not chronological. The first two deal with the post-Cyrus period when exiled Jews returned to Jerusalem; the last two deal with the same content found in Genesis through 2 Kings: from Adam until the fall of Jerusalem. What is even more important is that the hearers cannot miss the fact that the last book, 2 Chronicles, ends where the first book, Ezra, starts:

> Now in the first year of Cyrus king of Persia, that the word of the Lord by the mouth of Jeremiah might be accomplished, the Lord stirred up the spirit of Cyrus king of Persia so that he made a proclamation throughout all his kingdom and also put it in writing: "Thus says Cyrus king of Persia, 'The Lord, the God of heaven, has given me all the kingdoms of the earth, and he has charged me to build him a house at Jerusalem, which is in Judah. Whoever is among you of all his people, may the Lord his God be with him. Let him go up.'" (2 Chr 36:22-23)

> Now in the first year of Cyrus king of Persia, that the word of the Lord by the mouth of Jeremiah might be accomplished, the Lord stirred up the spirit of Cyrus king of Persia so that he made a proclamation throughout all his kingdom and also put it in writing: "Thus says Cyrus king of Persia, 'The Lord, the God of heaven, has given me all the kingdoms of the earth, and he has charged me to build him a house at Jerusalem, which is in Judah. Whoever is among you of all his people, may the Lord his God be

with him. Let him go up to Jerusalem, which is in Judah, and rebuild the house of the Lord, the God of Israel—he is the God who is in Jerusalem.'" (Ezra 1:1-3)

The intention is unmistakable. Unless the "returnees" understand that they are bound by the same divine Law as their brethren who did not return, they will end up in the same exile as their predecessors. Indeed, of Ezra we hear that "he was a scribe skilled in the law of Moses which the Lord the God of Israel had given ... Ezra had set his heart to study the law of the Lord, and to do it, and to teach his statutes and ordinances in Israel" (7:6, 10). Thus, the *Ketubim* finish on an open-ended note just as the Law and the Prophets did, making of them not a history but an instruction to all upcoming generations.

15

The Septuagint

In the Greek translation of the Hebrew Old Testament, known as the Septuagint, we find some extra books known traditionally as *anaginōskomena*, "good to be read aloud (in the gatherings),"[1] thus underscoring their instructional value in the same vein as their counterparts, the Writings, and the Law and the Prophets. The closeness between the Septuagint and the Hebrew canon is evident in the prologue to the Wisdom of Sirach, which indicates that the original work was in Hebrew. The Wisdom of Sirach and the Wisdom of Solomon follow the lead of the Books of Proverbs and Ecclesiastes and integrate their teaching into the "biblical story" since they both contain chapters that review the latter (Wisdom of Solomon 10-19; Wisdom of Sirach 44-49).

The Books of Maccabees follow another route since they assess the very questionable Maccabean armed revolt against the Seleucids. I should like to take some extra time to discuss these books given that, lately in the United States, the Maccabean revolt is hailed in the media as the "first struggle for religious freedom in history." The intention of the proponents of such a view is undoubtedly to strike a sensitive chord in the minds of the citizens of this country. What renders this matter even more serious is that the feast commemorating the event is Hanukkah, which falls close to the feast of Christmas commemorating the birth of the "Prince of Peace" who advocated the love for the

---

[1] These are—besides the additions to Esther, Daniel, and Psalms (Ps 151)—1 and 2 Esdras; Tobit; Judith; Wisdom of Solomon; Wisdom of Sirach; Baruch; Letter of Jeremiah; Prayer of Manasseh; 1, 2, 3, and 4 Maccabees.

enemies. The detrimental result is that the *alleged* message of Hanukkah is made to contradict that of Christmas and even take precedence in the minds of the American citizens who are keen about "religious freedom." A closer reading of these books will clearly show that their intention is a far cry from what is sold in the media nowadays.

While 1 Maccabees reviews the Maccabean revolt and its success, it does so with an inherent critique of the method used by Judas the Maccabee (Judas called Maccabeus; 2:4) and his brothers. First, the book refers repeatedly to the fact that Judas took the opportunity of an armed revolt to settle an old score with his neighbors "the sons of Esau in Idumea (Edom)" (5:3, 64), the Ammonites (v.6), the inhabitants of Galilee and Gilead (vv.9-62), and the Philistines (vv.66-68), which is reminiscent of the feats of King David. Secondly, the book repeatedly refers to the alliances Judas struck with the Romans (1 Macc 8) and with Egypt (10:51-66) to repel the opponents. Such alliances were abhorred by the prophets who taught that Israel and Judah were to rely solely on God; should he decide to punish them, no friendly foreign power would be able to save them from his punishment. That the previous two features were intended by the author is corroborated in his final note that is reminiscent of a comment repeatedly found in 1 and 2 Kings: "The rest of the acts of John and his wars and the brave deeds which he did, and the building of the walls which he built, and his achievements, behold, they are written in the chronicles (annals) of his high priesthood, from the time that he became high priest after his father." (1 Macc 16:23-24) The hearers cannot miss that the author is putting the success of the Maccabees on the same footing as that of their predecessors the kings of Israel and Judah. Military success is no guarantee of a safe future.

2 Maccabees follows suit and explores the caveat introduced at the end of 1 Maccabees by reviewing the same story while introducing in the narrative another perspective, that of martyrdom rather than armed opposition for the sake of one's commitment to God's law. Right in the middle of the book (2 Macc 6:18-31) we read about the martyrdom of "Eleazar, one of the scribes in high position, a man now advanced in age and of noble presence" who took a stand similar to Daniel's in that he refused to eat food forbidden in the Law (v.18). The epilogue of the pericope reveals the author's intention to make out of Eleazar's martyrdom an example to follow: "So in this way he died, leaving in his death an example of nobility and a memorial of courage, not only to the young but to the great body of his nation." (v.31) His demise is followed by the lengthy chapter 7 describing the martyrdom of a mother and her seven sons, pointing out that the seed planted by Eleazar (whose name means "God is my help" or "My God is (my) help") was already blossoming. What is impressive, however, is the author's "digression" immediately preceding the two stories in which he gives his assessment of martyrdom and its meaning:

> Now I urge those who read this book not to be depressed by such calamities, but to recognize that these punishments were designed not to destroy but to discipline our people. In fact, not to let the impious alone for long, but to punish them immediately, is a sign of great kindness. For in the case of the other nations the Lord waits patiently to punish them until they have reached the full measure of their sins; but he does not deal in this way with us, in order that he may not take vengeance on us afterward when our sins have reached their height. Therefore he never withdraws his mercy from us. Though he disciplines us with calamities, he does not forsake his own people. Let what we have said serve as a reminder; we must go on briefly with the story. (2 Macc 6:12-17)

The path of martyrdom as the more advisable alternative to resorting to arms is further developed in the Books of 3 and 4 Maccabees. In the former, the same fate that the Jews of Palestine suffered at the hands of the Seleucids is visited upon the Jews of Alexandria by Ptolemy IV Philopator, King of Egypt, which was the earthly power to whom the Maccabees appealed for help in 1 Maccabees. Thus, this book underscores the prophetic teaching against appeals to new alliances to repel opponents, since such alliances end up subjugating the people to the new powers:

> For they sow the wind, and they shall reap the whirlwind. The standing grain has no heads, it shall yield no meal; if it were to yield, aliens would devour it. Israel is swallowed up; already they are among the nations as a useless vessel. For they have gone up to Assyria, a wild ass wandering alone; Ephraim has hired lovers. (Hos 8:7-9)

> At that time Merodachbaladan the son of Baladan, king of Babylon, sent envoys with letters and a present to Hezekiah, for he heard that he had been sick and had recovered. And Hezekiah welcomed them; and he showed them his treasure house, the silver, the gold, the spices, the precious oil, his whole armory, all that was found in his storehouses. There was nothing in his house or in all his realm that Hezekiah did not show them. Then Isaiah the prophet came to King Hezekiah, and said to him, "What did these men say? And whence did they come to you?" Hezekiah said, "They have come to me from a far country, from Babylon." he said, "What have they seen in your house?" Hezekiah answered, "They have seen all that is in my house; there is nothing in my storehouses that I did not show them." Then Isaiah said to Hezekiah, "Hear the word of the Lord of hosts: Behold, the days are coming, when all that is in your house, and that which your fathers have stored up till this day, shall be carried to Babylon; nothing shall be left, says the Lord. And some of your own sons,

The Septuagint 209

who are born to you, shall be taken away; and they shall be eunuchs in the palace of the king of Babylon." (Is 39:1-7)

However, what is impressive about 3 Maccabees is that it reintroduces (the martyr) Eleazar as the true savior of his people, when upon his prayer (6:1-15) the oppressor Ptolemy repents and becomes the patron of the Jews he was persecuting (6:16-7:23).

Lastly, the martyrdom referred to in 2 Maccabees as the reasonable as well as right choice becomes the thesis of 4 Maccabees:

> I could prove to you from many and various examples that reason is dominant over the emotions, but I can demonstrate it best from the noble bravery of those who died for the sake of virtue, Eleazar and the seven brothers and their mother. All of these, by despising sufferings that bring death, demonstrated that reason controls the emotions. On this anniversary it is fitting for me to praise for their virtues those who, with their mother, died for the sake of nobility and goodness, but I would also call them blessed for the honor in which they are held. For all people, even their torturers, marveled at their courage and endurance, and they became the cause of the downfall of tyranny over their nation. By their endurance they conquered the tyrant, and thus their native land was purified through them. I shall shortly have an opportunity to speak of this; but, as my custom is, I shall begin by stating my main principle, and then I shall turn to their story, giving glory to the all-wise God. (1:7-12)

In order to drive home his point the author makes of the martyrs the prototype of the true Jew:

> By their endurance they conquered the tyrant, and thus their native land was purified through them. (1:11)

> These, then, who have been consecrated for the sake of God, are honored, not only with this honor, but also by the fact that because of them our enemies did not rule over our nation, the tyrant was punished, and the native land purified—they having become, as it were, a ransom for the sin of our nation. (17:20-21)
>
> O Israelite children, offspring of the seed of Abraham, obey this law and exercise piety in every way, knowing that devout reason is master of all emotions, not only of sufferings from within, but also of those from without. Therefore those who gave over their bodies in suffering for the sake of religion were not only admired by men, but also were deemed worthy to share in a divine inheritance. Because of them the nation gained peace, and by reviving observance of the law in the native land they ravaged the enemy. (18:1-4)

He even extols them to the highest possible degree by presenting them as joining the ranks of patriarchs living with God immediately upon their death, without having to wait for the final judgment, a thesis picked up by the author of the Book of Revelation:[2]

> O aged man, more powerful than tortures; O elder, fiercer than fire; O supreme king over the passions, Eleazar! ... O man of blessed age and of venerable gray hair and of law-abiding life, whom the faithful seal of death has perfected! If, therefore, because of piety an aged man despised tortures even to death, most certainly devout reason is governor of the emotions. Some perhaps might say, "Not every one has full command of his emotions, because not every one has prudent reason." But as many as attend to religion with a whole heart, these alone are able to control the passions of the flesh, since they believe that they, like

---

[2] See later below how this thesis will help us unveil the "mystery" of the Millennium or the Reign of Thousand Years spoken of in Rev 20, and understand it correctly.

our patriarchs Abraham and Isaac and Jacob, do not die to God, but live in God. (7:10, 15-19)

For when you and your sons were arrested together, you stood and watched Eleazar being tortured, and said to your sons in the Hebrew language, "My sons ... you ought to endure any suffering for the sake of God. For his sake also our father Abraham was zealous to sacrifice his son Isaac, the ancestor of our nation; and when Isaac saw his father's hand wielding a sword and descending upon him, he did not cower. And Daniel the righteous was thrown to the lions, and Hananiah, Azariah, and Mishael were hurled into the fiery furnace and endured it for the sake of God. You too must have the same faith in God and not be grieved. It is unreasonable for people who have religious knowledge not to withstand pain." By these words the mother of the seven encouraged and persuaded each of her sons to die rather than violate God's commandment. They knew also that those who die for the sake of God live in God, as do Abraham and Isaac and Jacob and all the patriarchs. (16:15-16, 19-25)

Part IV

The New Testament

16

The New Testament Writings

The Biblical Story

Before moving to the New Testament literature, and in order to understand how it functions and why it handles the topic of the promised earth the way it does, it is imperative here to review the biblical story of the Old Testament. After having shown that the predicament in which humanity put itself by disobedience to the will of the One who created it, scripture singles out one exemplar of this humanity, the children of Israel, and describes how this exemplar, although granted a special treatment through the gift of a detailed Law, continually misses the mark. The outcome is that the readers end up convinced that God's punishment visited upon the Kingdoms of Israel and Judah is just and well-deserved. Furthermore, they end up realizing that the only way to forego such a just judgment is to obey God's will. The Apostle Paul captures the scriptural teaching in his magisterial introduction to his Letter to the Romans. After having showed that humanity in general faltered in its dealings with God, he concludes his description of their attitude in the following terms:

> They were filled with all manner of wickedness, evil, covetousness, malice. Full of envy, murder, strife, deceit, malignity, they are gossips, slanderers, haters of God, insolent, haughty, boastful, inventors of evil, disobedient to parents, foolish, faithless, heartless, ruthless. *Though they know God's decree that those who do such things deserve to die, they not only do them but approve those who practice them.* (Rom 1:29-32)

Then, Paul proceeds *immediately* to follow the scriptural story line by showing that the Jews (Judahites) did not fare better and describes their failure in the same terms as those he used to refer to humanity in general:

> Therefore you have no excuse, O man, whoever you are, when you judge another; for in passing judgment upon him you condemn yourself, because you, the judge, are *doing the very same things*. We know that the judgment of God rightly falls upon those *who do such things*. Do you suppose, O man, that when you judge *those who do such things and yet do them yourself*, you will escape the judgment of God? Or do you presume upon the riches of his kindness and forbearance and patience? Do you not know that God's kindness is meant to lead you to repentance? But by your hard and impenitent heart you are storing up wrath for yourself on the day of wrath when God's righteous judgment will be revealed. *For he will render to every man according to his works*: to those who by patience in well-doing seek for glory and honor and immortality, he will give eternal life; but for those who are factious and *do not obey the truth, but obey wickedness*, there will be wrath and fury. (2:1-8)

Consequently, the Jews do not receive special treatment, as is very commonly assumed, because they have been "chosen." Their chosenness consists in that they are merely the trustees of the scriptural story where God's will is found for *all humanity*:

> Then what advantage has the Jew? Or what is the value of circumcision? Much in every way. To begin with, the Jews are entrusted with the oracles of God ... They are Israelites, and to them belong the sonship, the glory, the covenants, the giving of the law, the worship, and the promises; to them belong the

patriarchs, and out of them, according to the flesh, is the Christ *of which speaks scripture*.¹ (Rom 3:1-2; 9:4-5a)

But the scriptural story, as we saw, does not end with the punishment of the children of Israel and humanity in general. It ends with the promise that God will restore his *entire* creation to its original state where everything will revert to the way he willed it at the beginning. This is clear from the prophetic terminology where the new Zion, God's heavenly city, is depicted in terms encountered in the pre-Abrahamic period of the scriptural story which deals with humanity in general:

> For this is like the days of Noah to me: as I swore that the waters of Noah should no more go over the earth, so I have sworn that I will not be angry with you and will not rebuke you. For the mountains may depart and the hills be removed, but my steadfast love shall not depart from you, and my covenant of peace shall not be removed, says the Lord, who has compassion on you. O afflicted one, storm-tossed, and not comforted, behold, I will set your stones in antimony, and lay your foundations with sapphires. I will make your pinnacles of agate, your gates of carbuncles, and all your wall of precious stones. All your sons shall be taught by the Lord, and great shall be the prosperity of your sons. In righteousness you shall be established; you shall be far from

---

¹ I opted for this translation for the following reason. The original Greek has *ho Khristos to kata sarka* (the Christ according to the flesh) instead of *ho Khristos ho kata sarka*. The Greek relative pronoun *to* (before *kata sarka* [according to the flesh] is neuter while *ho* is masculine. What Paul is saying, then, is that all the "items" or "topics" he is referring to (patriarchs and Christ as well as sonship, glory, covenants, giving of the law, worship, promises) are found in scripture. Consequently, the idea is not that the Israelites possess these "items" as their *property*, but they are aware, and can speak, of them because they are found in scripture that was entrusted to them (Rom 3:2). See detailed comments on Rom 9:4-5a in my forthcoming *C-Rom*.

oppression, for you shall not fear; and from terror, for it shall not come near you. (Is 54:9-14)

Hearken to me, you who pursue deliverance, you who seek the Lord; look to the rock from which you were hewn, and to the quarry from which you were digged. Look to Abraham your father and to Sarah who bore you; for when he was but one I called him, and I blessed him and made him many. For the Lord will comfort Zion; he will comfort all her waste places, and will make her wilderness like Eden, her desert like the garden of the Lord; joy and gladness will be found in her, thanksgiving and the voice of song. (Is 51:1-3)

It is no wonder then that these promises are uttered in the scriptural story of the children of Israel in that period when they were punished and scattered among other nations. It is only in their punishment of exile that they will be able to realize that they are no better than the other nations that were punished by the same God. The equality in status between the punished Israel and the punished nations can be best seen in that Tyre itself, before she sinned, is referred to as having been originally a garden of Eden planted by God himself:

Son of man, raise a lamentation over the king of Tyre, and say to him, Thus says the Lord God: "You were the signet of perfection, full of wisdom and perfect in beauty. You were in Eden, the garden of God; every precious stone was your covering, carnelian, topaz, and jasper, chrysolite, beryl, and onyx, sapphire, carbuncle, and emerald; and wrought in gold were your settings and your engravings. On the day that you were created they were prepared. With an anointed guardian cherub I placed you; you were on the holy mountain of God; in the midst of the stones of fire you walked. You were blameless in your ways from the day you were created, *till iniquity was found in you.*" (Ezek 28:12-15)

In turn, this explains why the new heavenly city of God will encompass both Israel and the nations on an equal footing and that representatives of both will serve in God's sanctuary:

> Thus says the Lord: "Keep justice, and do righteousness, for soon my salvation will come, and my deliverance be revealed. Blessed is the man who does this, and the son of man who holds it fast, who keeps the sabbath, not profaning it, and keeps his hand from doing any evil." Let not the foreigner who has joined himself to the Lord say, "The Lord will surely separate me from his people"; and let not the eunuch say, "Behold, I am a dry tree." For thus says the Lord: "To the eunuchs who keep my sabbath, who choose the things that please me and hold fast my covenant, I will give in my house and within my walls a monument and a name better than sons and daughters; I will give them an everlasting name which shall not be cut off. And the foreigners who join themselves to the Lord, to minister to him, to love the name of the Lord, and to be his servants, every one who keeps the sabbath, and does not profane it, and holds fast my covenant—these I will bring to my holy mountain, and make them joyful in my house of prayer; their burnt offerings and their sacrifices will be accepted on my altar; for my house shall be called a house of prayer for all peoples. Thus says the Lord God, who gathers the outcasts of Israel, I will gather yet others to him besides those already gathered." (Is 56:1-8)

> And they shall bring all your brethren from all the nations as an offering to the Lord, upon horses, and in chariots, and in litters, and upon mules, and upon dromedaries, to my holy mountain Jerusalem, says the Lord, just as the Israelites bring their cereal offering in a clean vessel to the house of the Lord. And some of them also I will take for priests and for Levites, says the Lord. (Is 66:20-21)

This new divine city that reflects the situation extant in Genesis 1-11, where the ancestors of Israel were part and parcel of the nations created by God, is a reality that warrants being referred to as "the new heavens and the new earth" (Is 66:22), again harkening back to "the heavens and the earth" of Genesis 1:1.

The description of "my holy mountain Jerusalem" (Is 66:20), corresponding to the garden of Eden as well as God's entire creation and thus a city open to all humanity without differentiation, occurs at the beginning of the Book of Isaiah which started by announcing these good tidings with the following terms:

> It shall come to pass in the latter days that the mountain of the house of the Lord shall be established as the highest of the mountains, and shall be raised above the hills; and all the nations shall flow to it, and many peoples shall come, and say: "Come, let us go up to the mountain of the Lord, to the house of the God of Jacob; that he may teach us his ways and that we may walk in his paths." *For out of Zion shall go forth the law, and the word of the Lord from Jerusalem.* He shall judge between the nations, and shall decide for many peoples; and they shall beat their swords into plowshares, and their spears into pruning hooks; nation shall not lift up sword against nation, neither shall they learn war any more. O house of Jacob, come, let us walk in the light of the Lord. (Is 2:2-5)

God's law will be the trademark of that city, since it will be built on his justice that will ensure that only those who abide by his will shall find abode in it:

> Zion shall be redeemed by justice, and those in her who repent, by righteousness. But rebels and sinners shall be destroyed together, and those who forsake the Lord shall be consumed. (Is 1:27-28)

Given that God's justice applies to the nations as well as to the house of Jacob, it is imperative that his law be made known to all nations. This is precisely why the mission of God's ultimate messenger will entail that the propagation of the law governing the new Jerusalem be carried to all nations, as we hear in the second section of the Book of Isaiah.[2]

---

[2] See Is 42:1-7 and 49:1, 5-6 quoted earlier

17

The Mission of Jesus and the Apostles

The literature of the New Testament precisely describes the "light to the nations, that my salvation may reach to the end of the earth" (Is. 49:6). It begins with the Gospels that cover the activity of Jesus Christ as God's final messenger to both the Jews and the Gentiles living in Palestine, followed, after his resurrection, by the continuation of this mission by the Apostles throughout the Roman empire, as witnessed in the Book of Acts and the Epistles. The Roman empire, known as *oikoumenē gē* (the inhabited earth), was a kind of microcosm representing the entire earth since its boundaries included members of the surrounding nations, including those considered as barbarians, who were conquered by the Romans. That Paul had in mind to carry his apostolic mission to literally all nations after having reached the westernmost parts of the Roman empire (Rom 15:24-28) can be seen in his statement at the beginning of his letter to the Romans:

> I want you to know, brethren, that I have often intended to come to you (but thus far have been prevented), in order that I may reap some harvest among you as well as among the rest of the Gentiles. I am under obligation both to Greeks and to *barbarians*, both to the wise and to the foolish: so I am eager to preach the gospel to you also who are in Rome. (Rom 1:13-15)

We find the same all-encompassing vision in his letter to the Colossians, while he was still toiling in the eastern part of the Roman empire: "Here there cannot be Greek and Jew, circumcised and uncircumcised, *barbarian, Scythian*, slave, free man, but Christ is all, and in all." (Col 3:11) And it is no wonder that it should be so since this centrifugal movement was initiated by the Lord himself in his final commission:

> Now the eleven disciples went to Galilee, to the mountain to which Jesus had directed them. And when they saw him they worshiped him; but some doubted. And Jesus came and said to them, "All authority in heaven and on earth has been given to me. Go therefore and make disciples of all nations, baptizing them in the name of the Father and of the Son and of the Holy Spirit, teaching them to observe all that I have commanded you; and lo, I am with you always, to the close of the age." (Mt 28:16-20)

Jesus' universal interest is detected in Matthew's description of Jesus' beginnings: away from Jerusalem and Judah, and in a northern direction toward the heart of the Roman province Syria, a symbol of Rome and its peoples in the Eastern Mediterranean. Jesus, as the new David and the Suffering Servant,[1] is God's last messenger to the Gentiles as well as to the sheep of Israel, including the lost among them. As such, he inaugurates the new beginning, which will be consummated in God's "new heavens and new earth" at "the end of the age." It is with this purpose in mind that Matthew entitles his Gospel "the book of genesis,"[2] that is, of the (new) beginning, connected with "Jesus Christ, the son of David, the son of Abraham" (Mt 1:1); indeed Jesus' story is presented as a "genesis" (*genesis*; v.18) rather than a birth (*gennēsis*) although we are told that he was born of Mary (v.20) in Bethlehem (2:1). This new beginning starts with the exile of punishment visited upon the Kingdoms of Israel and Judah, because the first David, God's beloved, betrayed him. Consequently, what started as a promise to Abraham looked as though it was fulfilled in that David at the

---

[1] Mt 1:1-17; 12:14-21.
[2] Mt 1:1, 18.

end of the first fourteen generations,³ but David's era of fourteen generations ended up in the deportation to Babylon. Christ is introduced as the culmination of the new era of fourteen generations, which starts with that deportation (1:11, 12) without any mention of return! In order to underscore that the new David comes from God and is not a product of the "generations," Matthew presents him as the son of Mary through God's spirit, and not of Joseph, who is the end of the line of those generations (v.16). It is as if, although he was born in Bethlehem, David's city of birth and whence the Messiah was to come (Mic 5:2; Mt 2:1-8), he does not pertain to it, but rather to God's heavenly city, the new Jerusalem:

> And a great portent appeared in heaven, a woman clothed with the sun, with the moon under her feet, and on her head a crown of twelve stars; she was with child and she cried out in her pangs of birth, in anguish for delivery. And another portent appeared in heaven; behold, a great red dragon, with seven heads and ten horns, and seven diadems upon his heads. his tail swept down a third of the stars of heaven, and cast them to the earth. And the dragon stood before the woman who was about to bear a child, that he might devour her child when she brought it forth; she brought forth a male child, one who is to rule all the nations with a rod of iron, but her child was caught up to God and to his throne, and the woman fled into the wilderness, where she has a place prepared by God, in which to be nourished for one thousand two hundred and sixty days. (Rev 12:1-6)

This explains the rather unexpected reply of Jesus to his parents at the age of twelve: "How is it that you sought me? Did you not know that I must be dealing with my Father's matters (I must be in my Father's house)?" (Lk 2:49) Yet immediately thereafter we

---

³ From the same root as "genesis" in Greek.

are told that "he went down with them and came to Nazareth, and was obedient to them" (v.51).

Upon his return from the Roman province Egypt where he fled the Jerusalemite political and religious authorities who had intended to eliminate Jesus, Joseph tried to go back to "the earth of Israel" (Mt 2:20-21). He was, however, guided by divine intervention in a dream (v.22) to proceed away from "the earth of Israel" (v.21)[4] to "the areas of Galilee." Galilee will become Jesus' homeland as evident from the repeated statements to the effect that he was known commonly not as "Jesus of Bethlehem," but rather as "Jesus the Nazarene"[5] or "Jesus of Nazareth (of Galilee)."[6] Actually, in describing Jesus' permanent settling in Galilee, Matthew writes:

> Now when he heard that John had been arrested, he withdrew into Galilee; and leaving Nazareth he went and dwelt in Capernaum by the sea, in the territory of Zebulun and Naphtali, that what was spoken by the prophet Isaiah might be fulfilled: "The earth of Zebulun and the earth of Naphtali, toward the sea, across the Jordan, Galilee of the nations—the people who sat in darkness have seen a great light, and for those who sat in the region and shadow of death light has dawned." (4:12-16)

Thus, Jesus the Nazarene (2:23) pulls away from central Galilee toward the Sea of Galilee in order to pass more easily across the Jordan to the other side where the nations, herders of swine, resided (Mt 18:28-31). Notice Matthew's choice of the Isaiah quotation containing the phrase "Galilee of the nations." The term Galilee in Hebrew actually means "district, (surrounding) area." That Matthew had in mind the Roman

---

[4] These are the only two instances of that phrase in the entire New Testament.
[5] Mt 2:23; Mk 14:67.
[6] Mt 21:11; Mk 1:9; Acts 10:38.

province Syria is corroborated in the passage following closely after 4:12-16:

> And he went about all Galilee, teaching in their synagogues and preaching the gospel of the kingdom and healing every disease and every infirmity among the people. *So his fame spread throughout all Syria*, and they brought him all the sick, those afflicted with various diseases and pains, demoniacs, epileptics, and paralytics, and he healed them. And great crowds followed him from Galilee and the Decapolis and Jerusalem and Judea and from beyond the Jordan. (4:23-25)

Furthermore, the mention of Decapolis, a ten city Greco-Roman league extending along the eastern coast of the Jordan river, along with the phrase "from beyond the Jordan," also point to the importance of the nations in Jesus' purview. In Mark, the use of the Decapolis is clearly connected with the territory of the swine-herding Gerasenes who lived "on the other side of the sea" (Mk 5:1). Indeed, following Jesus' summons to "go home to your friends, and tell them how much the Lord has done for you, and how he has had mercy on you" (v.19), we are told that the healed Gerasene demoniac "went away and began to proclaim in the Decapolis how much Jesus had done for him; and all men marveled" (v.20). Finally, the last mention of the Decapolis in the New Testament, also in Mark, clearly links it with the region of Tyre and Sidon (Then he returned from the region of Tyre, and went through Sidon to the Sea of Galilee, through the region of the Decapolis; 7:31) where Jesus had just healed the demoniac daughter of a woman who is expressly introduced as "a Greek, a Syrophoenician by birth" (v.26). This interest in the province Syria and, by extension, the entire Roman empire is at its clearest in the way Luke introduces the birth of Jesus: "In those days a decree went out from Caesar

Augustus that all the world should be enrolled. This was the first census, when Quirinius was governor of Syria." (2:1-2) Since this general census was ordered by Caesar, there was no need to mention Quirinius except that Syria is the broader area around Galilee where Jesus' activity was taking place. Luke wanted to make sure that his readers understood that Jesus was the same servant of God referred to in Isaiah in terms that made him the ultimate divine messenger to both Israel and the nations. Luke's intent is corroborated in the way he introduces the public ministry of John the Baptist, Jesus' forerunner, which he sets within the larger boundaries of the Roman empire: "In the fifteenth year of the reign of Tiberius Caesar, Pontius Pilate being governor of Judea, and Herod being tetrarch of Galilee, and his brother Philip tetrarch of the region of Ituraea and Trachonitis, and Lysanias tetrarch of Abilene, in the high-priesthood of Annas and Caiaphas, the word of God came to John the son of Zechariah in the wilderness." (3:1-2) Furthermore, Ituraea, Trachonitis, and Abilene were outside Galilee but in the Roman province Syria (in the southern parts of actual Syria).

That Galilee was viewed as a springboard into the Roman province Syria where Jews lived among the nations is further evident in both Jesus' activity within Galilee and his ventures while in Galilee into the neighboring areas of the Decapolis where the Gerasenes or Gedarenes lived, and in Tyre and Sidon and Caesarea Philippi. In Galilee, Jesus heals outcasts and Gentiles as well as Jews. Having trained his disciples in this manner inclusive of all without differentiation, Jesus forces the reticent disciples into full Gentile territory. It is while there that he challenges them into confessing him, the Son of man, as the Jewish messiah (Mt 16:13-16). Still, in spite of his correctly stated confession, Peter misunderstands its meaning by assuming

The Mission of Jesus and the Apostles

that the Jewish messiah will subjugate the Gentiles under Jewish victory and hegemony in the manner of the uprising under Judas the Maccabee and his brothers. But Jesus immediately and sternly corrects Peter by presenting himself along the lines of the teachings of Ezekiel and Isaiah:

> From that time Jesus began to show his disciples that he must go to Jerusalem and suffer many things from the elders and chief priests and scribes, and be killed, and on the third day be raised. And Peter took him and began to rebuke him, saying, "God forbid, Lord! This shall never happen to you." But he turned and said to Peter, "Get behind me, Satan! You are a hindrance to me; for you are not on the side of God, but of men." Then Jesus told his disciples, "If any man would come after me, let him deny himself and take up his cross and follow me. For whoever would save his life will lose it, and whoever loses his life for my sake will find it. For what will it profit a man, if he gains the whole world and forfeits his life? Or what shall a man give in return for his life? For the Son of man is to come with his angels in the glory of his Father, and then he will repay every man for what he has done." (Mt 16:21-27)

As Son of man, he, like Ezekiel, delivers his teaching while living among and with the nations. As Isaiah's Suffering Servant—as Matthew presented him earlier (Mt 12:17-21)—Jesus teaches both Israel and the nations God's commandment of love, fellowship, and peace in God's perfect justice for all, and also lays down his life for all of them even though it is a shameful death on the Roman cross, that is, not the humanly glorious death of a military martyr like a Maccabee.

The intention of this message of peace in God's justice for all his children, the human beings he created, is presented at its clearest in the Gospel of Matthew. There we are told that, upon his correctly phrased confession, Peter was blessed with these words: "Blessed are you, Simon Bar-Jona! For flesh and blood has not revealed this to you, but my Father who is in heaven." (Mt 16:17) The Semitic "Bar-Jona" means "son of Jonah," that is, "son of the dove." Since the phrase "son of" means "someone pertaining to," Peter's acceptance of Jesus as the Jewish messiah while on a mission of peace and healing in Gentile areas makes of Peter someone of the kind of "Jonah" (the dove), the prophet of repentance and peace to the Ninevites who destroyed the kingdom of Israel. But Peter will have to abide by this position. Otherwise he would be like Jonah, an anti-prophet who, although forced by God through the medium of a whale to continue his mission, still felt unhappy about it:

> When God saw what they [the Ninevites] did, how they turned from their evil way, God repented of the evil which he had said he would do to them; and he did not do it. *But it displeased Jonah exceedingly*, and he was angry. And he prayed to the Lord and said, "I pray thee, Lord, is not this what I said when I was yet in my country? That is why I made haste to flee to Tarshish; for I knew that thou art a gracious God and merciful, slow to anger, and abounding in steadfast love, and repentest of evil. Therefore now, O Lord, take my life from me, I beseech thee, for it is better for me to die than to live." (Jonah 3:10-4:3)

And indeed, Peter followed Jonah's path when he rebuked Jesus (Mt 16:22) for wanting to be the messenger of forgiveness and peace, to the extent of accepting to die a shameful death in order to accomplish his mission (v.21). Therefore, Jesus retorted with the harsh rebuke of calling Peter Satan (v.23).

Just before Peter's confession ("You are the Christ, the Son of the living God" Mt 16:16), Jesus replied to the Pharisees and Sadducees who were still insisting on one more sign from heaven corroborating his authority (16:1): "An evil and adulterous generation seeks for a sign, but no sign shall be given to it except the sign of Jonah." (v.4) This sign of Jonah he had delivered earlier:

> Then some of the scribes and Pharisees said to him, "Teacher, we wish to see a sign from you." But he answered them, "An evil and adulterous generation seeks for a sign; but no sign shall be given to it except the sign of the prophet Jonah. For as Jonah was three days and three nights in the belly of the whale, so will the Son of man be three days and three nights in the heart of the earth. The men of Nineveh will arise at the judgment with this generation and condemn it; for they repented at the preaching of Jonah, and behold, something greater than Jonah is here." (12:38-41)

After his resurrection, the crucified, dead, and buried Son of man will be raised by God to appear again to his disciples in Galilee (Mt, Mk, Jn) and commission them to continue the mission he initiated in Galilee. Thus, his visit to Jerusalem and Judah was to encounter his demise at the hand of the leaders of Israel just as God's emissaries, the prophets, before him (Mt 21:33-40; 23:37-39). That is why Jerusalem is not the official place of Jesus' post-resurrection. It is just another unfaithful city that needs to repent and accept his message delivered to her by the disciples, as are all other cities of the world:

> Therefore I send you prophets and wise men and scribes, some of whom you will kill and crucify, and some you will scourge in your synagogues and persecute from town to town, that upon you may come all the righteous blood shed on earth, from the blood of innocent Abel to the blood of Zechariah the son of Barachiah, whom you murdered between the sanctuary and the altar. Truly, I say to you, all this will come upon this generation. "O Jerusalem, Jerusalem, killing the prophets and stoning those who are sent to

you! How often would I have gathered your children together as a hen gathers her brood under her wings, and you would not! Behold, your house is forsaken and desolate. For I tell you, you will not see me again, until you say, 'Blessed is he who comes in the name of the Lord.'" (Mt 23:34-39)

Luke preserves the same saying: "O Jerusalem, Jerusalem, killing the prophets and stoning those who are sent to you! How often would I have gathered your children together as a hen gathers her brood under her wings, and you would not! Behold, your house is forsaken. And I tell you, you will not see me until you say, 'Blessed is he who comes in the name of the Lord!'" (13:34-35) In that Gospel, although Jesus appears to the disciples in Jerusalem, their commissioning is delayed till the Book of Acts:

> Then he opened their minds to understand the scriptures, and said to them, "Thus it is written, that the Christ should suffer and on the third day rise from the dead, and that repentance and forgiveness of sins should be preached in his name to all nations, beginning from Jerusalem. You are witnesses of these things. And behold, I send the promise of my Father upon you; but stay in the city, until you are clothed with power from on high." (Lk 24:45-49)

The Mission of the Apostles

Still, the downplaying of Jerusalem and the centrality of Galilee are evident. In both Luke and Acts, Jesus does not ascend from Jerusalem, but from locations away from it:

> Then he [Jesus] led them out *as far as Bethany*, and lifting up his hands he blessed them. While he blessed them, he parted from them, and was carried up into heaven. And they returned to Jerusalem (Lk 24:50-52)

> And when he had said this, as they were looking on, he was lifted up, and a cloud took him out of their sight. And while they were

> gazing into heaven as he went, behold, two men stood by them in white robes, and said, "Men of Galilee, why do you stand looking into heaven? This Jesus, who was taken up from you into heaven, will come in the same way as you saw him go into heaven." Then they returned to Jerusalem from the mount called Olivet, which is near Jerusalem, *a sabbath day's journey away.* (Acts 1:9-12)

The centrality of Galilee is already apparent in the address "Men of Galilee" given to the disciples. But even more importantly, one will notice that in the commissioning statement (But you shall receive power when the Holy Spirit has come upon you; and you shall be my witnesses in Jerusalem and in all Judea and Samaria and to the end of the earth; Acts 1:8) Galilee is omitted, whereas Jerusalem and Judea are made recipients of the message on a par with Samaria and the entire earth whose capital, Rome, will be reached by Paul, the Apostle to the nations, at the end of the Book. The intention is clear: Galilee is both the place of origin of the gospel of the kingdom and functions as a springboard of its message to the entire Roman empire as well as to Judea and Samaria. In this way, Luke depicts the activity of the apostles, and especially that of Paul, as parallel to that of Jesus himself. Again in Acts, the interest in the province Syria as representative of the Roman empire is evident in that it was in the vicinity of Damascus that the commissioning of Paul, the Apostle par excellence, took place. Furthermore, the wording with which he is introduced makes of him a copy of Jesus, the Suffering Servant, who was to bring God's tidings to both Israel and the nations:

> But the Lord said to him, "Go, for he is a chosen instrument of mine to carry my name before the Gentiles and kings and the sons of Israel; for I will show him how much he must suffer for the sake of my name." (Acts 9:15-16)

The Book of Acts follows the apostles' journeys in Judea, Samaria and entire Palestine, then Paul's journeys over the eastern parts of the Roman empire. His letter to the Romans looks forward to his preaching the gospel to its western regions:

> In Christ Jesus, then, I have reason to be proud of my work for God. For I will not venture to speak of anything except what Christ has wrought through me to win obedience from the Gentiles, by word and deed, by the power of signs and wonders, by the power of the Holy Spirit, so that from Jerusalem and as far round as Illyricum I have fully preached the gospel of Christ, thus making it my ambition to preach the gospel, not where Christ has already been named, lest I build on another man's foundation, but as it is written, "They shall see who have never been told of him, and they shall understand who have never heard of him." This is the reason why I have so often been hindered from coming to you. But now, since I no longer have any room for work in these regions, and since I have longed for many years to come to you, I hope to see you in passing as I go to Spain, and to be sped on my journey there by you, once I have enjoyed your company for a little. (Rom 15:17-24)

18

The Absence of Canaan in the New Testament

If the biblical story begun in the Old Testament finds its end as well as its fulfillment in the New Testament, then it is imperative to take with utmost seriousness the fact that the latter does not deal at all with a "return" to the earth of Canaan. The reason is unmistakable: the believers, as the prophets taught, understand that they pertain to a city that is totally God's and not a city made by the hand of man like the unfaithful Jerusalem, the city of David, which was punished. As early as the Letter to the Galatians and as late as the Book of Revelation, this teaching is upheld. In Galatians Paul authoritatively asserts that the believers are children of "the Jerusalem above" (Gal 4:26), and in Revelation John describes it as "coming down out of heaven from God" (Rev 21:2) *after* the establishment of "the new heaven and the new earth" (v.1). Furthermore, it will be a city that does not look like any earthly city even by a stretch of the imagination:

> And I saw no temple in the city, for its temple is the Lord God the Almighty and the Lamb. And the city has no need of sun or moon to shine upon it, for the glory of God is its light, and its lamp is the Lamb. By its light shall the nations walk; and the kings of the earth shall bring their glory into it, and its gates shall never be shut by day—and there shall be no night there; they shall bring into it the glory and the honor of the nations. But nothing unclean shall enter it, nor any one who practices abomination or falsehood, but only those who are written in the Lamb's book of life. Then he showed me the river of the water of life, bright as crystal, flowing from the throne of God and of the Lamb through the middle of

the street of the city; also, on either side of the river, the tree of life with its twelve kinds of fruit, yielding its fruit each month; and the leaves of the tree were for the healing of the nations. There shall no more be anything accursed, but the throne of God and of the Lamb shall be in it, and his servants shall worship him; they shall see his face, and his name shall be on their foreheads. And night shall be no more; they need no light of lamp or sun, for the Lord God will be their light, and they shall reign for ever and ever. (Rev 21:22-22:5)

This is nothing else save a description of the restored garden of Eden, the earth where God originally intended the human being—all human beings—to live in the true peace secured by obedience to his will, which is precisely what the prophecies of the end times were looking forward to. But the garden of Eden is the entire human world, not a defined geographical location: it is the place where the human beings will live in full harmony with their peers, and with the animals and the vegetation God created, abiding by God's commandments that are subsumed in the love for each other.

It is of utmost importance to realize that this understanding was not special to the New Testament authors, but it was also the overall Jewish stand as I explained when discussing the Ketubim. The interest in a Jewish establishment in Canaan was the stand of a minority of Jewish Palestinian zealots. When these were crushed by the Roman army, the rest of the Jews were not affected. They continued to live wherever they were, congregating in the synagogues in order to listen to and to make the daily effort to abide by God's commandments that boil down to the care for any needy co-inhabitant. So the stand of Paul, the Apostle to the nations, was not anything special. He imposed upon his Gentile believers to remain where they were and congregate as church[1] in order to do the same thing: listen to and make the daily effort to abide by God's commandments. Indeed, taught he, "neither circumcision counts for anything nor uncircumcision, *but keeping the commandments of God*" (1 Cor 7:19). However, unlike the synagogues, the Pauline church communities were inclusive of both Jews and Gentiles. This is the stand he boldly defended against Peter and the men of James, and even Barnabas, in Antioch (Gal 2:11-14). He imposed on the Gentile believers full table fellowship with the Jews in spite of all the difficulties that this attitude entailed (Rom 14; 1 Cor 8:7-13). He could not afford anything less since God's heavenly Jerusalem, who is the mother of all believers, is the garden of Eden where "man (*'adam*) lives by bread (from the garden God has planted; Gen 2:8)" as well as "by everything that proceeds out of the mouth of the Lord" (Deut 8:3). As children of that heavenly Jerusalem, the believers were bound by its rule, God's law, according to which every "man (*'adam*)" shall be judged:

> For God shows no partiality. All who have sinned without the law will also perish without the law, and all who have sinned under the law will be judged by the law. For it is not the hearers of the law who are righteous before God, but the doers of the law who will be justified. When Gentiles who have not the law do by nature what the law requires, they are a law to themselves, even though they do not have the law. They show that what the law requires is written on their hearts, while their conscience also bears witness and their conflicting thoughts accuse or perhaps excuse them on that day when, according to my gospel, God judges the secrets of men by Christ Jesus. (Rom 2:11-16)

---

[1] Church and synagogue are the two classic terms for the congregation "Israel of God" in the Old Testament.

This, in turn, explains why Jesus' ministry was delivered in "the Galilee of the nations," a stepping stone to the entire Roman empire and through it to the inhabited earth.[2] There in Galilee, Jesus taught about the Kingdom of God, where accession to it depended on implementing the righteousness required by its Law (Mt 6:33).

This is how both Jews and Christians continued to live in and around synagogues and churches, listening to the Word of God inscribed in scripture—just, as later, Muslims will do in and around their mosques.[3] Both Jews and Christians understood that scripture did not contain the history of the Jewish people before and until Christ. They understood that scripture is the Word of God unto their instruction in the times in which they lived in order for them indeed to be and thus to behave as children of the heavenly Zion and eventually accede to it. For how long? Until Judgment Day, as endorsed in the three monotheistic religions, when God will judge the dead he will have raised as well as the living. And the judgment will be based on whether one will have done God's will to care for the needy, any needy (Mt 25:31-46) since Jesus said: "Not every one who says to me, 'Lord, Lord,' shall enter the kingdom of heaven, but he who does the will of my Father who is in heaven." (7:21) Furthermore, those who will enter the kingdom are neither Jesus' blood kin nor those who sit in his company—Judas shared with

---

[2] The inhabited earth (*hē oikoumenē [gē]*) was an appellation the Roman empire was known by.

[3] Mosque is the translation of the Arabic *jami'* (gatherer; the one bringing together). It actually corresponds to the Hebrew *qohel* (the one who calls a gathering). The Book of Ecclesiastes (the one who calls to order the *ekklēsia* [church gathering]) is known as Qohelet (the feminine of *qohel*) in Hebrew, which is translated as *jami'at* (feminine of *jami'*) in Arabic.

him the same dish and betrayed him!—but those who do God's will:

> While he was still speaking to the people, behold, his mother and his brothers stood outside, asking to speak to him. But he replied to the man who told him, "Who is my mother, and who are my brothers?" And stretching out his hand toward his disciples, he said, "Here are my mother and my brothers! For whoever does the will of my Father in heaven is my brother, and sister, and mother." (Mt 12:46-50)

That is why, in the meantime and until the close of the age, a true disciple is the one who keeps the raised Jesus alive in this world by heeding his last commission: "All authority in heaven and on earth has been given to me. Go therefore and make disciples of all nations, baptizing them in the name of the Father and of the Son and of the Holy Spirit, *teaching them to observe all that I have commanded you*; and lo, I am with you always, to the close of the age." (Mt 29:19-20) This is what Paul, the Apostle to the nations, referred to as "the law of Christ" (Gal 6:2) and "the law of the Spirit of life" (Rom 8:2).

19

Scripture: History of the Jewish People or Word of God?

If the biblical story ends with Jesus' teaching being carried out to all nations until the end of the age, then the story is complete and does not have a sequel. To consider that it does is sheer blasphemy since the assumption would be that there is still something of value for the human beings besides or over and above the teaching Word of God in the Old Testament and the teaching Word of Jesus in the New Testament. The fact that the biblical story is complete and closed as the Word of God and the Word of his ultimate messenger is reflected in that it forms a "canon," which is a Greek term (*kanōn*) meaning "rule" or "ruler," that is, an authoritative reference. Notice how the last words of Jesus in Matthew are prefaced with "All authority in heaven and on earth has been given to me" (Mt 20:18). One should not fall in the trap of understanding the scriptural "canon" as being "canonized" by an outside authority; that would be in plain contradiction to the statement by Jesus at the end of Matthew. Rather, the believers are to accept and to acknowledge it as a "rule" for their daily lives.

The term *kanōn* is found in the New Testament in two instances. The first occurs in 2 Corinthians in reference to the rule assigned by God, the senior, to Paul, the junior, regarding his apostolic commission:

> But we will not boast beyond limit, but will keep to the assigned field (*kanōn*) God has apportioned us, to reach even to you. For we are not overextending ourselves, as though we did not reach you; we were the first to come all the way to you with the gospel of

Christ. We do not boast beyond limit, in other men's labors; but our hope is that as your faith increases, our assigned field (*kanōn*) among you may be greatly enlarged, so that we may preach the gospel in regions beyond you, without boasting of work already done in another's assigned field (*kanōn*). "Let him who boasts, boast of the Lord." For it is not the man who commends himself that is accepted, but the man whom the Lord commends. (10:13-18)

The other instance reflects the same thought: a rule imposed by a senior, the Apostle Paul, on his subordinates, the Galatian believers:

> For neither circumcision counts for anything, nor uncircumcision, but a new creation. Peace and mercy be upon all who *walk* by this rule (*kanōn*), upon the Israel of God. (Gal 6:15-16)

The latter instance is very telling for our investigation. First, the rule is to be "walked by," that is, a rule of behavior. Secondly, the Greek verb translated as "walk" is *stoikheō* whose meaning is "walk in line, in order" as in the military. It is the same verb Paul used earlier to ask the Galatians to "walk" by the Spirit (5:25). The conclusion is evident: the "rule" Paul is imposing on the Galatians has divine authority and its value is not bound by their decision to accept it or not. Thirdly, this same verb is used in Acts 21:24 in parallel with "keeping the Law." This is precisely what Paul is imposing on the Galatians: his teaching as a divine law by which they are to abide. This can be gathered from the following two points: (1) Paul refers to walking by the Spirit as the "law of Christ" (Gal 6:2) and (2) he presents this "rule" as "written down by his own hand" (6:11), that is, with his apostolic seal, just as the divine Law was "ordained by the hand of Moses" (3:19). This same verb "ordain" is the one that Paul uses to speak of the regulations he orders in his churches (1 Cor 7:17; 11:34; 16:1). When we take into consideration all of the above, then it becomes clear that Paul wrote his Epistle to the Galatians as the divine law of Christ in the same vein as the Book of Deuteronomy. Anyone who follows this written rule will have peace and mercy (Gal 6:16) secured by the divine blessing (3:14). Anyone who does not follow it will be under curse (1:8-9). The conclusion is incontrovertible. Scripture does not have a "canon" assigned to it by an outside authority, but is itself the "canon" by which we have to abide. We do not judge scripture; it judges us. The scriptural canon is not created by us believers; it is rather received and accepted as we hear in the Synodikon we recite every year on the first Sunday of Lent known as Sunday of Orthodoxy: "As the prophets have seen, as the apostles have taught, *as the Church has received.*"

Thus the Church does not decide on "the truth of the gospel." It receives it, without any addition or subtraction, as inscribed for the ages in the Old and New Testaments. The reason is that the scriptural God "in many and various ways spoke of old to our fathers by the prophets; *but in these last days* he has spoken to us by a Son, whom he appointed the heir of all things, through whom also he created the world" (Heb 1:1-2), a Son whose mission was accomplished "once and for all," after which we are not faced with a continual history, but with the judgment of the coming age:

> For Christ has entered, not into a sanctuary made with hands, a copy of the true one, but into heaven itself, now to appear in the presence of God on our behalf. Nor was it to offer himself repeatedly, as the high priest enters the Holy Place yearly with blood not his own; for then he would have had to suffer repeatedly since the foundation of the world. But as it is, he has appeared once for all at the end of the age to put away sin by the sacrifice of

himself. And just as it is appointed for men to die once, and after that comes judgment, so Christ, having been offered once to bear the sins of many, will appear a second time, not to deal with sin but to save those who are eagerly waiting for him. (Heb 9:24-28)

And how do we prepare for that judgment? Not by trying to figure out what God is "still up to"—he has already done it all through his Son!—but by living according to his will:

> The death he died he died to sin, once for all, but the life he lives he lives to God. So you also must consider yourselves dead to sin and alive to God in Christ Jesus. Let not sin therefore reign in your mortal bodies, to make you obey their passions. Do not yield your members to sin as instruments of wickedness, but yield yourselves to God as men who have been brought from death to life, and your members to God as instruments of righteousness. For sin will have no dominion over you, since you are not under law but under grace. What then? Are we to sin because we are not under law but under grace? By no means! (Rom 6:10-15)

Thus, what ensues is a teaching not about the future actions of God or deciphering the precursor signs of the end times, but an instructional teaching that requires *obedience*:

> Do you not know that if you yield yourselves to any one as obedient slaves, you are slaves of the one whom you obey, either of sin, which leads to death, or of obedience, which leads to righteousness? But thanks be to God, that you who were once slaves of sin have become obedient from the heart to the standard of teaching to which you were committed, and, having been set free from sin, have become slaves of righteousness. (vv.16-18)

Notice the awkward wording "obedient slaves ... of obedience." The reason for this is that the "standard of teaching" to which the believers are committed has been defined by Paul not as a compendium of theology, but as "the gospel through his [God's] prophets in the holy scriptures, concerning his Son" (Rom 1:1-3) that requires a "full trusting obedience" (faithful obedience; v.5). It is no wonder then that Paul refers to his apostolic message as a "divine and thus incontrovertible law" to follow: "There is therefore now no condemnation for those who are in Christ Jesus. For the law of the Spirit of life in Christ Jesus has set me free from the law of sin and death." (8:1-2) In Galatians, he calls it "the law of Christ" (6:2) which requires that we *walk* in it as though we are following the divine Spirit's orders (5:16, 25).[1] And this teaching, "the truth of the gospel" (2:5, 14) that is, "the only true gospel," which we are to obey (You were running well; who hindered you from obeying the truth? 5:7), has been consigned for all subsequent ages in writing by the Apostle's hand: "See with what large letters I am writing to you with my own hand." (6:11) And it is none other than Paul's oral teaching that is now consigned once and for all as scripture for the ages, as is evident in his statement:

> But even if we, or an angel from heaven, should preach to you a gospel contrary to that which we preached to you, let him be accursed. *As we have said before, so now I say again*, If any one is preaching to you a gospel contrary to that which you received, let him be accursed. (Gal 1:8-9)

This Pauline approach has impacted the entire New Testament literature, making out of it a "canon" with the same authority as the Old Testament. The clearest case is the Book of Revelation:

> I warn every one who hears the words of the prophecy of this book: if any one adds to them, God will add to him the plagues *described in this book*, and if any one takes away from the words of

---

[1] See above my comments on Gal 5:25 where the verb used (*stoikheō*) means "walk in line as a marching army."

the book of this prophecy, God will take away his share in the tree of life and in the holy city, which are *described in this book*. He who testifies to these things says, "Surely I am coming soon." Amen. Come, Lord Jesus! (Rev 22:18-20)

However, the same is also evident in the rest of the New Testament. This is illustrated through two of its latest books, the Gospels of John and Matthew, where the hearers are bound by what is *written* and are not allowed any addition or subtraction "until the close of the age:"

> Now Jesus did many other signs in the presence of the disciples, which are not written in this book; but these are written that you may believe that Jesus is the Christ, the Son of God, and that believing you may have life in his name … This is the disciple who is bearing witness to these things, and who has written these things; and we know that his testimony is true. But there are also many other things which Jesus did; were every one of them to be written, I suppose that the world itself could not contain the books that would be written. (Jn 20:30-31; 21:24-25)

> And Jesus came and said to them, "All authority in heaven and on earth has been given to me. Go therefore and make disciples of all nations, baptizing them in the name of the Father and of the Son and of the Holy Spirit, teaching them to observe all that I have commanded you; and lo, I am with you always, to the close of the age." (Mat 28:18-20)

It is precisely this New Testament feature which gave rise to the traditional explanation behind the closing of the New Testament canon: the death of the last apostle.

Consequently, as I have shown earlier in discussing the Old Testament, the teaching which applied to Israel, who reneged on it, still applies to it and to the nations as well, as we can see in the following telling passages:

You are the light of the world. A city set on a hill cannot be hid. Nor do men light a lamp and put it under a bushel, but on a stand, and it gives light to all in the house. Let your light so shine before men, that they may see your good works and give glory to your Father who is in heaven. *Think not that I have come to abolish the law and the prophets; I have come not to abolish them but to fulfill them.* For truly, I say to you, till heaven and earth pass away, not an iota, not a dot, will pass from the law until all is accomplished. Whoever then relaxes one of the least of these commandments and teaches men so, shall be called least in the kingdom of heaven; but he who does them and teaches them shall be called great in the kingdom of heaven. For I tell you, *unless your righteousness exceeds that of the scribes and Pharisees, you will never enter the kingdom of heaven.* (Mt 5:14-20)

I want you to know, brethren, that our fathers were all under the cloud, and all passed through the sea, and all were baptized into Moses in the cloud and in the sea, and all ate the same supernatural food and all drank the same supernatural drink. For they drank from the supernatural Rock which followed them, and the Rock was Christ. Nevertheless with most of them God was not pleased; for they were overthrown in the wilderness. *Now these things are warnings for us, not to desire evil as they did.* Do not be idolaters as some of them were; as it is written, "The people sat down to eat and drink and rose up to dance." We must not indulge in immorality as some of them did, and twenty-three thousand fell in a single day. We must not put the Lord to the test, as some of them did and were destroyed by serpents; nor grumble, as some of them did and were destroyed by the Destroyer. *Now these things happened to them as a warning, but they were written down for our instruction, upon whom the end of the ages has come.* (1 Cor 10:1-11)

For the believer, with the advent of Jesus Christ, God's last and final emissary, the biblical story comes to a close. The next step is

God's final advent to judge all humans. In the meantime one is given a chance to fulfill his law by which he will judge all living:

> For God shows no partiality. All who have sinned without the law will also perish without the law, and all who have sinned under the law will be judged by the law. For it is not the hearers of the law who are righteous before God, but the doers of the law who will be justified. When Gentiles who have not the law do by nature what the law requires, they are a law to themselves, even though they do not have the law. They show that what the law requires is written on their hearts, while their conscience also bears witness and their conflicting thoughts accuse or perhaps excuse them on that day when, according to my gospel, God judges the secrets of men by Christ Jesus. (Rom 2:11-16)
>
> Owe no one anything, except to love one another; for he who loves his neighbor has fulfilled the law. The commandments, "You shall not commit adultery, You shall not kill, You shall not steal, You shall not covet," and any other commandment, are summed up in this sentence, "You shall love your neighbor as yourself." Love does no wrong to a neighbor; therefore love is the fulfilling of the law. Besides this you know what hour it is, how it is full time now for you to wake from sleep. *For salvation is nearer to us now than when we first believed; the night is far gone, the day is at hand.* Let us then cast off the works of darkness and put on the armor of light; *let us conduct ourselves becomingly as in the day*, not in reveling and drunkenness, not in debauchery and licentiousness, not in quarreling and jealousy. But put on the Lord Jesus Christ, and make no provision for the flesh, to gratify its desires. (Rom 13:8-14)

In other words, starting with and after Jesus Christ, whose preaching required that we "repent, for the kingdom of heaven is *at hand*," "the day of the Lord" is always *at hand*, around the corner, as it were. Consequently, chronological time and human history are not at all negated, but they function as a *kairos*, an opportune time, an opportunity, for us to do God's will before his day:

> Do not be deceived; God is not mocked, for whatever a man sows, that he will also reap. For he who sows to his own flesh will from the flesh reap corruption; but he who sows to the Spirit will from the Spirit reap eternal life. And let us not grow weary in well-doing, for in due season we shall reap, if we do not lose heart. So then, as we have opportunity (*kairos*), *let us do good to all men*, and especially to those who are of the household of faith. (Gal 6:7-10)

One should not then imagine that the historical events after Christ "lead" to the end of times, rather every age and generation is at the same level, at a moment where it is under the judgment of the Lord's Day that always and ever "is at hand," "upon" every age and generation which is judged in the "light" of the teaching that speaks of that Day. And no one is exempt, not even the Apostle:

> This is how one should regard us, as servants of Christ and stewards of the mysteries of God. Moreover it is required of stewards that they be found trustworthy. But with me it is a very small thing that I should be judged by you or by any human court. I do not even judge myself. I am not aware of anything against myself, but I am not thereby acquitted. It is the Lord who judges me. Therefore do not pronounce judgment before the time, before the Lord comes, who will bring to light the things now hidden in darkness and will disclose the purposes of the heart. Then every man will receive his commendation from God. (1 Cor 4:1-5)

The so-called "signs" of the end are *accompanying*, not preceding, signs. Were they indeed preceding, then they would not be signs. Even more, one could be fooled; hence the Lord's cautionary statements that we not be "led astray." The signs function as the clerk of the court who heralds the entrance of the judge into the courtroom. There is no functional time between the announcement and the procession of the judge. The attendees' standing up is also a sign of the judge's entrance, but their rising can hardly be considered as a sign that would allow anyone to take action or prepare oneself. A sign is not a countdown; a countdown can stop at the last second as often happens at the launching of a rocket or a space shuttle. Notice how, throughout the twentieth century, people who have considered the signs as the beginning of a countdown have been fooled time and again. A sign is rather the *assurance* that what has all along been expected has come. When the sign is there it is already too late for anyone or anything. Indeed, the end does not come by stages, but "in a moment, in the twinkling of an eye" (1 Cor 15:52), "like the lightning" (Mt 24:27; Lk 17:24), "like the thief in the night" (1 Thess 5:2); the sign comes *unexpectedly*:

> But know this, that if the householder had known in what part of the night the thief was coming, he would have watched and would not have let his house be broken into. Therefore you also must be ready; for the Son of man is coming at an hour you do not expect. (Mt 24:43-44)

> But know this, that if the householder had known at what hour the thief was coming, he would not have left his house to be broken into. You also must be ready; for the Son of man is coming at an unexpected hour. (Lk 12:39-40)

Still, among those accompanying signs, at no point is there reference in the New Testament to the Jews returning to Palestine, let alone to it being their own deeded country! If the Lord Jesus Christ himself and Paul, God's Apostle to the nations, deemed it not necessary to discuss the Jews' return to Palestine, there must be a reason. And the reason is clear: there is, as we have seen, no such thing in the prophetic teaching. The biblical story is a linear one that has a beginning and an end, albeit an end with a promise. The return is to God's heavenly city, Zion, to which is invited every man (*'adam*)—whether Jew or from among the nations—who will have abided by God's will. This, as I have extensively shown, is the prophetic teaching. If there is mention of a return to "the earth of Israel" (*'eretz yisra'el*), it is, as Ezekiel makes abundantly clear, as "the ground of Israel" (*'admat[2] yisra'el*), in clear reference to the ground out of which man (*'adam*) is made. It is another way to challenge the Jews to understand that the earth granted them to live on, wherever they might be, is never their deeded possession, but the place of their testing as to whether they will deal with it as a ground to be shared with all the other inhabitants as in a perpetual jubilee year. And what applied to the Jews now applies to the nations. With the advent of Jesus Christ, according to the New Testament, the entire earth of the Roman empire is to be viewed by the believer as God's *'adamah* (ground) to be shared equally by every *'adam* (man) formed out of it by God. Every earth and the fullness thereof is the Lord's, indeed the whole world and those who dwell therein (Ps 24:1). Actually the biblical lesson after Christ is now valid for all who inhabit God's earth: the citizens of both the Kingdoms of Israel and Judah were punished by God to death and into exile precisely *because* they thought that the earth they were living on and the cities they were abiding in were theirs by an inalienable right, and that even their God would not dare to contradict such, even if they continually disobeyed his commandments:

> Amend your ways and your doings, and I will let you dwell in this place. Do not trust in these deceptive words: "This is the temple of

---

[2] This is the form *'adamah* takes when followed by a noun complement.

the Lord, the temple of the Lord, the temple of the Lord." For if you truly amend your ways and your doings, if you truly execute justice one with another, if you do not oppress the alien, the fatherless or the widow, or shed innocent blood in this place, and if you do not go after other gods to your own hurt, then I will let you dwell in this place, in the earth that I gave of old to your fathers for ever ... Will you steal, murder, commit adultery, swear falsely, burn incense to Baal, and go after other gods that you have not known, and then come and stand before me in this house, which is called by my name, and say, "We are delivered!"—only to go on doing all these abominations? Has this house, which is called by my name, become a den of robbers in your eyes? ... And now, because you have done all these things and when I spoke to you persistently you did not listen, and when I called you, you did not answer, therefore I will do to the house which is called by my name, and in which you trust, and to the place which I gave to you and to your fathers, as I did to Shiloh. And I will cast you out of my sight, as I cast out all your kinsmen, all the offspring of Ephraim. (Jer 7:3-15)

The Bible: A Lesson for All Nations and All Ages

That the biblical story has a beginning and an end, and consequently cannot be considered as the history of a people to be continued beyond the limits of the scriptural canon, is borne by the content of scripture itself. I shall single out three compelling features.

First and foremost, the traditional nomenclature of the biblical books and sections do not reflect an interest in human history. Rather, the titles of the first two main parts of the Old Testament reflect an interest in the teaching: Law and Prophets, that is, God's rule for human behavior and his repeated critique and chastening through his prophets in order to bring the people back into obedience of his law. Even the biblical books themselves are titled mainly after God's prophets (Samuel, Isaiah, Jeremiah, Ezekiel and each of the twelve prophets) or his representatives (Joshua, Judges, Samuel); even the Pentateuch, the five Books of Moses, are referred to also simply as "Moses."[3] The title of the third section, the Writings or Books, reflect the same intent since they are clearly teaching material whose main point is to show that the Law contains the full divine wisdom sought after by the nations. On the other hand, the only "history" they contain is a repeat of the biblical story, as is the case in the Wisdom of Sirach (chs.44-49) and the Wisdom of Solomon (chs.10-19).

Secondly, the previous nomenclature is not haphazard, but rather reflects fully the intention of the biblical authors themselves. They were clearly not interested in any historical events except to show that the Kings of Israel and Judah were unfaithful to God's law. In this regard, it is worth noting that the original title of the Books is "Kings," rather than "Kingdoms" as in the Septuagint. In each case, however, the author highlights those aspects of the monarch's reign that relate to the overarching theme, namely, the kings' faithlessness to Yahweh's law. Other aspects of each monarch's reign are dismissed with the stereotype formula: "The rest of the acts of [name of king] and all that he did, are they not written in the Book of the Chronicles of the Kings of Judah, Israel respectively?"[4] Even if we assume that the author had access to written official

---

[3] See Lk 16:29 (But Abraham said, "They have Moses and the prophets; let them hear them"); 24:27 (And beginning with Moses and all the prophets, he interpreted to them in all the scriptures the things concerning himself).
[4] 1 Kg 14:19; 15:7, 23, 31; 16:5, 14, 20, 27; 22:39, 45; 2 Kg 1:18; 8:23; 10:34; 12:19; 13:8, 12; 14:15, 18, 28; 15:6, 11, 15, 21, 26, 31, 36; 16:19; 20:20; 21:17, 25; 23:28; 24:5.

documents of those reigns, he opted not to use them. Instead he prepared his "own" work, one that approached the existing material from the perspective of Deuteronomy, the last Book of the Law. Consequently, the story of the Kingdoms of Israel and Judah was not foremost on his mind, but rather the dilemma of kingship that was expected to abide by the requirements of God's law.

Finally, although the biblical story of the kingdoms ends with their demise, as is the case with all earthly political powers, still their rise is not linked to any human valor, but rather to God's willingness and mercy. Whenever the human factor intervenes with its hubris, as in the case of David and Solomon, it is always to the detriment of mankind and is a harbinger of a disastrous future. The same applied earlier to the rise of the children of Jacob as a people in the Pentateuch. God intervened to raise them from under the oppression of a Pharaoh who did not know Joseph, yet they self-destruct in the wilderness through their revolt against that God. The same pattern continues and repeats itself endlessly in the period of the Judges. Thus, in contradistinction to all other histories of peoples and nations, in the Bible the glorious deeds are not done by the people or by heroes. The glorious deeds are God's work. A classic example of the biblical story is Psalm 78 that presents that story as one of God's merciful deeds and the people's stubbornness in their disobedience toward him. What is more important though is that this "story" is presented clearly as a teaching and a lesson to be heeded, just as is scripture in its entirety, Law, Prophets, and Writings:

A Maskil[5] of Asaph. Give ear, O my people, to my teaching; incline your ears to the words of my mouth! I will open my mouth in a parable (*mashal*); I will utter riddles (*ḥidot*) from of old, things that we have heard and known, that our fathers have told us. We will not hide them from their children, but tell to the coming generation the glorious deeds of the Lord, and his might, and the wonders which he has wrought. He established a testimony in Jacob, and appointed a law in Israel, which he commanded our fathers to teach to their children; that the next generation might know them, the children yet unborn, and arise and tell them to their children, so that they should set their hope in God, and not forget the works of God, but keep his commandments; and that they should not be like their fathers, a stubborn and rebellious generation, a generation whose heart was not steadfast, whose spirit was not faithful to God. (vv.1-8)

Indeed, the same phraseology is found in Ezekiel, who also presents the story of the promiscuous Jerusalem and Samaria in a similar way in chapters 16 and 23: "The word of the Lord came to me: 'Son of man, propound a riddle (*ḥidah*), and speak a parable (*mashal*) to the house of Israel.'" (Ezek17:1-2). Actually, Ezekiel's fame among his opponents was that he was "a speaker in parables (a maker of allegories; *memashshel meshalim*)" (20:49).

The message is clear: it is God's law, i.e., his instruction, which grants and secures life. Indeed, although it seems as though the city is merely the reality within which divine law is applicable, in actuality it is the divine law that founds, builds, and maintains the existence of the city.[6] And if so, then it was the Law granted in the wilderness of Sinai that brought Israel into existence and main-

---

[5] The Hebrew *maskil* means actually a wisdom teaching.
[6] For more detail see *OTI₃* 59-67.

tained it, insofar as Israel remained obedient to it. But, as we saw, instead of the Law, Israel sought food and water for its sustenance, forgetting that the former was brought down from heaven, the divine domain,[7] and the latter was made to gush out from a dead and barren rock.[8] These events should have been sufficient to prove that God alone was necessary for Israel's sustenance. In fact it was necessary for God to perform such miracles to prove that fact. For if God had destroyed Israel in the wilderness, that could—*would*— have been misinterpreted as though Israel merely succumbed in the wilderness due to the lack of food and water. So God waited until Israel was settled as a nation, in a city-state, and there, in the domain of secure existence, he unleashed his anger against it, thus showing Israel and everyone else that it is he, and only he, who makes and breaks his people whenever they contravene his law that is subsumed in the care for the needy co-inhabitant.

Thus, the biblical story is in no way the story of Israel—let alone its history. It is the story of God. A story—or a history—is related through deeds; according to the biblical story, however, had Israel's deeds been allowed to take their course, they would have nipped Israel in the bud, in which case there would have been no Israel and no story to tell about it. It is rather God's deeds, which are anti-deeds from the human perspective,[9] that created the biblical story as we have it. This story tells us that life, human and any other kind of earthly life—be it vegetation, oasis, king, city, or temple—proceeds *directly* from God, without any intermediary. His kingship lies in his shepherding role.[10] And whoever has witnessed the activity of shepherds in the Near East will have noticed two things: (1) shepherding takes place at the fringes of

---

[7] Ps 78:23-25.
[8] Ps 78:15-16.
[9] Since they work against the will of the people.
[10] Ps 78:70-72. See also Ezek 34.

settled life, where wilderness, the domain of death and nonexistence, is daily experienced; and (2) the flock is not an agglomeration of sheep, but rather a creation of the shepherd. Without him the sheep would scatter and ultimately perish. The existence of the individual sheep is literally bound to the reality we call a flock, and there is a flock only where there is a shepherd who walks *ahead* of the sheep that recognize the sounds emitted by him and thus "follow his voice."

20

The Second Coming

The biblical story is then not so much a description of what happened between the creation of the world and the coming of Jesus Christ as God's promised Messiah and Son of man, but rather a proposition that were it not for God's mercy again and again, to which he bound himself through his one-sided covenant with Noah, humanity and all life on earth would have been swept into oblivion according to the words of Genesis:

> The Lord saw that the wickedness of man was great in the earth, and that every imagination of the thoughts of his heart was only evil continually. And the Lord was sorry that he had made man on the earth, and it grieved him to his heart. So the Lord said, "I will blot out man whom I have created from the face of the ground, man and beast and creeping things and birds of the air, for I am sorry that I have made them." (6:5-7)

The same proposition tells us that "Noah found favor in the eyes of the Lord" (v.8) and that he "was a righteous man, blameless in his generation" and "walked with God" (v.9). It then tells us *how* he did that. Unlike Adam who did not do what "God commanded him" (2:16), Noah kept *doing* "whatever God commanded him" (6:22; 7:5, 9, 16). However, according to the same proposition, all other human beings continued to contravene God's commands. So, he decided to punish them unto instruction, for their own good, but to no avail:

> "I gave you cleanness of teeth in all your cities, and lack of bread in all your places, yet you did not return to me," says the Lord. "And I also withheld the rain from you when there were yet three months to the harvest; I would send rain upon one city, and send

no rain upon another city; one field would be rained upon, and the field on which it did not rain withered; so two or three cities wandered to one city to drink water, and were not satisfied; yet you did not return to me," says the Lord. "I smote you with blight and mildew; I laid waste your gardens and your vineyards; your fig trees and your olive trees the locust devoured; yet you did not return to me," says the Lord. "I sent among you a pestilence after the manner of Egypt; I slew your young men with the sword; I carried away your horses; and I made the stench of your camp go up into your nostrils; yet you did not return to me," says the Lord. "I overthrew some of you, as when God overthrew Sodom and Gomorrah, and you were as a brand plucked out of the burning; yet you did not return to me," says the Lord. (Amos 4:6-11)[1]

Being the just God, he could not possibly allow unrighteousness into his kingdom. So, the biblical proposition goes, he decided for "what no eye has seen, nor ear heard, nor the heart of man conceived" (1 Cor 2:9), to *willfully* raise someone who would have the traits of Noah to the full extent of completeness and absoluteness, the obedient servant par excellence:

> The Lord God has given me the tongue of those who are taught, that I may know how to sustain with a word him that is weary. Morning by morning he wakens, he wakens my ear to hear as those who are taught. The Lord God has opened my ear, and I was not rebellious, I turned not backward. I gave my back to the smiters, and my cheeks to those who pulled out the beard; I hid not my face from shame and spitting. (Is 50:4-6)

> Surely he has borne our griefs and carried our sorrows; yet we esteemed him stricken, smitten by God, and afflicted. But he was wounded for our transgressions, he was bruised for our iniquities; upon him was the chastisement that made us whole, and with his

---

[1] See also Is 1:2-10.

stripes we are healed. All we like sheep have gone astray; we have turned every one to his own way; and the Lord has laid on him the iniquity of us all. He was oppressed, and he was afflicted, yet he opened not his mouth; like a lamb that is led to the slaughter, and like a sheep that before its shearers is dumb, so he opened not his mouth. By oppression and judgment he was taken away; and as for his generation, who considered that he was cut off out of the earth of the living, stricken for the transgression of my people? And they made his grave with the wicked and with a rich man in his death, although he had done no violence, and there was no deceit in his mouth. *Yet it was the delight (good pleasure) of the Lord to bruise him; he has put him to grief;* when he makes himself an offering for sin, he shall see his offspring, he shall prolong his days; the will of the Lord shall prosper in his hand; he shall see the fruit of the travail of his soul and be satisfied; by his knowledge shall the righteous one, my servant, make many to be accounted righteous; and he shall bear their iniquities. (53:4-11)

With the sending of that servant the biblical story comes to an end, putting every human being at the threshold of God's heavenly city, which is now open to all creation and whose children will be taught by the Lord just as his special servant is:

Sing, O barren one, who did not bear; break forth into singing and cry aloud, you who have not been in travail! For the children of the desolate one will be more than the children of her that is married, says the Lord. Enlarge the place of your tent, and let the curtains of your habitations be stretched out; hold not back, lengthen your cords and strengthen your stakes. For you will spread abroad to the right and to the left, and your descendants will possess the nations and will people the desolate cities … All your sons shall be taught by the Lord, and great shall be the prosperity of your sons. In righteousness you shall be established; you shall be far from oppression, for you shall not fear; and from terror, for it shall not come near you. (Is 54:1-3, 13-14)

However, again according to the biblical proposition, this city will not materialize until the end of time and *after the last judgment*:

> Then I saw a great white throne and him who sat upon it; from his presence earth and sky fled away, and no place was found for them. And I saw the dead, great and small, standing before the throne, and books were opened. Also another book was opened, which is the book of life. And the dead were judged by what was written in the books, by what they had done. And the sea gave up the dead in it, Death and Hades gave up the dead in them, and all were judged by what they had done. Then Death and Hades were thrown into the lake of fire. This is the second death, the lake of fire; and if any one's name was not found written in the book of life, he was thrown into the lake of fire. Then I saw a new heaven and a new earth; for the first heaven and the first earth had passed away, and the sea was no more. And I saw the holy city, new Jerusalem, coming down out of heaven from God, prepared as a bride adorned for her husband. (Rev. 20:11-21:2)

The questions that then arise are: "What is the factual difference between the Old and the New Testaments if both end by pointing to the coming Kingdom?"; "In which sense does the New Testament close the story begun in the Old Testament?" My readers will recall that I showed that the Old Testament story is basically interested in the entire realm of God's earth. That is why starting with Genesis 1-11 it shows that all human beings are basically disobedient and behave in an ungodly manner. The general trait of all human beings is to say or, at least, think as the Pharisee of the parable does: "God, I thank thee that I am not like other men, extortioners, unjust, adulterers." (Lk 18:11) So, in order to make its point, starting with Genesis 12 up to and including the Prophets, the Old Testament story zeroes in on a specific human unit who, in spite of God's special attention, ends up performing as poorly, if not more so, than the rest of the nations:

> Hear, O heavens, and give ear, O earth; for the Lord has spoken: "Sons have I reared and brought up, but they have rebelled against me. The ox knows its owner, and the ass its master's crib; but Israel does not know, my people does not understand." (Is 1:2-3)

> Therefore I still contend with you, says the Lord, and with your children's children I will contend. For cross to the coasts of Cyprus and see, or send to Kedar and examine with care; see if there has been such a thing. Has a nation changed its gods, even though they are no gods? But my people have changed their glory for that which does not profit. Be appalled, O heavens, at this, be shocked, be utterly desolate, says the Lord, for my people have committed two evils: they have forsaken me, the fountain of living waters, and hewed out cisterns for themselves, broken cisterns, that can hold no water. (Jer 2:9-13)[2]

> And he said to me, "Son of man, go, get you to the house of Israel, and speak with my words to them. For you are not sent to a people of foreign speech and a hard language, but to the house of Israel—not to many peoples of foreign speech and a hard language, whose words you cannot understand. Surely, if I sent you to such, they would listen to you. But the house of Israel will not listen to you; for they are not willing to listen to me; because all the house of Israel are of a hard forehead and of a stubborn heart." (Ezek 3:4-7)

Once the Law and the Prophets have convinced the hearers that the behavior of the children of Israel is that of dismal failure, the Wisdom literature is introduced to offer to the nations the same chance as Israel had by inviting them to abide by God's fatherly instruction inscribed in the Law, the only true wisdom

---

[2] See also Jer 7:25-28; 18:13-18.

those nations are yearning and looking for. However, the last part of scripture, the New Testament writings, especially, those of Paul, the Apostle to the nations, reflects the same bleak situation among the Gentiles. One need only read his first Letter to the Corinthians to be convinced of that. Consequently, he can make his point without hesitation: "I have already charged that all men, both Jews and Greeks, are under the power of sin" (Rom 3:9); "As sin came into the world through one man and death through sin, so also death spread to all men because all men sinned." (5:12) It is no wonder then that he keeps reminding the Gentiles who accepted his message not to be deceived since God, the judge of all, cannot be mocked (Gal 6:7), and that they have actually to *do* his will to inherit his coming kingdom:

> Do not be deceived; God is not mocked, for whatever a man sows, that he will also reap. For he who sows to his own flesh will from the flesh reap corruption; but he who sows to the Spirit will from the Spirit reap eternal life. And let us not grow weary in well-doing, for in due season we shall reap, if we do not lose heart. (Gal 6:7-9)

> Now the works of the flesh are plain: fornication, impurity, licentiousness, idolatry, sorcery, enmity, strife, jealousy, anger, selfishness, dissension, party spirit, envy, drunkenness, carousing, and the like. I warn you, as I warned you before, that those who do such things [the works of the flesh] shall not inherit the kingdom of God. (Gal 5:19-21)[3]

---

[3] See also 1 Cor 6:9-10 (Do you not know that the unrighteous will not inherit the kingdom of God? Do not be deceived; neither the immoral, nor idolaters, nor adulterers, nor sexual perverts, nor thieves, nor the greedy, nor drunkards, nor revilers, nor robbers will inherit the kingdom of God).

Biblical Story and Human History

From the preceding, it becomes clear that the Bible is neither a book describing the history of a given people nor one containing the decipherment of future events. It is intended to be an instruction, a lesson. Again, this instruction is not to allow us to figure out God. It is an instruction showing us how to behave during our life according to the "way" that will eventually lead us into the state in which he always wanted the human beings to be. Yet, they refused this by contravening God's will, as we hear at the beginning of the "prayer of remembrance and offering" of the Liturgy of St Basil the Great:

> With these blessed Powers, O Master, Lover of man, we sinners also do cry out and say, Holy art thou, in truth, and all-holy, and there is no measure to the magnificence of thy holiness, and holy art thou in all thy works, for in righteousness and true judgment hast thou brought about all things for us. When thou hadst fashioned man, taking dust from the earth, and hadst honored him with thine own image, O God, thou didst set him in a paradise of plenty, *promising him life immortal and the enjoyment of eternal good things in the observance of thy commandments. But when he disobeyed thee, the true God, who had created him, and was led astray by the deceit of the serpent, and was slain by his own trespasses, thou didst banish him, in thy righteous judgment, O God, from Paradise into this world,* and didst turn him back to the earth from which he was taken.

In view of this coming kingdom and in order for us not to wander away, the Lord Jesus Christ taught us his prayer which is a compendium of what we should be asking for and also how to ensure that we are on the right track:

> And in praying do not heap up empty phrases as the Gentiles do; for they think that they will be heard for their many words. Do

> not be like them, for your Father knows what you need before you ask him. Pray then like this: "Our Father who art in heaven, hallowed be thy name, thy kingdom come, thy will be done, on earth as it is in heaven. Give us this day our daily bread; and forgive us our debts, as we also have forgiven our debtors; and lead us not into temptation, but deliver us from evil." For if you forgive men their trespasses, your heavenly Father also will forgive you; but if you do not forgive men their trespasses, neither will your Father forgive your trespasses. (Mt 6:7-15)

God's kingdom is closely linked to his will being done on earth as it is in heaven since there is going to be "a new heaven and a new earth." And what is his will except to behave "divinely" by forgiving others as he himself repeatedly did throughout the biblical story. *Otherwise, we shall not be forgiven* and, consequently, we shall not inherit his kingdom or, if we imagine that we have it "in our pocket," we shall be thrown out. The seriousness of the matter is underscored in the parable we hear later in the same Gospel of Matthew:

> Then Peter came up and said to him, "Lord, how often shall my brother sin against me, and I forgive him? As many as seven times?" Jesus said to him, "I do not say to you seven times, but seventy times seven. Therefore the kingdom of heaven may be compared to a king who wished to settle accounts with his servants. When he began the reckoning, one was brought to him who owed him ten thousand talents; and as he could not pay, his lord ordered him to be sold, with his wife and children and all that he had, and payment to be made. So the servant fell on his knees, imploring him, 'Lord, have patience with me, and I will pay you everything.' And out of pity for him the lord of that servant released him and forgave him the debt. But that same servant, as he went out, came upon one of his fellow servants who owed him a hundred denarii; and seizing him by the throat he said, 'Pay what you owe.' So his fellow servant fell down and besought him,

'Have patience with me, and I will pay you.' He refused and went and put him in prison till he should pay the debt. When his fellow servants saw what had taken place, they were greatly distressed, and they went and reported to their lord all that had taken place. Then his lord summoned him and said to him, 'You wicked servant! I forgave you all that debt because you besought me; and should not you have had mercy on your fellow servant, as I had mercy on you?' And in anger his lord delivered him to the jailers, till he should pay all his debt. So also my heavenly Father will do to every one of you, if you do not forgive your brother from your heart." (Mt 18:21-35)

The lesson is clear: in order for us to pass the test on Judgment Day, which we pray God not to lead us into too soon—the Greek term *peirasmon* which is translated as "temptation" actually means "test"[4]—, we must be "perfect" in our mercy as God is in his (Mt 5:48 and Lk 6:36).[5] Put otherwise, the Lord's prayer that we are to recite daily functions as God's law in Deuteronomy. It is intended for life, but it might end up witnessing against us unto our condemnation. And we had better check on ourselves daily as the Apostle warned: "Be angry but do not sin; do not let the sun go down on your anger, and give no opportunity to the devil." (Eph 4:26-27) Why? Here again Paul gives us the answer:

> Repay no one evil for evil, but take thought for what is noble in the sight of all. If possible, so far as it depends upon you, live peaceably with all. Beloved, never avenge yourselves, but leave it to the wrath of God; for it is written, "Vengeance is mine, I will repay, says the Lord." No, "if your enemy is hungry, feed him; if

---

[4] This goes hand in hand with the parallel petition that we be delivered form "the evil one," that is, Satan, the opponent, who will be heaping counter-arguments against our righteousness as he does against Job (Job 1).

[5] See earlier my discussion of this matter.

he is thirsty, give him drink; for by so doing you will heap burning coals upon his head." Do not be overcome by evil, but overcome evil with good. (Rom 12:17-21)

But, if the kingdom is coming, then also the divine judgment preceding it is still ahead. In the meantime, we are to live on God's earth *as though* it is God's heaven, where his will is perfectly implemented. A garden is after all a garden; it is only God's will that makes it his garden and our paradise:

> You have heard that it was said, "You shall love your neighbor and hate your enemy." But I say to you, Love your enemies and pray for those who persecute you, so that you may be sons of your Father who is in heaven; for he makes his sun rise on the evil and on the good, and sends rain on the just and on the unjust. (Mt 5:43-45)

Furthermore, in view of the coming Kingdom, it is necessary to practice on a daily basis God's will of being as merciful as he is. The stake could well be no less than finding ourselves thrown out of his Kingdom, *even if we are allegedly entitled to it and even if we are already seated*:

> And while they [the maidens] went to buy, the bridegroom came, and those who were ready went in with him to the marriage feast; and the door was shut. Afterward the other maidens came also, saying, "Lord, lord, open to us." But he replied, "Truly, I say to you, I do not know you." Watch therefore, for you know neither the day nor the hour. (Mt 25:10-13)

> But when the king came in to look at the guests, he saw there a man who had no wedding garment; and he said to him, "Friend, how did you get in here without a wedding garment?" And he was speechless. Then the king said to the attendants, "Bind him hand and foot, and cast him into the outer darkness; there men will weep and gnash their teeth." For many are called, but few are chosen. (Mt 22:11-14)

On the other hand, we should not try to judge and foresee who will be in the Kingdom, since the Lord himself warned us:

> Judge not, that you be not judged. For with the judgment you pronounce you will be judged, and the measure you give will be the measure you get. Why do you see the speck that is in your brother's eye, but do not notice the log that is in your own eye? Or how can you say to your brother, "Let me take the speck out of your eye," when there is the log in your own eye? You hypocrite, first take the log out of your own eye, and then you will see clearly to take the speck out of your brother's eye. (Mt 7:1-5)

An unpleasant surprise may well be waiting for us: "Truly, I say to you, the tax collectors and the harlots go into the kingdom of God before you." (Mt 21:31)

21

The Millennium

Despite the repeated warnings by both Jesus (Mk 13:5-10, 32-37) and the Apostle (1 Thess 5:1-7) not to try to figure out the timetable of the end times, people as far back as the 2nd century B.C. were fascinated with doing so. If such people would do it for the right reason namely, to help prepare for the event by repenting of their sins and asking others to do the same, as the Baptist and the Lord summoned (Repent for the kingdom of heavens is at hand; Mt 3:2; 4:17), then the result would still be beneficial. Unfortunately, however, those who are interested in end time calculations are often the self-righteous who assume that they are assuredly among the 144,000 "chosen" who will "reign" on earth for one thousand years before the advent of God's kingdom (Rev 20:1-7), and then enjoy eternal bliss in that kingdom with the rest of the people whose names are inscribed in the Book of Life (vv.12-15). Let me point out the inanity of such a view:

1. If we were to accept the word of all those who trust that they are among the 144,000, then the actual count would be larger than this number. It ensues then that some of those who feel "chosen" are actually not so and thus are proven wrong. If some are proven wrong, then all are potentially so. Also, if some of those who consider themselves to be in that number die before the Lord's coming—which actually happens time and again—how could they undergo rapture? At any rate, we shall never be sure who those 144,000 are. The fact is the number 144,000 is fluid

and is intended as a metaphor, which I shall discuss below.

2. Reigning entails an inhabited realm. To say that someone is king assumes that he is ruling over subjects. That is why, in scripture, the Lord is not simply king, but "King of Israel" or "King of the Nations" (Jer 10:7). So, to say that the 144,000 will reign or rule *with* Christ (Rev 20:4, 6), we have to ask, whom will they be ruling over since the rest of mankind will not be around? They will be watching one another, ruling over no one for one thousand years!

3. What would be the big deal about reigning on earth for one thousand years and then enjoying God's kingdom for eternity? How will the extra thousand years affect the status of the 144,000 elect when they will be sharing the kingdom for eternity equally with all the others whose names are inscribed in the Book of Life? What can an extra thousand years add to eternity except a feeling of superiority over other colleagues, which would not be worthy of those admitted into God's Kingdom.

4. The population of a good size town in the United States is 144,000. Where will these 144,000 people reside? In one town? Spread all over the globe? If the latter, then each of them will be bored to death by oneself for a thousand years.

5. Those who endorse the literal understanding of the thousand year reign also speak of the rapture of those "left behind" (1 Thess 4:17) who will join "the dead

in Christ who will have risen first" (v.16). Since the 144,000 are said to be raised from the dead (Rev 20:4, 6), then questions arise: "Are those who undergo rapture part of that total number or in addition to it?" "Given that the Lord has been delaying time and again, will those who considered themselves at one point 'left behind' and then died be still counted in that number?"

6. How does this interpretation reconcile with 1 Corinthians where we hear that those "left behind" will be transformed at the same time as when *all* the dead will be raised and *both parties* will be made "imperishable" and thus will look alike (15:51-53)?

The questions could go on and on, but I hope my readers have realized by now the absurdity of such a view.

In order to understand correctly the millennium reign, which is mentioned only in the Book of Revelation, one needs to know what the book is talking about and how the author is saying it. On the one hand, the author is using traditional terminology when, for example, he is speaking of the resurrection and the final judgment. On the other hand, however, he is introducing a new approach in handling some of the traditional terms. I shall concentrate on one such feature that is related to our topic since it appears in conjunction with the millennium. It is only in Revelation that we hear about a first and a second resurrections from the dead (20:5-6, 13). If this was to be taken literally, then it would contradict the rest of the New Testament as well as the Old Testament, and it would be a heresy. The solution for a correct understanding, therefore, lies elsewhere. The noun "souls" (*psykhas*) occurs only four times in Revelation, twice to speak generally of all human beings (8:9; 18:13), and twice to refer to the souls of those who were sacrificed, that is, the martyrs, for the sake of their commitment to the word of God:

> When he opened the fifth seal, I saw under the altar the souls of those who had been *slain* for the word of God and for the witness they had borne; they cried out with a loud voice, "O Sovereign Lord, holy and true, how long before thou wilt judge and avenge our blood on those who dwell upon the earth?" Then they were each given a white robe and told to rest a little longer, until the number of their fellow servants and their brethren should be complete, who were to be killed as they themselves had been. (6:9-11)

> And I saw thrones, and seated on them were those to whom judgment was committed. Also I saw the souls of those who had been *beheaded* (*pepelekismenōn*) for their testimony to Jesus and for the word of God, and who had not worshiped the beast or its image and had not received its mark on their foreheads or their hands. They came to life, and reigned with Christ a thousand years. The rest of the dead did not come to life until the thousand years were ended. This is the first resurrection. Blessed and holy is he who shares in the first resurrection! Over such the second death has no power, but they shall be priests of God and of Christ, and they shall reign with him a thousand years. (20:4-6)

The parallelism is unmistakable. Although Revelation 20:4 is the only instance of the Greek verb *pepelekismenōn* (beheaded) in the New Testament, the verb "slain" occurs repeatedly in chapter 5 in reference to the Lamb (vv.6, 9, 12). Thus, the souls spoken of in the two quoted passages do not pertain to all dead believers, as is commonly assumed, but rather specifically to those who were "slain," just as Jesus was, as martyrs for the sake of their commitment to God. This is corroborated in the following text where the "slain" are singled out as a separate entity from the rest

The Millennium

of the believers who are known as "saints" in the New Testament: "And in her [Babylon] was found the blood of prophets and of saints, and of all who have been slain on earth." (18:24)[1] The conclusion is inescapable: it is specifically and only the martyrs who are spoken of in the passage about the reign of thousand years. And the martyrs can in no way, by any stretch of the imagination, be considered as being "left behind" and still living. So how are we to understand the passage?

It would behoove us to digress here and say a few words about the metaphoric language and the symbolic numerology encountered in the Book of Revelation. This does not mean that those devices are special to it, since we encounter them throughout the Bible, but the author uses them profusely in a way that makes them the fabric with which the entire work is woven.[2] To illustrate this I shall limit myself to two matters: the time factor and the numerals associated with the number 144,000.

---

[1] The difference between the prophets and the saints lies in that the former are the leaders of the Christian communities as we hear in 1 Corinthians: "And God has appointed in the church first apostles, second prophets, third teachers" (12:28); "Make love your aim, and earnestly desire the spiritual gifts, especially that you may prophesy. For one who speaks in a tongue speaks not to men but to God; for no one understands him, but he utters mysteries in the Spirit. On the other hand, he who prophesies speaks to men for their upbuilding and encouragement and consolation. He who speaks in a tongue edifies himself, but he who prophesies edifies the church. Now I want you all to speak in tongues, but even more to prophesy. He who prophesies is greater than he who speaks in tongues, unless some one interprets, so that the church may be edified." (14:1-5) We find the same differentiation between the prophets, of whom John is one, and the saints at the end of Revelation: "I am a fellow servant with you and your brethren the prophets, and with those who keep the words of this book." (22:9)

[2] For more detail see *NTI₃*.

The basic mistake when trying to understand the Book of Revelation is to assume that the book is describing events that extend over a long period of time. This is practically impossible if it is referring to the "last days" inaugurating the Kingdom. Indeed, there seems to be no movement between the beginning and the end of the book since its entire message is bracketed with these statements:

> The revelation of Jesus Christ, which God gave him to show to his servants what must soon take place; and he made it known by sending his angel to his servant John, who bore witness to the word of God and to the testimony of Jesus Christ, even to all that he saw. Blessed is he who reads aloud the words of the prophecy, and blessed are those who hear, and who keep what is written therein; for the time is near. (1:1-3)

> And he said to me, "These words are trustworthy and true. And the Lord, the God of the spirits of the prophets, has sent his angel to show his servants what must soon take place. And behold, I am coming soon." Blessed is he who keeps the words of the prophecy of this book. I John am he who heard and saw these things. And when I heard and saw them, I fell down to worship at the feet of the angel who showed them to me; but he said to me, "You must not do that! I am a fellow servant with you and your brethren the prophets, and with those who keep the words of this book. Worship God." And he said to me, "Do not seal up the words of the prophecy of this book, for the time is near ... "Behold, I am coming soon, bringing my recompense, to repay every one for what he has done... "I Jesus have sent my angel to you with this testimony for the churches. I am the root and the offspring of David, the bright morning star." ... He who testifies to these things says, "Surely I am coming soon." Amen. Come, Lord Jesus! (22:6-10, 12, 16, 20)

Many of those who misunderstand and misuse the book do so because they believe it speaks of the times we are now living and thus could not have been fully understood until our present days. Consequently, they say, although its meaning was hidden throughout the centuries, it was nevertheless miraculously preserved in the biblical canon in order for us who are now living these "last days" to understand the signs preceding the end. However, this is contrary to what the seer John was told: "*Do not seal up the words of the prophecy of this book*, for the time is near." (22:10) That is to say, the meaning of the book he wrote was not intended to be hidden from his readers, but rather evident and pertinent, and, if so, then this book, just as all the other books of the Bible, was written unto instruction and exhortation for each and every upcoming generation. Indeed, as I indicated earlier when discussing the New Testament literature, the Day of the Lord is always and ever "at hand."

So, then, the Book of Revelation "looks" special only because it is an expanded version of Mark 13 (also Luke 21, and Mathew 24), which speaks of the "last days," and at the end of which the Lord Jesus warns:

> But of that day or that hour *no one knows, not even the angels in heaven, nor the Son, but only the Father.* Take heed, watch; for you do not know when the time will come. It is like a man going on a journey, when he leaves home and puts his servants in charge, each with his work, and commands the doorkeeper to be on the watch. Watch therefore—for you do not know when the master of the house will come, in the evening, or at midnight, or at cockcrow, or in the morning—lest he come suddenly and find you asleep. And *what I say to you I say to all*: Watch. (Mk 13:32-37)

The message is to *all* upcoming generations of disciples and is no different than what Jesus said to his first disciples. Consequently, the Book of Revelation cannot be adding anything, but merely expanding on what has already been said.

The reason behind this extensive expansion is that it is addressed to hearers who are facing a new situation: persecution and threat of death on a larger scale than their predecessors. The author was inviting his hearers to martyrdom, which is no easy task. To do so, however, he had predecessors in the Books of Daniel and Maccabees. More than that, he had even what the authors of those books did not have: the image of the crucified and resurrected Christ proclaimed by Paul and the other apostles. Indeed, Christ figures in Revelation as the prototypical martyr to whom all new martyrs will be likened and with whom they will reign in the coming Kingdom of God. That such was on the author's mind right from the beginning can be seen in that the first title given by him to Jesus Christ—even before those of "first-born of the dead" and "ruler of kings on earth"—is "the faithful martyr (witness; *martys*)"[3] (1:5). That is why the writer John introduces himself three verses earlier as the one "who bore witness (*emartyrēsen*) to the word of God and to the testimony (witness; *martyrian*) of Jesus Christ" (v.2).[4] The hearers of John's message (Blessed is he who reads aloud the words of the prophecy, and blessed are those who hear, and who keep what is written therein; for the time is near; v.3) could not have missed the point of this intensive repetition. This thought controls the entire book which is bracketed between the notion of witness, here and in 22:18 (I bear witness [testify; *martyrō*] to every one who hears the words of the prophecy of this book), and the notion that "the time is near" (1:3 and 22:10).

The martyrs—and only the martyrs because of their sacrificial death—are assured partnership with Christ "the faithful martyr"

---

[3] In Greek *martys* becomes *martyros* when in the position of complement to another noun.
[4] All three Greek words are from the same root *marty(r)*—.

The Millennium

in the coming Kingdom, and it is only they who will not have to undergo judgment. The reason for this is that they have already been tested and found worthy because they totally and completely fulfilled God's law by doing what Jesus did, obeying God until death! All others will undergo judgment on the basis of their deeds, meaning they will be judged on whether or not they will have implemented God's ordinances (Rev 20:12-15). This is what is expressed in imagery in chapters 5 and 6:

> And between the throne and the four living creatures and among the elders, I saw a Lamb standing, as though it had been slain, with seven horns and with seven eyes, which are the seven spirits of God sent out into all the earth; and he went and took the scroll from the right hand of him who was seated on the throne. And when he had taken the scroll, the four living creatures and the twenty-four elders fell down before the Lamb, each holding a harp, and with golden bowls full of incense, which are the prayers of the saints; and they sang a new song, saying, "Worthy art thou to take the scroll and to open its seals, for *thou wast slain* and by thy blood didst ransom men for God from every tribe and tongue and people and nation, and hast made them a kingdom and priests to our God, and they shall reign on earth." (5:6-10)

> When he opened the fifth seal, I saw under the altar *the souls of those who had been slain* for the word of God and for the witness they had borne; they cried out with a loud voice, "O Sovereign Lord, holy and true, how long before thou wilt judge and avenge our blood on those who dwell upon the earth?" Then they were each given a white robe and told to rest a little longer, until the number of their fellow servants and their brethren should be complete, who were to be killed as they themselves had been. (6:9-11)

Yet, although the martyrs were slain just as Jesus was, they do not stand in the glory of God's kingdom as Jesus does. They have to wait until their "number" is complete, and that complete number is 144,000 since it is those "from all tribes and peoples and tongues" who "have washed their robes and made them white in the blood of the Lamb:"

> And I heard the number of the sealed, a hundred and forty-four thousand sealed, out of every tribe of the sons of Israel ... After this I looked, and behold, a great multitude which no man could number, from every nation, from all tribes and peoples and tongues, standing before the throne and before the Lamb, clothed in white robes, with palm branches in their hands, and crying out with a loud voice, "Salvation belongs to our God who sits upon the throne, and to the Lamb!" And all the angels stood round the throne and round the elders and the four living creatures, and they fell on their faces before the throne and worshiped God, saying, "Amen! Blessing and glory and wisdom and thanksgiving and honor and power and might be to our God for ever and ever! Amen." Then one of the elders addressed me, saying, "Who are these, clothed in white robes, and whence have they come?" I said to him, "my lord, you know." And he said to me, "These are they who have come out of the great tribulation; they have washed their robes and made them white in the blood of the Lamb. Therefore are they before the throne of God, and serve him day and night within his temple; and he who sits upon the throne will shelter them with his presence. They shall hunger no more, neither thirst any more; the sun shall not strike them, nor any scorching heat. For the Lamb in the midst of the throne will be their shepherd, and he will guide them to springs of living water; and God will wipe away every tear from their eyes." (7:4, 9-17)

Besides the reference to this multitude as being those who "have washed their robes and made them white in the blood of the Lamb," another oblique indication that we are dealing with the martyrs is that the plural "sealed," in Greek *esphragismenoi* (7:3, 4, 5, 8), sounds extremely close to the plural "slain" (*esphagmenoi*). Later we hear again that all 144,000 are in a situation similar to the martyrs described in chapter 6:

> Then I looked, and lo, on Mount Zion stood the Lamb, and with him a hundred and forty-four thousand who had his name and his Father's name written on their foreheads. And I heard a voice from heaven like the sound of many waters and like the sound of loud thunder; the voice I heard was like the sound of harpers playing on their harps, and they sing a new song before the throne and before the four living creatures and before the elders. No one could learn that song except the hundred and forty-four thousand who had been redeemed from the earth. It is these who have not defiled themselves with women, for they are chaste; it is these who follow the Lamb wherever he goes; these have been redeemed from mankind as first fruits for God and the Lamb, and in their mouth no lie was found, for they are spotless. (14:1-5)

This Mount Zion is nothing other than the new Jerusalem that will descend from heaven at the end, as one can see from the similar phraseology:

> Then I saw a new heaven and a new earth; for the first heaven and the first earth had passed away, and the sea was no more. And I saw the holy city, new Jerusalem, coming down out of heaven from God, prepared as a bride adorned for her husband; and I heard a loud voice from the throne saying, "Behold, the dwelling of God is with men. He will dwell with them, and they shall be his people, and God himself will be with them; he will wipe away every tear from their eyes, and death shall be no more, neither shall there be mourning nor crying nor pain any more, for the former things have passed away." (21:1-4)

The martyrs—and only they—are described as *already* being where the rest of the saints who will have done the deeds required by God's law (20:12-15) will accede.

What is one to make of all this? First, the number 144,000 is symbolic since it is the number the seer "heard" (7:4) and yet could not count since there was a great multitude (v.9). Ten and multiples of ten—hundreds, thousands, etc.—are generally used in reference to numbers of people and to suggest a large number that represents a totality. Twelve, of course, refers to the twelve tribes of biblical Israel and so serves to allude to the totality of the selected by God for a purpose. Doubling a number, as in the case of the twenty four elders (Rev 4:4), indicates assuredness in the sense that it is borne by the witness of at least two as required in the Law (Deut 17:6). Squaring a number ($12 \times 12 = 144$) would thus bring such assuredness to the highest possible level. Indeed, as promised, God will bring to completion the total number of the martyrs in order to show his total control over the dragon and its beast whom he will have proven to be impotent even though they slay those who are willing to be killed for God and his Christ, the prototype of all "faithful martyrs."

Secondly, God's kingdom is revealed at the end of times, although Christ already reigns for those who have accepted the gospel preaching him as the ruling Lord. The martyrs, whose number is not yet complete—otherwise, the end would have come!—are reigning with Christ, in an unseen way. They will be revealed as such together with Christ upon God's coming.

Thirdly, just as the "thousand" in the 144,000 represents a totality, so does the "thousand" (years) in the period describing the reign of the martyrs with Christ. It refers to the total period between the preaching of Christ, which posited the coming kingdom as being "at hand" and the actual coming of that Kingdom.

The conclusion imposes itself. Since no human history or time can be outside the realm of the impending Kingdom, the one thousand year reign "on earth" of the martyrs with Christ is not in a different, let alone subsequent, time frame than that of human history, but rather it is superimposed on it. It is throughout the centuries that the dragon will be chained, that is, made ineffective against the martyrs who time and again are slain by him, yet conquer him: "He who conquers, I will grant him to sit with me on my throne, as I myself conquered and sat down with my Father on his throne." (3:21) This statement is actually the opening of the sequence where we hear of the divine throne (chapter 4), of the Lamb's access to it (chapter 5), and the martyrs' souls being protected under its altar *until their number is complete* (chapter 6).

This "superimposition" is so much inherent to the message of the apostolic preaching (God's kingdom is at hand) that John the seer, in expanding the message concerning the end times from a chapter in Mark (13)[5] to an entire book, was forced to use this literary device. A close examination of the content and structure of the Book of Revelation will corroborate that. After the introductory three chapters, the rest of the book reveals the contents of the scroll, a bewildering array of seals, trumpets, bowls, plagues, riders, hallelujahs, thunders, and strange imagery. Although it may be difficult at first to see any structure in this mélange, structure there is. First we have a series of seven "seals," each except the last associated with a particular vision (chs.6-7). The seventh seal introduces a series of seven "trumpets," each except the last likewise associated with a vision (8:1-11:18). The seventh trumpet heralds the third and final

---

[5] See also the parallel chapters: Lk 21 and Mt 24.

sequence of seven: seven "bowls" containing seven "plagues" (15:6-16:21) following a long interlude (11:19-15:5) bracketed by references to the opening of God's heavenly temple. Chapter 17 goes on to describe the bowls and plagues in greater detail (notice how it opens with "Then one of the seven angels who had the seven bowls came and said to me ..."). This is done in two sets of three: three woes against Babylon proclaiming its imminent fall (17:1-18:24),[6] followed by three hallelujahs heralding God's victory (19:1-10). The hallelujahs bring us back to the beginning of the whole series of visions as the seer again beholds the white horse and its victorious rider (19:11-21) with whom the cycle began (6:2). The rider, Jesus Christ himself, will be joined in his victory by those who by then will have undergone martyrdom (20:1-6), thereby having defeated Satan themselves (20:7-10). The last judgment (20:11-15) then follows with the establishment of the new Jerusalem (21:1-22:5), and the book closes with an exhortation to all who read it or hear it read to look for Christ's coming (22:6-21).

Although at first glance all this may appear to chronicle a long series of future events, such was not the author's intent. A forecast of a long wait would not have been good news for his beleaguered audience, and the repeated expression *erkhomai takhy* (I am coming soon; 2:16; 3:11; 11:14; 22:7, 12, 20) explicitly belies the idea of a long delay. Why then so many different descriptions of things to come? As in all ancient literatures, which did not have the luxury of changing type faces or sizes, italicizing, underscoring, or even punctuating, repetition served to underscore a point the author considered important. Extended repetition conveys the notion of assuredness: it is as

---

[6] The woes are preceded by an introduction decrying the great city's power and wickedness in ch.17.

though the author is insisting over any and all doubts that what he says will indeed come to pass. And the main message is that bad things will happen, but regardless of what happens, Christ "is coming soon." In other words, the Book of Revelation is about the end time that is at hand for those hearing John's words and not about something that will happen later on, something that will take a long time to get here and will last a long time after it gets here.

Consequently, each successive set of seven does not depict new and different events that chronologically follow its predecessors. What is going on is a repeat presentation of the same message in different terms. The sets of seven may be compared to a set of Russian or Ukrainian dolls: as you open each one and find the one inside it, you are seeing something fundamentally similar. Notice how the seventh elements of the first two sets do not contain any information as do the preceding six, but open the following set of seven (8:1 introduces 8:2; 11:15-19 introduces 15:6[7]). So one does not move ahead in time, but rather move deeper in one's assuredness of God's superiority over one's foes.

Each group of seven may be subdivided into a set of four followed by a set of three. The sets of four are composed of visions that are complementary in that they provide related elements that add up to a whole: the first four seals present four horses, the first four trumpets herald calamities that all happen to "thirds" of the earth;[8] the first four bowls are poured out upon earth, sea, rivers, and sun. This fits perfectly with the common

---

[7] As noted above, despite the long digression, the link between the 7th trumpet and the 7 plagues is evident in the mention at both places of the opening of the temple (11:19; 15:5).

[8] And 8:13 explicitly draws a line of demarcation between the first four and the last three trumpets.

symbolic meaning of the number four which points to the entirety of a universe that was conceived as extending in the four directions of east, west, north, and south. That is why, besides being complementary, the content of these sets of four is general and stereotyped. The white horse of the first seal goes out "conquering and to conquer"; the first trumpet announces fiery destruction of "a third of the earth"; the first bowl is poured "on the earth"; and so on. The author's purpose is to impress upon the mind of his readers and hearers that whatever happens in the four corners of the universe is ultimately under God's control and according to his plan. This, of course, is a generality that must already be present to some degree in the minds of believers, and John merely needs to reinforce it. Yet he needs to do that to move on to an assertion that is not so easily believed: that God is in control here and now, despite the believers' hardships under Roman persecution, which would seem to indicate that God's enemies have the upper hand. In other words, the first four of each group of seven express God's control over events in general terms that will not be difficult to believe, then, having built up the hearers' confidence, the final three elements move on to say that God also has control over what is going on here and now. Within the last three of each set of seven there is a progression between the fifth element and the sixth, which makes them a kind of succession leading to the seventh and fulfilling element.[9] For today's readers of scripture, who tend to read it as though it were in effect a newspaper article chronicling events of the future instead of the past, recognition of this structure should go a long

---

[9] See, for instance: "After two days he will revive us; on the third day he will raise us up, that we may live before him" (Hos 6:2); "Behold, I cast out demons and perform cures today and tomorrow, and the third day I finish my course. Nevertheless I must go on my way today and tomorrow and the day following; for it cannot be that a prophet should perish away from Jerusalem." (Lk 13:32-33)

The Millennium

way toward making sense of what otherwise might seem a long list of calamities to be lived through by countless future generations.

Let me reiterate: those who pertain to the one thousand year reign are exclusively the martyrs who, because they look like the sacrificed Lamb, are assured of a seat in the coming Kingdom. That is why they are presented as seated on thrones of judgment (20:4) instead of undergoing it as the rest of us will, whether we are dead or "left behind"(vv.12-15). Indeed, the "left behind" and thus living, cannot possibly be martyrs. Consequently, anyone reading these lines, including myself, cannot be already reigning with Christ. Those living "souls" who present themselves as part the 144,000 souls who will reign for one thousand years with Christ are simply wretched "souls" who had better get their act together and do some good deeds toward their needy fellows in order to ensure that, indeed, their names be found in the Book of Life, since they cannot be sure that they would eventually be martyred. Actually, the connotation in Revelation is actual physical death for commitment to the biblical God. Since most people who believe they are part of the 144,000 live in the United States, where individual beliefs are dearly respected and protected, it would be very rare to hear about people being martyred. In fact, the opposite is true: I am a Christian Orthodox priest and every so often my collar has saved me from being ticketed for a potential traffic violation!

Epilogue

Epilogue

For many centuries, both Jews and Christians lived together, side by side, hoping that when God would establish the "new heavens and new earth," they would be numbered among those who would be invited in:

> For as the new heavens and the new earth which I will make shall remain before me, says the Lord; so shall your descendants and your name remain. From new moon to new moon, and from sabbath to sabbath, all flesh shall come to worship before me, says the Lord. (Is 66:22-23)

In the 19th century, with the rise of nationalism in Europe, anti-Jewish sentiments were on the rise, especially in Russia and France. Some leading European Jews realized that the mood presented an opportunity for them to establish a "Jewish homeland." The culmination of their efforts, and especially those of Theodore Herzl, a Viennese Jew, was the First Zionist Congress convened in Basel, Switzerland in 1897. Until 1905, Argentina and Uganda were considered as possible sites for the establishment of a "homeland." So, the idea of a "return" to Palestine and Jerusalem was not as essential then as it is presented nowadays. Even when the choice eventually tilted toward Palestine, this cannot be taken, per se, as a proof that it was a de facto realization of a perennial dream or even triggered by the "obvious" understanding of "Next Year in Jerusalem" and the *'aliyah*. If Jews were genuinely interested in the "return" to Jerusalem for religious reasons, they could have done so over past centuries. They did not do so because they fared well or preferred to stay, for other reasons, wherever there were dwelling.

The 20th century saw biblical scholars producing colossal works with titles such as *Theology of the Old Testament* and *Theology of the New Testament*. The intention, to be sure, was to underline the primacy of the Bible in any theological endeavor; still the titles betrayed the underlying reality that the Bible was indeed considered a "theological" endeavor. The factual result was that these scholars viewed themselves as the heirs of the prophets and apostles, and thought they could bring to fruition the intellectual discourse started by the prophets and apostles. To my mind, this way of perceiving matters is none other than the Hegelian view that controlled not only theology but also philosophy and the writing of history from the beginning of the 19th century. An example of this influence is the approach to world history predominant among British and then U.S. historians and politicians, who view their own time and country as the end which previous world history converges and culminates into, and that their own commonwealth is the paradigm to be sought after by the rest of the world communities.[1] In spite of all appearances, this is not a new phenomenon. It did not originate with Hegel; he just sanctified it. This approach actually originated in Athens, was then taken over by imperial Rome, then by imperial Constantinople—the new Rome, and then by Charlemagne. Each of those societies saw itself as the highest expression of human civilization.

From the beginning of the 20th century, governments that supported the establishment and later the policies of the state of Israel did so and still do for political reasons. Their interest then and now lies in the control of that region for its geo-political and oil-related economical importance. But, here again, while Jews

---

[1] Even Pierre Teilhard de Chardin with his Point Omega and Noosphere theory is not immune to Hegel's influence.

and super-powers look to their interests, which can be explained on a human level, it is the religious factor that complicates the matter in an unprecedented manner. The introduction of an unwarranted divine element makes the situation of the Middle East even more complex. The most pernicious aspect of this factor is that it is affecting policy making for and in the region. Such an attitude becomes dangerous when people believe they have figured out God's ongoing activity on the historical realm from the perspective of their specific group or nation, their collective. In doing so, they create a monster, if not an idol, to which they chain God. But the biblical premise, as I have repeatedly shown, is that history is still trailing along not because of man's realizations, but out of God's mercy and longsuffering.

Throughout the Bible, God's law summons its hearers to love and care for anyone in need living on his earth. It even asks them to behold God's face, that is, his presence, in that of their presumed enemy, as Jacob was taught in his encounter with God and Esau. This divine commandment is pushed to its ultimate meaning in Jesus' teaching about love, which is magisterially summed up in the words of John:

> He who does not love does not know God; for God is love ... Beloved, if God so loved us, we also ought to love one another. No man has ever seen God; if we love one another, God abides in us and his love is perfected in us ... If any one says, "I love God," and hates his brother, he is a liar; for he who does not love his brother whom he has seen, cannot love God whom he has not seen. And this commandment we have from him, that he who loves God should love his brother also. (1 Jn 4:8, 11-12, 20-21)

In its turn, Islam proceeds along these same lines when it makes almsgiving, that is, the care for the needy neighbor, one of its pillars, thus putting it on the same footing as the "confession of faith in God and the words of his messenger." Actually, almsgiving is referred to as *zakat* and *tzadaqah*. *Zakat* is from the root *zakah*, the same as in Hebrew, meaning "make pure, atone," while *tzadaqah* is from the root *tzadaq*, again the same as in Hebrew, meaning "be righteous, innocent, legally correct, truthful." Consequently, the one who performs almsgiving is both cult-wise pure, that is, worthy of serving in God's temple, and legally at no fault in God's court of law.

Virtually all the residents of the Middle East pertain to the three monotheistic religions that worship the God of Abraham. In this sense, they all confess to be children of Abraham and, thus, indeed brethren. Love among brethren entails the challenge to abide by one's belief as the point of reference for one's behavior. Such can be and is done on a daily scene in the Arab countries as well as in Israel, as anyone following the news should know.

Unfortunately, the way to a peaceful co-existence for and by the residents of the Middle East is complicated by two main factors related to our study. First, powers foreign to the region, especially the United States, are meddling in and with that region for what they label as "their interests." But this is not new, since the Middle East has had its share, if not its fill, of such behavior by the Romans, the Byzantines, the European Latins, and more recently by the British and the French. World powers are world powers with their own patented psyche and behavior.

However, from the perspective of our concern in this study, it is the other, more pernicious, factor that proves deadlier, and that involves interference by Christians from outside the Middle East. By consistently appealing to their "brotherhood" with Middle Eastern Christians, they force the latter into a double-edged dilemma:

1. Since the Christians of the West form the majority of Christians in the world, and control the world media, they function as the de facto sole speaker for Christianity, and thus marginalizing the Christians of the Middle East. Christians of the West behave as "Big Brother" silencing "little brother" and speaking for him even to the latter's own detriment: little brother is suffering the whiplashes while big brother is counting them. It would behoove "Big Brother" to remember that it was "in Antioch (that) the disciples were for the first time called Christians" (Acts 11:26).

2. The result of the influence and interference of Western Christians is that the Jews and the Muslims in the Middle East view their counterparts, the Christians of that region, as an alien entity and not a vital part of it. Instead of being brethren sharing the same earth and its destiny, the Christians of the Middle East are made to be outsiders and viewed with suspicion. What the majority of the Christians in the West cannot understand is a very simple reality: the Christians of the Middle East are brethren with the Jews and Muslims in the same patrimony of the earth they live in, the same way that Anglicans, Catholics, and Protestants in the United Kingdom are British.

By sharing the same religion, the Christians of the Middle East and those of the West are one entity. However, as citizens of the region, Middle Eastern Christians feel and factually are more "brethren" with the Jews and Muslims of that area than they are with the European or American Christians. Indeed, one is first born as citizen and then baptized into the faith, and not vice-versa. God has willed that all three—Jews, Muslims and Christians—live together in the Middle East. If the Christians of the West are indeed "brethren in Christ" with the Christians living in the Middle East, they ought to help the latter as such. Otherwise, the Christians of the West would be behaving as an in-law jealous of the original family of his or her spouse.

The Christians of the Middle East, citizens of its countries including Palestine, have always viewed and still view—correctly so—the Bible as a religious, and not historical, document inviting its hearers to behave in a manner after God's heart. To phrase it scripturally, as in Deuteronomy, and as Jeremiah and Paul underscore, belonging to God—being his people—is a matter of the "heart," that is, the "mind," and not of the "flesh." Consequently, holiness is not spatial, inherent to a piece of real estate or a building. It is behavioral: "Become ye holy, for I am holy" (Lev 11:44-45). This, translated into everyday life, is a command to "be merciful, even as your Father is merciful" (Lk 6:36).

The earth—every earth—is the Lord's as are *those who dwell therein*. The Middle East, as any other part of the earth, is the patrimony of those who have lived there for centuries. It is their duty, regardless of their religious affiliation, to make it a better

Epilogue

place for the upcoming generations. More specifically, the earth of Palestine is the patrimony of the Palestinians, and they alone have the last word in its future. Others are welcome to help, but not to dictate. This scriptural teaching does not apply solely to the Middle East. Our entire planet would be a better place if that rule was applied in every earth on our planet.

Whether Palestine will prove to be a "holy land," is up to God, and him alone, to decide when he comes to judge the living and the dead. The nations of the world and, more importantly, the Christians of the West, are to extend a helping hand for the purpose of committing the Palestinians to the Lord's peace. They are not, through their self-serving policies and attitudes, to force Palestine into a bloodbath and then use the situation they create as a renewed opportunity to intervene. To live in peace, the Palestinians need to be left in peace!

www.ingramcontent.com/pod-product-compliance
Lightning Source LLC
Chambersburg PA
CBHW031135160426
43193CB00008B/148